The Modern
Jewish Experience

The Modern Jewish Experience

Advisory Editor

Moses Rischin

Editorial Board

Arthur A. Goren

Irving Howe

CHILDHOOD IN EXILE

BY SHMARYA LEVIN

ARNO PRESS

A New York Times Company

New York / 1975

Reprint Edition 1975 by Arno Press Inc.

Reprinted from a copy in
  The Newark Public Library

THE MODERN JEWISH EXPERIENCE
ISBN for complete set: 0-405-06690-2
See last pages of this volume for titles.

Manufactured in the United States of America

—————◦◦◦◦————

Library of Congress Cataloging in Publication Data

Levin, Shmarya, 1867-1935.
    Childhood in exile.

    (The Modern Jewish experience)
    Reprint of the 1929 ed. published by Harcourt, Brace,
New York.
    The first part of the author's autobiography; the
second of which has title: Youth in revolt, and the
third: The arena.
    1. Levin, Shmarya, 1867-1935. 2. Zionists--Corre-
spondence, reminiscences, etc. 3. Jews in Russia--
Social life and customs. I. Title. II. Series.
DS151.L44A33 1975   956.94'001'0924 [B]
ISBN 0-405-06724-0   74-27997

CHILDHOOD
IN EXILE

CHILDHOOD
IN EXILE

BY SHMARYA LEVIN

TRANSLATED BY
MAURICE SAMUEL

NEW YORK

HARCOURT, BRACE
AND COMPANY

PRINTED IN THE UNITED STATES OF AMERICA
BY QUINN & BODEN COMPANY, INC., RAHWAY, N. J.

CONTENTS

CHILDHOOD
IN EXILE

CHAPTER ONE: THE FAMILY

WHENEVER I sit down with closed eyes and turn my gaze inward in an effort to recall the past, the skein of my life unwinds with the swiftness of a spool on a loom: and always at the last point, which is the first point of my memory, one figure emerges—my mother. In that image, clear and sharp as if she were still before me, moving about the house or bending over the cradle of her newest-born in silent prayer— an unofficial addition to her daily religious services—in that image I recognize the beginning of my life and feel the first pulse-beat of my being.

Hers is the first memory, and next to hers is that of my father, with his grave, severe, and intellectual face. The next places are taken up by my two grandfathers and my grandmother (the other grandmother, on my mother's side, I never knew), and around them are grouped uncles and aunts, cousins and second cousins, the young and the old, relatives of all degrees. A characteristic image springs out of the groups: my mother and my father, my grandfathers and my grandmother, are like a colonnade of trees planted at equal distances, each in its own destined place. The relatives are like an irregular grove scattered about the colonnade, one tree elbowing its neighbour eagerly, a second standing darkly aside: the complete knoll serving as a background to the stately colonnade.

Beyond the farther end of the colonnade, in the shadow

of which I press close to my mother's side, I see the last glimmer of sunset. The night rises slowly and covers with her dark mantle the men and women and incidents that were before me. The past sleeps there, in the Dwelling of Eternity: the hard memorial stones serve for cushions, and over the unknown figures a sheet is drawn, sparkling with golden stars. But between me and the Dwelling of Eternity, there is some sort of relationship—dark and obscure, but authentic. Beyond my living parents and grandparents (living because I still evoke them as living beings) stretches the long line of my great-grandfathers and great-great-grandfathers. I see the beginning of the line near me, but not the end of it: I run toward it, I try to overtake the vanished generations, but the more eagerly I pursue them the more swiftly they withdraw. And at last my strength gives out, my young feet fail under me: the line curves over and disappears like the trail of a meteor on the farther side of the sea, or like a thunderclap which loses itself among distant mountains.

This image which haunted my childhood acquired a singular meaning for me in later years. In measure as I grew older and entered into more intimate contact with life, in like measure did the colonnade of the dead unveil itself before me, as though fragment after fragment were coming up for the resurrection. I know well that this is only the play of my fancy. But it is in this manner that I perceive my life, and I do not believe myself to be an exception. On the contrary, I believe with all my strength that we carry within ourselves more of a *living* past than we suspect: and if we gave the right degree of attention to this truth, and exerted ourselves to create some sort of harmony between our present and our past, we should avoid many of the spiritual conflicts which torment us.

My mother, Elke the daughter of Mendel, of the family Astrakhan, was exactly fourteen years old when she was married to my father, Samuel Chaim, son of Solomon Salkind Ha-Levi, of the family Levin: and my father was just one year older than my mother. I have often heard my mother tell that she suffered a great deal during the first year of her marriage. Not, God forbid, because the match did not please her, but because for a whole year she was ashamed to look my father straight in the eyes. Whether my father suffered likewise I do not know. My mother used to add, to these memories, that it was wrong to marry children off so early. It was pitiful, she said. After all, we were no longer living in the days of the Terror, when the agents of the Czar might descend at any moment on the unmarried boys of a Jewish family and send them off to distant military service for twenty-five years or more. One ought to wait, my mother said, until the brides were at least fifteen and the bridegrooms sixteen years of age. My mother was never a shrewd bargainer, and she was content to nibble off one year. There was a natural modesty in our parents.

The meaning of the Terror, the Boholoh, was already known to me in my childhood: and the epoch was still fresh in the memory of millions of the living. During those days there would be marriages between children of twelve years of age, for the horror of those military schools, which were chosen at the most distant points from the home of the child-recruit (they would send them as far as Orenburg in Siberia), hung over every Jewish family. Even Nicholas the First would not go so far as to take the married children. That word Boholoh, the Terror, has a fearful ring to Jewish ears: more successfully than volumes of description, it conjures up a world of agony and fear. But a people does not describe. It creates a primitive song, a word—and that suffices.

On my mother's side I belong to the mystic and passionate sect of the Chassidim: on my father's side I am a cool, logical Misnagid, or opponent of the Chassidim. My grandfather Mendel Astrakhan was a fiery adherent of the Lubowitch dynasty of wonder-working rabbis: he did not let a single High Holiday pass without a visit to the "Court," nor a year without payment of tithes. My grandfather Solomon Salkind was a dry, cool Misnagid, an eternal student of our sacred books. He made it a point to surround himself with the wandering preachers and rabbis and emissaries sojourning in our little town. Naturally our house as such was typically Misnagid, and my education was planned and carried out under the direction of my father. But the Chassidic stories and legends which my mother would tell us exerted a profound influence on me: and even more powerful than the lore of the Chassidim was the manner of her life, her individual style. Toward my father my attitude was one of the deepest respect: but in that respect there was not lacking an element of fear. Toward my mother my relationship was one of pure love. She was in my eyes the personification of all that is loveliest and most lovable. She was widely known as a gentle, charitable, and God-fearing woman. In my eyes she was a saint. There were thus two distinct and opposed influences in my life: the severe intellectual Misnagid influence on my father's side, and the gentle and mystic Chassidic influence on my mother's side.

My father had, as the phrase goes, "a good head on him." He was especially clever at figuring, and in later years, when I was a student in the upper classes of the Realschule or Secondary School in Minsk, I convinced myself that my father had a real grasp of the elements of algebra and geometry, subjects he had never studied. He frequently astounded me by the manner in which he approached a problem in either subject: the problem, it is true, would not be a very advanced one, but he had an extraordinary way of resolving it into its first elements by sheer dint of business acumen, or, I am tempted to say, by a sort of instinct for what was logical and just. It was from my father that I inherited a gift for mathematics which in later years was to enable me to overcome some of the heaviest obstacles placed in the way of my education. My mother was, in every fibre of her being, a woman of mood and intuition. In all that she did or said—even if the matter was some daily commonplace—she made evident such depth of soul, such fineness of feeling, such sympathy and compassion, that she drew me to her with magic power. If it could be put so crudely, I would say that my father's influence was to intellectualize me, my mother's to inspire me: from my father streamed a cool, clear light: from my mother, warmth and emotion. My head was drawn toward my father, my heart toward my mother, and I was forever swinging like a pendulum between these two forces. Which of these forces finally came to dominate? Did I finally emerge a Chassid, with a Misnagid background, or was the contrary the case? The answer will have to be given by others than myself. For my part I can only say that both of my parents played a great part in my life.

But the mere fact that a Chassidic and a Misnagid family had entered into an alliance by marriage showed that the crest of the wave of enmity between the two sects had already passed; I do not believe that the difference in character between my father and mother created actual inner conflicts along the path of my development.

It was not, however, by virtue of their religious divisions that my grandfathers Mendel and Solomon belonged to two different groups. Their social standing was about the same. They both belonged to the upper middle class, but for all that my grandfather Solomon was a grade higher. The reason is to be found in the difference between the two townlets from which they came respectively. Grandfather Mendel lived in the townlet of Beresin, on the river of the same name, not far from Borisow, where the great Napoleon met disaster. Grandfather Solomon lived in Swislowitz, which is also on the Beresina, but has a second river, namely, the Swisla, which after half encircling the town falls into the Beresina. I remember that the possession of two rivers was a source of much pride to us. Nor was the feeling entirely academic. In the first place two rivers, both of them easily accessible, meant a great deal when fire broke out, and periodic fires played an important rôle in the history of our towns. It was the custom with us to date events before or after "the great fire." In the second place, there was the matter of our ritual of divorce, which cannot be observed in a town without a river. So they would come to us from Lapitz and from Choloi and from other forlorn and God-forsaken villages without a river, to get their divorces. And then, finally, there was the great ceremony of Taschlich on the Jewish New Year, when the Jew goes down to the river and empties his sins into the flowing waters. Two rivers to choose from. If you liked you could patronize the Beresina, and if you liked, you went to the Swisla, flung your transgressions into it, and had them carried down to the far-off Dnieper, thence to the Black Sea, to be lost at last in the oceans which encircle the globe.

A matter of fifty kilometres separated the townlets of Beresin and Swislowitz, yet the two Jewish communities differed radically in their structure and character. Beresin prided itself on its metropolitan—almost its megalopolitan—

character, and looked down with tolerance on provincial Swislowitz. Eight hundred Jewish souls and as many non-Jewish made up the population of the latter. There were no magnates in Swislowitz, and only a handful of comparatively rich men. Below these, in descending order, were a few score shopkeepers and small merchants, and two or three hundred artisans and labourers. These last were mostly trained in the special craft of raft-binding, and were generally regarded as the most skilful in their line. The fact that there were no magnates in Swislowitz contributed a great deal to the democratic character of the community. It is almost impossible for us Jews of the modern western world to realize the rôle that was played by the Jewish magnate in the small community. The distinction between the magnate and the merely "rich" Jew was enormous: it was at least as great as—to borrow a parallel from the English social hierarchy—that between the baronet and the ordinary knight.

The transition from the rôle of the well-to-do burgher to that of the magnate was difficult, for the latter status was a distinct rank, conferred after recognition not only by the middle classes, but by the established body of magnates. And as a rule the latter closed their ranks obstinately against the social ambitions of newcomers.

Thus Swislowitz was a healthy, middle-class, democratic Jewish community, organically bound up through all its parts by family alliances. The place of honour in the Synagogue, the seats by the eastern wall, did not necessarily coincide with the place of honour in our social life. Wherever a birth or marriage was celebrated, the invitation went out tacitly to every Jew in the townlet. And every Jew came to a funeral, whosesoever it might be.

Now Beresin was a much larger community in point of numbers, and it was completely dominated by a family of magnates—the Seldovitches. This was the family which ordered, regulated, and supervised its social and communal life. The Seldovitches were the true counterpart of the feudal lords of the Middle Ages. Not a step was taken without their knowledge and permission. No man dared utter a word in their presence, much less express a strong opinion. In brief, Beresin represented a small absolute monarchy, with the Seldovitches at the head.

The family consisted of two collateral branches, each with its patriarch at the head—respectively Wolf and David Seldovitch. Both of them were timber merchants on a large scale. They bought up the forests of the Polish provincial aristocracy, cut down the trees, prepared them for shipment, and sent them off in two directions, floating their rafts by way of Kiev and Kerson down to Odessa on the one side, or up to Danzig on the other. Their business connections in Danzig brought them in contact with German culture, which took a strong hold on the younger generation. Each of the two patriarchs, Wolf and David, had a Synagogue of his own, and when I first came to Beresin as a boy of fourteen I still found in existence the following custom: whenever, during the sacred services, a relative of the Seldovitches was called up to read out a portion of the Law, he was invited by the honorific title of "Rav," while every one else was plain Mister. Immediately after the Seldovitches and their relatives came their employés, under the general and sonorous title of "agents." Theirs was the second place in the hierarchy. Third on the list were the independent burghers, the merchants and shopkeepers. Last came the artisans and labourers. The intellectual life of the community was supplied by the doctor, the pharmacist, two lawyers, and a few teachers.

By all rights the independent burghers should have taken

precedence over the "agents" of the Seldovitches. But so powerful was the pressure of the family that this little world was separated into two camps: the Seldovitches and the non-Seldovitches. Woe to him who made any attempt to upset this natural order of classes. I say "classes." I should perhaps use the word "caste," in its Indian sense. The magnate, in a word, was ruler and overlord. Learning and family standing, those two controls of our traditional Jewish aristocracy, played no part in this case. The genealogy of the Seldovitches was of the humblest, and they never achieved the slightest distinction in the world of learning. It was only in later years that by a series of marriages they allied themselves with the aristocracy of scholarship. Of the two brothers Wolf and David—the double heads of the Seldovitch eagle—the latter was widely celebrated as an almost illiterate ignoramus. He was unable to read from the Hebrew prayer-book: he had to have some one read out to him, while he repeated the words. Even this he did so badly, twisting words and verses into such grotesque combinations, that the howlers of David Seldovitch became classics in that part of the world, travelling as far as Minsk at one boundary and Mohilev at the other.

My grandfather Mendel was agent for one of the brothers Seldovitch—I no longer remember which. It was his task to make the rounds of the forests put up for sale, and estimate the value of the timber. The work was exacting and responsible. In those days the price of wood was absurdly low, leaving little or no room for speculation on the sale. If, therefore, the Jewish merchants made money, it was less by skilful selling than by shrewd buying. When the Russian government sold its forests, it would fix the price according to the number, height, and girth of the trees. The Polish nobles had not yet acquired the system. They sold forests in the lump. In making purchases from the Polish nobles, it was therefore necessary to employ a man who was reliable on two counts, first as to his level-headedness, second as to his absolute honesty. He had to have the feel of the quantity of timber in a forest: and he had to be free from temptation to make deals either with competitors or with the noble.

My grandfather qualified on both counts. He was a first-class expert on forests, and his honesty was above suspicion. When I first saw my grandfather he was already an old man, tall, well built, with a handsome snow-white beard and with unusually heavy eyebrows, which stood out like rustic hedges above his deep eyes. Something in him spoke of the countless forest trees which he had felt and examined for so many years; he was himself like a powerful old oak planted in the centre of a winter landscape. I looked upon him with awe, and resented the fact that he was merely an agent for the Seldovitches. In my young imagination that title was far beneath his merits and his dignity.

But in this respect my grandfather Solomon Salkind did satisfy my pride. He was not as imposing as Grandfather Mendel, but he did not have to submit to the name of "agent." He was an independent man, also engaged in the timber trade, though on a smaller scale. This trade had been in our family for many, many generations. Our townlet was the property of a Polish nobleman named Ostrovsky: more correctly, of his wife. They themselves lived in Warsaw, and the management of the estate was handed over to a commissar or administrator. My grandfather was a *persona grata* at the petty court of the estate, held in the highest esteem by the commissar. But the most important merchant, in the commissar's eyes, was my father. To my grandfather belonged the monopoly on the supplying of material for binding the rafts. Placed as our town was, at the junction of

two rivers, it was well adapted for the building and floating
of the rafts which were sent down the Beresina to the
Dnieper. Instead of ropes, branches of willow were used,
after having been softened in fire. The monopoly provided a
decent income for my grandfather. The work was seasonal;
it began with the festival of Purim, in the early spring,
when the rivers thawed out, and lasted until Pentecost, at the
beginning of the summer. For the rest of the year there was
nothing to be done. But even during the season my grandfather occupied himself little with this monopoly. He had
turned over the management of it to his son, my uncle Meyer,
a plain, simple Jew who by long intercourse with the peasants had himself become something of the earthy peasant
type. My grandfather spent the days of his life in study and
prayer. He gave his nights to those special midnight vigils
of lamentation which we call Chtzoth—mourning for the
exile of the Divine Glory from the Holy Land, and for the
destruction of the Temple. Across all these years there comes
to me the sound of the old man weeping in his lonely room.
And I still remember the tears which, with childish terror,
I sometimes saw rolling down his cheeks. He carried on his
studies in the night by the light of a special candle—a long
woollen wick passed through a ball of wax. Every two or
three minutes he would suspend his studies, draw the woollen
wick a little further through the wax, and return to his
sacred books.

My grandfather was not a great scholar. I seldom saw him
engaged on the deep works of the Talmud or on the complicated juridical and religious decisions of our legal authorities. His favourite books were those of the wise sayings and
moral disquisitions of our sages. Indeed, he was more the
pietist than the scholar. During the day, if he left his
studies, it was mostly to engage in charitable work: he gave

to the limit of his means, and persuaded others to give. Himself no scholar, it was with him a point of pride to place himself at the service of scholars.

Our town possessed no inn or hotel. Our only communal institution was the Hekdesh, a bleak lodging-house for the accommodation of poor wanderers—mostly beggars travelling on foot. It consisted of a single vast room, in the centre of which stood a tremendous stove. Above the stove was a *lieszanka*, or alcove, in which a dozen men could lie comfortably on winter nights. Asher Pakess, the humble Jewish water-carrier, was caretaker of the Hekdesh. He received no payment for these duties, but he enjoyed a number of privileges. First, he and his wife lived in the Hekdesh rent-free. Second, the Synagogue and the Beth Hamidrash or Study House attached to it were obligated to buy their water from him. He lugged it uphill from the Beresina, and charged one kopeck (half a cent) for two buckets. Third, he was the communal purveyor of willow withes for the festival of Tabernacles. Fourth, every firstling kid and calf which acquired a blemish was his property. And fifth, he was permitted to buy all the meat he could eat without paying the *karobka*—the Kosher meat tax which was collected by the wealthy Jew to whom it had been farmed out by the Government. As Asher never had the price of a meat dinner, tax or no tax, this last privilege was purely honorific.

The Hekdesh was the asylum of the *déclassés*—the outcasts. Mostly it was used by lonely beggars; now and again, though very rarely, it would shelter an entire family travelling in its cart. Travellers with any sort of standing—such, for instance, as the emissaries of minor, backwoods Yeshivoth or academies, second-class itinerant preachers, respectable unfortunates, refugees of a fire, or such Jewish fathers as

were travelling from city to city piously gathering a dowry
for their unmarried daughters, were lodged not in the Hekdesh, but in the annex to the Synagogue. For important
travellers, the emissaries of great Yeshivoth, pilgrims from
the Holy Land, preachers of repute, and, of course, travelling Rabbis, the doors of my grandfather's house stood wide
open, with drink, food, lodging, and service: and from none
of these would he accept a kopeck. My grandfather observed with special passion the laws of hospitality to the
stranger, and took it as a personal affront if some one in the
town snatched from his friendly clutches a traveller of importance. His house, a large one with two wings, was always full of guests, and on the verandah which faced the
street travellers, wandering scholars, itinerant Rabbis and
preachers, would often be seen on summer days discussing
the affairs of this world and of the next with the worthies
of our town. In later years, when I went to *cheder* (elementary Hebrew school), I learned how Abraham, our father,
had been specially given to the practise of hospitality, and
how his tent had always had four entrances, north, east,
south, and west, so that the footsore traveller might not have
to wander round and round for admittance, but find it
straightway. And I pictured the patriarch to myself in the
form of Grandfather Solomon, though I was compelled to
add, from an early sense of fitness, the snow-white beard and
vast eyebrows of Grandfather Mendel. I was much chagrined
by the fact that Grandfather's house fell short of the glorious
model set up by the 'father of our people: it had only two
doors, one to the street and one to the courtyard in the rear.
It symbolized to me the mournful fact that even my grandfather could not attain to the standard of hospitality which
our patriarchs had set. And to my chagrin was added dis-

15

appointment: it was my ambition that in the next world my grandfather's seat should be set next to the golden thrones on which the patriarchs of our people sit forever.

Not only was my grandfather's house the largest in the town, but it also had the largest courtyard, with long rows of stables for such as came travelling in their own carts or diligences. The house had, in addition, a private well and—unique possession in the town of Swislowitz—an ice cellar. There were no trees at all in my grandfather's yard. But the adjoining yard, belonging to a gentile, was well provided, chiefly with pear trees. The nearest of these was within reach from the stable roof, with the result that the grandchildren of the family became as agile as cats. More than once, however, our neighbour caught us red-handed, with disastrous consequences. The actual value of our booty may be gauged from the fact that a basket holding forty pounds of these small pears sold for between five and ten kopecks. Of course we had to do all of our pilfering before the fruit became ripe and was shaken down by the owner. However, if my grandfather's courtyard had no trees, it had another treasure: right in the centre of it was a muddy pool. In the summer we sailed paper boats on it or took off shoes and stockings and waded in it. But it was in the winter, when the pool was frozen over, that the full value of it was uncovered. It became then an inexhaustible source of joy. We spent every moment of freedom sliding on the ice. Not plain sliding, of course, but the highly ornamented sliding of the virtuoso, in postures and with gestures borrowed from the occupations of our elders; sliding with eyes closed and hands stretched before us, like Mother standing in front of the Sabbath candles: sliding in an almost kneeling position, like Father when he bowed himself in the Synagogue; sliding while performing complicated motions with the right hand round the left, like Father binding on the phylacteries: and, finally, sliding seated, most difficult and most dangerous.

I reach now the last of my childhood recollections of my family—the last, that is, in point of treatment. I have left it to the end because it occupies a special place in my memory, in a compartment of its own; it concerns my Grandmother Toibe, the wife of Grandfather Solomon. She was his first and only wife, lived out all the years of her life with him, and bore him many children, the last three at a single birth. (One of the three remained living, namely, my youngest uncle, Yechiel, whose three children are today in New York.) She was a mother and a grandmother in a widely ramified family. It was my good lot to have known her for fifteen years. And yet, for all her earthly bonds, she always made the strange impression of a thing apart, a spirit from another world fulfilling a definite earthly mission and never becoming an organic part of the life in which it moved and worked. We respected her, and to a certain degree even loved her. But there was never the feeling of intimacy. It seemed to us that our love and respect were being offered to some far-off person, some shadow of a grandmother. I once heard Bialik, the poet, speak in New York on the subject of the Bible in translation as compared with the original: and he likened the former to a kiss which a son might receive from his mother through the thickness of a veil. Automatically, I thought of Grandmother Toibe. My grandmother was, physically, an exception in our family; she was small and lean, and her parchment face was covered with innumerable wrinkles. Yet, as I remember her, she was barely sixty years of age. Hers was the face of one who had suffered and borne much. From one point of view her shadowy detachment was easily intelligible. It was enough that a woman so frailly built should have brought so many children into the world, all of them ten times as strong as herself. But I do not know what other sorrows there were in her life. I have never heard even a suspicion of ill-treatment on the part of my grandfather, or of lack of respect on the part of her children. Something I do understand. My grandfather's was a strong, imperious personality. My grandmother was as gentle, as quiet as a lamb. I never once heard her raise her voice. Her motions were timid, almost furtive, as if she were afraid of being in some one's way. Her eyes had a submissive look in them, begging for something she could not formulate. In brief, she was of those human beings upon whose forehead are clearly written the words, "Good people, merciful people, forgive me that I take up room in this world." My grandmother was extremely pious, but not "well instructed." In the Synagogue she had to rely on the "leader," the woman who reads aloud from the prayer-book so that the less educated may repeat the prayers after her. She was widely known for her charitable works, so that my grandfather had to put some restraint on her not to give away too much at once. For it was a proverb in the town that any one could go to Toibe, the wife of Solomon, and get from her every penny there was in the house. Nor were the needy slow to take advantage of this weakness. Not Jews alone, but non-Jewish neighbours too, were forever coming for favours, and were never turned back empty-handed.

In my time my grandfather and grandmother already lived separately in the two wings of the house. Grandmother suffered from chronic headaches, and kept her bed a great deal. Grandfather used to snatch a few hours' sleep in the day, and would pass most of the nights in vigils of lamentation and prayer. They seem to have realized that headaches and vigils do not go together—so they divided the house between them. My grandmother thought the world of her husband. Just before she died she called him to her bedside and asked him for a fraction of the glory which was set aside for him in Paradise. My grandfather promised it to her, and gave her his hand, perhaps—who knows?—for the first time in his life.

CHAPTER TWO: MEN AND NATURE

Swislowitz stands on a "mountain." We called it a mountain though at its highest point it is less than a hundred feet above the surrounding country. But I want to remain faithful to the spirit of my childhood, and so a mountain it must remain. On three sides the town has to be approached uphill. Along one side runs the Beresina, and along the other, parallel with it, the Swisla, which first finds historic mention in the famous chronicles of the Monk Nestor, who speaks of "Minsk, on the river Swizlotz." For the Swisla also runs through Minsk, but much nearer its source, so that it has a premature look about it, and suggests an irrigation channel dug by human hands; there are in fact quite a number of Minskers who do not even know that their town possesses a river called the Swisla. It is best known among the poor, for it passes through their quarter; and often enough, in the early spring or late autumn, the quiet, unassuming rivulet suddenly takes on character, lifts itself above its banks, and pours into the huts and hovels on either side, in revenge for the contempt it suffers in normal times.

In our town, however, the Swisla is as good a river as any. There it does not have to wait for floods in order to make known its presence. Its waters are full, steady, and tumultuous the whole year round. For a certain distance it runs parallel with the Beresina, then it makes a graceful half turn and pours into the mother-stream, proudly, as if to say, "True, I am younger and smaller, but I bring you plenty of sustenance." The Beresina, broad and majestic, swallows her up without noticing her, and flows on undisturbed to join the Dnieper.

Thus Swislowitz is a peninsula, surrounded by water on three sides. Certain of the elders of the city, still unsatisfied, grumbled at the incompleteness of the job. "Look you," they argued, "why couldn't the Swisla join the Beresina somewhere upstream, then detach itself again, pass round the town, and rejoin the Beresina farther down?" The advantage? Why, Swislowitz would be an island: it would not then be necessary to put up a long row of Sabbath markers—posts and wires within the limits of which the pious Jew might safely carry a parcel on the Sabbath day. Not that we ever did put up that fence on the landward side of the town: it would have had to pass through the non-Jewish quarter. You would never be sure that it had not been torn down; and there you would be, carrying something on the Sabbath, and no fence standing to complete the ritualistic enclosure.

Each of the rivers had a virtue and a fault. The Beresina was broad and splendid: in some places imposing enough to rank with Grandfather Dnieper. But in some places it was miserably shallow; in fact, you could wade clear across. I was ashamed and mortified to see peasants drive their cattle through without any precautions. The thing was a shameless deception practised on the public: above, a real river, wide as a lake, serene, magnificent: underneath, just a shallow pool. It was immoral—like offering a poor man a vast plate of soup one-eighth of an inch deep. The Swisla, though narrower, was deeper and swifter. We made the best of the situation by allocating the rivers—one to the men, the other to the women. So, on a midsummer Friday afternoon, the women would be lying in the shallow Beresina, cooling off, and the men swimming about in the deep Swisla. Between the two naked crowds the town lay deserted and patient, waiting for its inhabitants to put on their holiday attire and flock to the Synagogue for the prayers which usher in the Sabbath.

The Jews of Swislowitz were passionately fond of river bathing. Young and old waited for the approach of Pentecost, hoping always for an early summer, so that the bathing might begin. The gentiles were not given to the pastime, and it was the rarest thing to see one of them bathing or swimming in the river. I wonder whether this weakness on the part of the Jews had anything to do with the passage in the Talmud which bids every Jewish father train his son to a trade—or at least teach him how to swim! In any case, the fact remains that the Jews of Swislowitz were excellent swimmers. There were two favourite local tricks: the first was to lift one arm after the other out of the water, and use it like an oar. This made for speed. The second was for show: the swimmer had to keep himself afloat perpendicularly while holding both his hands clear of the water. The best swimmer among us was old Joseph Bear Schatz, the cantor. He used to swim not only with both hands clear of the water, but a knee too! While swimming he would pare the nails of his hands, and let the parings fall on to a sheet of paper which he balanced on his knee. This was no plain feat, because he did the paring according to the somewhat complicated instructions prescribed in the Talmud for the super-pious.

To the farther side of both rivers lay meadows. The land was unfit for cultivation, because twice a year—almost without exception—the rivers flooded it, and most of the time it remained impossibly marshy. The meadows produced one thing—hay. Thus the levels round the town went through three transformations in the course of the year. In the spring, and sometimes in the autumn, the meadows were covered with water. Then Swislowitz looked like a tiny island in the midst of a tremendous sea. In the summertime the townlet was surrounded by an ocean of green. And in the winter the stretches on all sides of it were covered with one vast mantle of white, smooth as a clean bed-sheet and dotted here and there with tiny pyramids—the frozen haystacks. It happened more than once that on a night toward the close of summer one of these pyramids would burst into flame, and fiery tongues would leap out of it toward the dark sky. The townlet knew that these tongues spoke the language of revenge: some one had set fire to the haystacks of his enemy. The government was very severe in cases like these—but the culprits were seldom caught.

Far beyond the meadows the forests began, but between them lay the wheat fields of the peasants. They were fat, rich fields, soft to the foot, breathing an odour of fruitfulness and sustenance. That odour interpreted the Russian phrase Matiushka Zemlya—Mother Earth, a mother giving suck from bountiful breasts to countless children. When the peasants spoke of Matiushka Zemlya their eyes, usually dull and expressionless, were flooded with love, like the eyes of children who see their mother at a distance.

The forests belonged in part to the local Polish nobility and in part to the government. They were scores of miles deep—in fact, no one knew where they really ended. The nobles, making their homes in Warsaw, lived the life of spoilers, denuding their forests stretch by stretch. The government forests were more carefully managed, and were therefore always in better condition. It was only in the eighties that the government began to control the ruthless destruction of the private forests. Until then the nobleman was free to do whatever he liked with his own forests—and he did it. The trees were cut down mercilessly, the young with the old. The old were cut into logs, the young into smaller pieces, for general use. We had a dozen names to indicate the various sizes of logs. The big ones were bound together into rafts, and the smaller ones floated on top of them. Within the forest the small trees used to lie about like young fowl dead before their time.

Jews and gentiles alike lived on terms of intimacy with the forest, their best friend. It provided them gratis with countless fruits and plants, with berries, mushrooms, and wild apples (we used to lay these on straw, wait till they began to rot, then eat them with great relish), wild pears, nuts of all kinds, and guelder-roses. In the things that grew in the soil Jew and gentile shared alike. But the gentile had something in addition—the hunt: hare, marten, mink, and occasionally even a bear. The Jews had nothing to do with the animals: that is, they would not shoot them. But they would buy the carcases from the peasants for the furs. However, as against this, the Jews had two uses for the forest which were unknown to the gentiles. They got from it their willow withes for the fifth day of the festival of Tabernacles, and the fir branches to cover the booths.

But something more explained the bond between the inhabitants of Swislowitz and the forest: they were dependent on the forest for their daily bread. If the winter was a good one, with plenty of snow and frost, and many rafts were put together and floated down the river, there was prosperity in Swislowitz. But if the winter was mild, and there was not time enough to carry the cut-down trees to the river brink, Swislowitz hungered. The forests were primaeval, virgin, thickly tangled. Their owners neglected them, and let them grow wild. More than once a fearful storm would burst through the forest, leaving in its wake little hillocks of broken branches and overturned roots. In the winter, when the snow lay deep on the ground, and a powerful frost held it together, it was possible to drag the logs down to the river on sleds. But in the summer it would have been necessary to cut a path through the tangle and roll the logs down on wheels. And prices being what they were in those days, this did not pay.

A picture rises again in my mind. It is early morning, in the winter. I see the shadowy figures of Jews passing down the street on their way to the Synagogue. Prayer-books, praying-shawls, and phylacteries are bundled under their arms. Every now and again a figure stops, stoops, and feels the snow with careful, thoughtful hand, to make sure that it is neither too soft nor too hard. In their hearts they carry a prayer, that God might send a good snow, and enough of it, and after it a good frost, and enough of that, in order that the snow might not melt too soon. With this prayer in their hearts they enter the Synagogue, don their prayer-shawls, and wind their phylacteries round their bared left arms. And when they come to that part of the daily prayers which speaks of God as the One "that causeth the wind to blow and the rain to fall," and further, to the passage which implores the All-Merciful to send down His blessing on the land and drench it in "dew and rain," a second, unuttered prayer rises in their hearts, a silent contradiction: and they beseech God for snow and frost. Two parallel prayers, antagonistic and stubborn; the one born of the daily struggle for bread, the other born thousands of years ago in a land of hot suns. Which prayer, I often wondered, came up before the throne of Grace?

Thanks to its topography—a long, elevated strip between two rivers—the townlet of Swislowitz was well planned. It had no crooked and broken streets. It lay as on a chess-board (chess being unknown then in our town, our simile was, "straight as a kneading-board"), six long streets parallel with the river, and ten shorter ones at right angles. One street only had achieved the dignity of a proper name—the Beresina street. All the others were alluded to by the names of their most prominent residents. But as degrees of prominence were not fixed, any more than its causes, a street might be known by a couple of names or more. One and the same street might be indicated as Pessye the candle-maker's street, or Joseph the chicken-slaughterer's street, or simply as Stepan Harnai's street. Every one was free to express his own taste and preferences through the medium of the streets. As a matter of fact street names were quite unnecessary. In Swislowitz everybody knew who everybody was and where everybody lived.

Of the six long streets one was the artery of Swislowitz. It was very broad. It began at the Swisla, climbed uphill, passed through the marketplace with its public well, and then split north and south. It was impossible to leave or enter Swislowitz without passing along the broad street. It was our link with the great outside world. But if you were to ask me what on earth we needed such a broad, luxurious street for, I could not tell you. Nor could any other townsman. But it would be quite wrong to imagine that the modest Swislowitzers ever used the whole of that boulevard. Trodden paths ran only down the two sides of it. The middle was taken up by patches of wild grass and innumerable mud-puddles, which were knee-deep in the summer. On week-days the children would play in the grass, but on Sabbath afternoons the burghers themselves would lie there, face down-

ward, enjoying life. The mud-puddles were the happy meet-
ing-grounds of all the pigs of our gentile neighbours on the
side-streets. For that matter, the "Jewish" animals, too, were
fond of the puddles. It was a homelike place. They sprawled
their bulk cosily in the ooze and were happy. More than once
they settled so thickly on the street that it was impossible
to drive through.

The broad street was the residence of the most important
burghers, most of whom had their own homes. A family
which had to rent rooms with another could hardly be reckoned among the social élite. In the same street, too, was
housed the complete local administration, the *stanovoi*, or
district commissioner, the postmaster, the village healer, the
volostnoi or community clerk, the public school teacher, and
the clergy—whom we instinctively looked on as part of the
civic administration: two priests and a reader. These were
the representatives of the powers that were.

The district commissioner was a little emperor. The entire
population, Jew and gentile, trembled in his presence. All
adults would rise from their seats and remain standing when
he passed down the street, and the children at play would
scatter at his aproach. "Look out! Here comes the *stanovoi!*"
When this cry was heard, they disappeared as if by magic,
to emerge again only when he had passed out of sight. He
very seldom ventured forth alone. Nearly always he was
accompanied by his retinue, which consisted of his clerk, the
sergeant, and two policemen. His rule was stern and severe.
In his private office or chancellery no one dared to sit
down without special permission. And this permission he
was seldom gracious enough to give. He addressed nearly
every one in the familiar and contemptuous second person
singular. And yet, marvellously enough, it was an open
secret that the commissioner was an eager bribe-taker. He

thirsted after every kopeck he could lay hands on, and could be bought body and soul for a five-rouble note. Yet this did not seem to trouble him in his strange rôle of the stern, unbending administrator appointed by the powers above as the incorruptible guardian of the law. Of one such official in our neighbourhood, a curious story was told. This commissioner, like the one in Swislowitz, was an eager taker of bribes, so eager, in fact, that whatever came up before him in the course of his duties he saw only in the form of coin. On a certain day the corpse of a murdered peasant was found in the woods near his village. On receiving the news, the commissioner at once proceeded to the place indicated, to prepare his report. "On the murdered man," he wrote, "were five wounds, two of which were on his head. Of these two, one was the size of a copper ten-kopeck piece, the other the size of a silver half-rouble." So, one by one, he described the wounds, and set down their size, in terms of some corresponding coin, in a separate column. Finally he drew a line under the column, added the total, and reported that the murdered man had died of wounds to the extent of one rouble and sixty-five kopecks. It was said that the public prosecutor at Babrusk was furious when he received the report, and demanded the instant dismissal of the official.

The community clerk had little to do with the Jewish population, for the Jews were not peasants, but of the *petite bourgeoisie*, and had a separate administration and a clerk of their own, who used to get their passports for them and act as their representative before the government. We therefore knew very little at first hand of the evil ways of the clerk. It was told of one such fellow, however, that he was inordinately fond of beer, and whenever he had to set down the personal description of some peasant who came to him for a travel document, he would invariably enter, opposite the word "Eyes," the description "Beer-coloured." More than one peasant got into fearful difficulties when occasion called for a closer scrutiny of the document and the description did not tally.

The official village healer gave medical attention only to the gentiles. It was not his duty to cure Jews. But whenever he was invited professionally to a Jewish home, he would be paid a fee. There was a "Jewish" doctor, Schwartz by name, who, however, did not happen to be a Jew. He was looked upon as a doctor of higher standing. But if the village healer served no useful purpose for the Jews in his regular profession, he had another which was placed freely at our disposal. He was an inveterate card-player, and among the pupils whom he instructed in his favourite game —Préférence—there were also a few of the young Jewish bloods of Swislowitz. Préférence was looked upon as the aristocratic game, standing as far above our favourite, "Sixty-six," as auction bridge does above poker. As Préférence players some of our young men actually broke into the Russian "aristocratic" society of Swislowitz, and were finally invited to the house of the priest and even of the commissioner himself.

The two town priests, Yuremitch and Matzkevitch, lived on pretty much the same terms as two Jewish Rabbis in a village about large enough for the services of half a Rabbi— that is to say, like two cats in one sack. They were already elderly men in my time. Matzkevitch was a simple priest of low rank: Yuremitch stood somewhat higher in the ecclesiastic scale. He was a Blagatschini. Matzkewitch was long and lean, and resembled an Egyptian mummy. Yuremitch was plump, with an imposing head of hair, black and silver, drawn into a pigtail behind, and an Assyrian beard. Above all, he had a splendid face, the face of a true prelate. Matzkevitch's parish was the poorer one, Yuremitch's the richer. Matzkevitch lived the life of a peasant labourer: worked in the field, ploughed, harvested and threshed, fished, gathered berries and mushrooms. Yuremitch lived the life of a nobleman, was addicted to card-playing, drank the rarest wines, and used to arrange great receptions and even dances. Matzkevitch was an ascetic, rigorously orthodox, severe in his interpretation of religious duty. Yuremitch was liberal, easygoing, with a happy-go-lucky relation toward his church. But his cheerful looks and his graceful gestures carried him further than his embittered colleague. I remember that even we, the Jewish children, were fond of Yuremitch, and though he was a priest of the Greek Orthodox Church we often went up to him shyly and kissed his hand. He had a charming way of stretching out his hand: it was a plump and pretty hand, which seemed to invite the kisses of the faithful. But we were afraid of Matzkevitch. There was not a glimmer of friendliness in his harsh features. But the older Jews, the pious ones particularly, reserved their respect for Matzkevitch. True, a Greek Orthodox priest, a superstitious "remitter of sins," but an ascetic nevertheless, an honest servant of his God.

The following were the grandest buildings in Swislowitz: the Synagogue—which was also the Beth Ha-Midrash or Study House, for it was only after my time that they built the plain Shuhl, or Synagogue, a place for prayer, but not for study: two Greek Orthodox churches in Byzantine style, the churches of Yuremitch and Matzkevitch: a Catholic cloister in Gothic style, dilapidated, almost collapsing, with age. The government would not permit the Catholics to build a new cloister. Nor did Swislowitz possess a Catholic priest of its own. It may have done, at one time, for I remember, as in a dream, a house opposite the cloister, and a white-robed figure issuing from it. Very seldom were the doors of the cloister open. It happened only when the visiting priest came all the way from Babrusk.

In addition to the above, there were the two government buildings on the same street—the police headquarters and the public school. All these buildings were of wood, the great logs lying horizontally. But in the case of the churches and the cloister, the logs stood up perpendicularly.

At the end of the southern spur of the broad street was the "Castle Hill," and on top of it stood the only real structure in town, five stories high and built of crude cut stones. To be exact, only the first two stories were built of stone: the upper three, in the form of a hexagon, were of wood, and out of them four gigantic wings, ruined and motionless, protruded. For the building was originally intended as a windmill, and it was put up by a half-mad magnate of the locality. There was a rumour that at one time the mill had actually worked, and had ground out flour. But I remember it only as a ruin. On top of that hillock there stood, next to the windmill, an empty house—for the manager. And next to the house stood the tumble-down stables, as empty as the house.

The only guardians of the ruin were four old birches in the foreground, at the foot of the hillock, with wooden benches in their shadow. Sabbath afternoons we used to take a walk to the ruin, and ascend Castle Hill. The prospect was beautiful: two rivers running parallel, each on one side of the town, then a graceful bend in one of the rivers, where it turns to pour itself into the other: beyond the rivers the green, soft meadows, and beyond the meadows the dark forests. At night no one went near the ruin, for then it was full of doleful creatures; owls dwelt there, and satyrs danced there. There were some who told that in the dead of night, when the town lay wrapped in sleep, they had seen lights moving through the rooms, and the vast wings suddenly began to revolve, and the millstones to grind. . . . In later years, however, I learned that there were boys and girls of spirit in our town, whom stories of ghouls and satyrs could not frighten away: and they spent many a happy hour in the late evenings among the ruins on the hill—and, astonishingly enough, always in the darkest and most terrifying corners.

The Jewish population of Swislowitz lived in the upper half of the town, near the ruined windmill, and the gentile population in the lower half, in the direction of the Minsk road. But the division was not exact, for it so fell out that right in the midst of the Jewish quarter were the homes of the gentile "aristocracy," and more than one Jewish family took rooms in the gentile section.

The Jewish houses were, as a rule, handsomer and better built than those of the gentiles; as against this, however, the gentile courtyards were thickly planted with trees of all kinds, fruit-bearing and others. Among us the love of nature seldom carried us further than the care of a vegetable garden, but even this was relegated to the women. An exception was made, of course, when the vegetable garden was cultivated as a matter of business, and therefore called for more attention.

There must have been very few idlers in our town, for I cannot remember any one who did not work hard. In the summer the gentiles worked in their fields, in winter in the forests. Out of one hundred and fifty families there were perhaps a dozen paupers, i.e. such as did not have their own little plot. But the Jews, too, were hard workers. And among them the two families which were most distinguished for industry, endurance, and thrift were the Poliessukes and the Kanarkes.

The Poliessukes were the chief raft-binders in the town, and controlled the monopoly on the labour for this industry. It had been theirs for many generations, and they were considered the most skilful in the trade. During the winter they were peddlers, and used to wander, often in the most fearful weather, from village to village, carrying huge packs on their backs. The family was divided into a large number of branches, but they lived an extraordinarily clannish life, like some Arab tribe with the sheik at the head. The elders ruled with an iron hand, and the younger people obeyed. The Poliessukes were famous for their physical strength. All of them were hardened by labour and exposure, of magnificent build and with muscles like the roots of old trees. They lived the simple, penurious life of peasants, adding to their savings kopeck by kopeck. I remember how one of them, a young man by the name of Ari Vol, who had just married and set up housekeeping for himself, came before Passover into the store of my older sister to buy wheat flour for the festival. We used to reckon that ten pounds of meal was about the right portion per head for the duration of the festival. Among the "genteel" five pounds a head was thought sufficient. The family of Ari Vol consisted, of course, of himself and his wife: he demanded a sack of flour weighing five *pud* —two hundred pounds. A number of people who happened to be in the store burst into a shout of laughter. Whereupon the young giant blushed, and stammered, "It's very hard, you know, to fill yourself up on wheat." I don't believe that any member of the Poliessuke family had ever eaten his fill of wheat meal, for they looked upon wheat as one of the greatest luxuries. Even the loaf which ornamented the table on the Sabbath eve was baked of corn, and it was only on the most important festivals that they adorned their table with wheat bread.

The second family, the Kanarkes, had a monopoly of their own on the supply of butcher's meat. Though they too were famous for their skill in saving their kopecks, they had already achieved a higher standard of living and ate wheat bread every Sabbath. Further than this their imagination did not carry them.

The names by which these families were known, by the way, were in reality descriptive, and had nothing to do with their genealogy. The former were called Poliessukes (*poliessie*, a forest) because of their association with the timber trade, and the latter Kanarkes (canaries) because of their diminutive size.

I come now to the last point in our townlet—the cemetery, the Dwelling of Eternity.

The Jewish cemetery lay at a remove of two kilometres beyond the fields of the peasants, and on the road to Minsk. The cemetery of the gentiles lay closer to the town, but in the opposite direction, on the way to Babrusk. As children we were taken to visit the cemetery only on Tisha d'Ab, the ninth day of the month of Ab, the day of the Black Fast, when we mourn for the destruction of both Temples, the first and the second. For the children, however, the day of mourning was a joyous festival. The very young ones did not fast. The outing, too, was a marvellous affair. We ran about in the cemetery in our stockinged feet; we made ourselves little wooden swords, painted them in gay colours, and girded them on like warriors of old. And then there was the actual pilgrimage to the cemetery and back, the stops on the road, when we dived into the woods in search of nuts, already half ripe at that time of the year, and black apples which we did not dare to eat, but which could be squeezed out for their juice and made the best kind of ink—just as good as you can buy in a shop. And then there were blackberries, raspberries, blueberries, wimberries and other fruits, some of which were forbidden, but which it was none the less a pleasure to pluck and throw around.

During the rest of the year we might see the body of a dead Jew carried, amidst lamentations, toward the cemetery —but we children were forbidden to go. And we were mortally afraid of the cemetery too. But we were on most familiar terms with the cemetery of the gentiles. It lay on this side of the woods, and on many a pleasant summer afternoon, just before evening prayer, we used to climb on its fence and sit there telling stories, not a whit frightened either by the monuments or the crosses. The explanation may be found in the ideas which were planted in our young minds with regard to death and the soul and the next world. In our little world it was an accepted fact among Jews that gentiles have no souls: they have only a spirit. If I were asked today what precisely was the difference between a "soul" and a "spirit" I could not answer. But as a little boy it was quite clear to me that a "soul" lives after death, and a "spirit" does not. And since the gentiles had no souls, what was there to be afraid of?

The roads which led to Minsk in the one direction, and Babrusk in the other, were planted with colonnades. There were four lines of birches, making three alleys, two at the sides for foot-travellers, and a wide one in the centre for carts and carriages. The colonnades were planted in the time of Catherine the Great. They were the Great Road, the Route du Roi.

The way to Babrusk lay over a long bridge which crossed the Swisla. The river itself was narrow enough, but because of the floods we had to make the bridge a great deal wider than the river. To the villages beyond the Beresina we went by a ferry, which had been leased by the landowner to Akiba David Dvaretzer. Dvaretz was the settlement or hamlet on the other side of the lake. It consisted of two houses: the inn, where Akiba David lived with his large family, and the cottage which belonged to the peasant who used to pull the rope of the ferry. Akiba David was a gigantic Jew, and of his two sons one was renowned for his stature, the other for his incredible strength. In our town they were despised as earthy peasants. What business had Jews to be either so gigantic of stature or so incredibly strong? They must have got their strength from Esau, the *goy*, the gentile. Not thus were the sons of Jacob. But if they were looked down on by the Jews, Akiba David and his sons were thoroughly respected by the peasants of the surrounding villages, none of whom ever dared to make themselves obstreperous round the ferry. They knew that on the place where Akiba David or a son of his once placed a hand the grass never grew again.

Later, when I went to *cheder* (elementary Hebrew school), I learned in *chumesh* (the Pentateuch, or Five Books of Moses) that there had once been an Aram Naharaim, the Land of the Two Rivers (Mesopotamia), and that beyond the river had dwelt Terah, the Father of Abraham, and therefore the grandfather of our people—Terah, an ignorant man, who worshipped idols. The picture then became clear to me. For Mesopotamia was our own little town of Swislowitz, lying between two rivers; and there sure enough, on the other side of the river, was Terah, father of Abraham, none other than Akiba David Dvaretzer.

As far as I remember, the relations between the Jews and the gentiles in our town were friendly enough. Until the

36

death of Alexander the Second I do not think that we knew what it was to be afraid of a gentile. True, we lived in two distinct worlds, but it never occurred to us that *their* world was the secure one, while the foundations of *ours* were shaky. On the contrary, we accounted our world the nobler, the finer, and the higher. Of course we learned even as children that we Jews were a people in exile, such being the divine decree, but that had nothing to do with the details of our daily life. The exile would come to an end when the Messiah would appear, riding on his white ass: but in the interim we did not stand on a lower level than the gentiles. We had a country in common, and we also had in common an Emperor who, seated on his throne, stretched his protecting hand over Jew and gentile alike. True, we were afraid of the police sergeant and the commissioner—but were not the gentiles just as much afraid as we?

The Rav (Rabbi) of our town never alluded to the country and to the Emperor except as "our" country and "our" Emperor. As evidence of the fact that the Emperor was good and wise, dispensing justice to all, we were told that under his outer garments he wore the Arba Kanfoth—the four-fringed ritualistic undergarment. In the Emperor's case, however, the two twisted fringes which fell behind were in perfect order, according to all the religious prescriptions of the Rabbis: while the two fringes which fell in front were torn out: one half of the shawl (behind) was therefore valid, and the other half was void. With the first half he reigned over the Jews, with the second half over the gentiles.

I cannot remember the first touches of the fingers of life, waking me in the dawn of memory. More than once I have tried my hardest to pierce the mist beyond a certain point, to carry the thread of recollection one inch farther back.

All my efforts have been vain. Sometimes I have felt that Nature sets as definite a term to our beginning as to our end, and just as we cannot hold open the book when the hands of death begin to close it, so we cannot open it as long as the hands of life are determined still to keep it closed.

Two incidents flicker on the fringes of my mind, the first vague acknowledgments of the sense of motion in life—the wedding of my older sister, the death of my younger sister. I cannot even tell how much older I was than my younger sister. I only know that her death occurred before I had been enrolled as a *cheder* boy—that is, before I was four years old. My older sister, Hannah Breine, married into a Jewish family of Babrusk.

Of the wedding I remember nothing, except the great reception arranged on the auspicious afternoon when the bridegroom came over from Babrusk, in the company of the stately retinue of parents, relatives, and friends of the family. All the rest I must rebuild out of my own fancy: the bridal canopy, under which the young couple became man and wife, lifted on its four poles in the courtyard of the Synagogue: the music that went with pomp and parade through the streets of Swislowitz and all the other appurtenances of a "rich" wedding. Nor do I remember my younger sister, little Esther. I remember only the terror which seized me when they uttered the word "death!" I remember also the burning tears that ran down my cheeks, and I remember running out, horrified, bewildered, to tell my new brother-in-law, Samuel Hirsh, that little Esther was dead. Most of all I remember the chill that came over me when he did not burst into tears, and the anger which followed the chill, and then the shame which followed both. But I cannot remember how my parents bore the death of their baby. I suppose they bore it as all good, pious Jews bear similar bereavements.

It is forbidden to mourn too deeply and to weep too long, and if the tears still persist in rising from the heart, they must be choked back before they reach the eyes and brim over.

But the third great incident of my early, pre-*cheder* life is quite clear in my mind: it stands, as it were, with feet planted firm on the threshold of my memory, on this side of the mists. My father made preparations for a journey to the vast, tumultuous city of Babrusk. He had already packed his portmanteau, and had put on his wide travelling mantle. All this time I had stood on one side, watching closely and silently. But no sooner did Are, the drayman, come driving up with his cart, than I shot from the house like an arrow, wound myself into the spokes of one of the wheels, and began to scream at the top of my voice that I wanted to go with Father to Babrusk. My father was usually a stern man, but the hunger in me to see the city of Babrusk, concerning which we little ones had heard innumerable and incredible marvels, overcame my fear of him. And neither the angry reproaches of my father, nor his softer promises to bring me a wonderful present from the city of Babrusk, were of any avail. I refused to be intimidated or comforted, and continued screaming that I wanted to go with him.

This was my first serious battle with my father: "You are a big, strong man, but I can cry: let's see who'll win." Today Freud explains on totally different grounds the conflicts between father and child. I remember that this particular battle was long and obstinately contested; for some reason my father, stern and severe as he was, could not bring himself to leave me in tears. Seeing that he was powerless, he sent for my grandfather, and when I perceived the latter approaching, a sweet feeling of revenge and satisfaction welled up in me. I thought, "Ha! Big and strong as you are, you could not conquer me alone. You had to call Grandfather." My grandfather took me in his arms and began to tell me seriously that little children dared not travel to Babrusk; there were big forests in between, full of wild beasts; and there was only one protection—to repeat a certain secret, sacred verse which children did not know. He therefore proposed something else: he would have another drayman harness a wagon, and drive me not, God forbid, to Babrusk, through those terrible forests, but to the Count's estate which lay at a distance of only one kilometre from the town, and which was reached through open fields where there was nothing to fear. There, he promised me, he would let me play in the nobleman's own garden, where all sorts of trees grew, pears and apples of every size, and even grapes under glass covers.

The picture that my grandfather drew was so charming, so enticing, that all of a sudden I was flooded by a feeling of pity for my father, who had to journey to Babrusk through forests infested with fierce creatures. So I begged my father not to go on this dangerous journey, but instead to come with me and Grandfather to the Count's estate. And finally we arrived at a clever compromise. My father was to go to Babrusk and I with my grandfather to the estate. I accepted everything in good faith, and even gave my father permission to set out on his journey to Babrusk. But my father would not have it so. He waited until a second drayman had appeared, had harnessed the horse, and had made all the preparations for my own unpremeditated journey. Then, sitting at my grandfather's side on the wagon, I called out to my father to start, and above all not to forget the magic verse which alone could conquer the wild beasts. My grandfather pinched my cheek, recommended me to the bystanders as a clever little rascal—and we set off for the Count's estate.

This was my first, my very first journey. The wings of fancy carried me a thousand times faster than the plodding horse. I had the feeling that I was sweeping through the air. And every two or three minutes I turned around and observed, to my amazement and disgust, that the town of Swislowitz was still quite visible. And I wanted it to disappear. I wanted to find myself at the point where earth and heaven meet, where, according to the accounts of playmates, a window opens into the skies. This is the window through which the tired sun crawls at night and lies down to sleep.

When at last we did reach the gardens, the houses of Swislowitz were no longer to be seen, and I was a happy child. On every side of me were countless fruit trees, with the first fruit of the year on them. My grandfather told me that I could pluck all the pears and apples that I wanted: but something in me, a mingling of happiness and a tender regard for the young, innocent fruit, kept me back. I was satisfied with the fruits which had fallen prematurely from the twigs. My grandfather kept his second promise, too. He led me to a house that was covered all over with glass, and there I saw, for the first time in my life, grapes, real grapes, the kind we got only in the late summer at home, actually growing on thin, tangled bushes. I did not dare to pluck any of them. I only fondled them. Who would dare to pluck so rare a fruit?

Of other individual incidents in my pre-*cheder* years I remember nothing. One general memory I have, however, and that is that I was a merry child. I liked to play, to joke, to tease, with older people not less than with children of my own age. My mother told me that even in the cradle I was the merriest of all her children, always in good humour and full of life. In one respect only I caused her much trouble: I would resist with stubborn energy her efforts to rock me to sleep: and I would close my eyes only when I had exhausted myself completely. So much my mother told me. What I myself remember is that I took full advantage of my healthy and powerful young frame, and saw to it that my playmates should treat me with the right degree of respect. Not that I actually wanted to hit them till it hurt. Such was not my nature. But I did like to hand out a punch, or a thump, playfully, *en passant* as it were. As against this, however, my friends knew that I could be very useful to them. Whenever a quarrel broke out, I was always on the side of the weaker. And this rôle of the elder, administering justice, tickled me mightily.

I shall have to confess here that what pleased me most was not the opportunity to dispense justice in a wicked world, but the simple fact that my playmates obeyed me. A feeling of pride came to me very early, and I began to look upon myself as one who stood on a higher level. I do not think that I became offensively haughty. For as a counterweight against this dangerous circumstance there was the powerful democratic influence of my home, and the behaviour of my father and my mother. As often as occasion presented itself, my mother would tell me that pride was a great fault, and that one ought to play with all children equally. But something even stronger contributed to keep me fairly healthy in mind: I was exceedingly fond of company, and could not play alone. And the first requisite of the haughty spirit is to be able to do without those whom it holds in contempt. As I could not do without my friends, I had to treat them in a way which kept them at my side. And the fact was that I was in my element only when I was surrounded by a small army of playmates.

I was almost as happy with the older folk as in the company of my own kind. Among these my physical prowess counted for nothing, of course. I therefore had to create a place for myself by means of something else—my tongue. There was company in the house at almost every hour of the day, neighbours who dropped in for a chat, for business, or for a glass of tea. I knew every one of them almost as well as I knew the members of my own family, and I listened with delight to the stories which they told. Unlike those stories which were the diversion of the peasants, the ones I heard in my home had little to do with robbers, murderers, thieves, and bandits. Instead they dealt with the deeds of pious Jews, the prodigies of famous scholars, the achievements of saints and sages, their sayings and their sufferings. Whatever I heard I translated into my own language, and gave it forth again as my own. It was my special way of finding myself at home among the older people, a participant in their conversations.

And my memory, which fails me in detail, still reproduces the wonder and the freedom and the joy of those first years, soon to end when I achieved the status of the *cheder* boy. From morning till night I was my own master. Father and mother both were busy. The idea of a governess was quite unknown in Swislowitz, and the very suggestion would, I am convinced, have been scorned as a sign of decadent extravagance. The truth is that at the age of four I was treated like a big boy. Whenever I forgot to put on my Arba Kanfoth (the four-fringed ritual under-garment), my mother would speak to me seriously, as to a grown-up, and tell me how shameful it was for an adult Jew to be running about like a heathen, without the reminder of his Jewishness hung about his body. There were grounds for fear that I would grow up into a wild rascal, no credit to a pious Jewish home: and the chief ground was that I had too sharp a head and too quick a tongue. The source of worry was also a source of family pride. My particular forte was arithmetic, and my father taught me a trick (I have long since forgotten it) of putting the fingers together in some special way to facilitate multiplication. His pride frequently got the better of his common sense, and he used to show me off before our friends.

The days of my freedom, my unrestrained happiness, drew to a close. I remember clearly the evening which was the overture to the second act in the drama of my life. At the close of one Sabbath, when the farewell prayer to the holy day had already been intoned, and we sat with friends round the samovar, my father drew me over to him, and said, "My son: most children begin their *cheder* at the age of five. I think yours is a better head than most, and we'll start you a year earlier. From tomorrow on, you will be a *cheder* boy. Enough of this wild freedom. It is time for you to begin learning Torah."

The news, coming so unexpectedly, was like a light that broke upon my soul. At a single bound I changed in my own eyes, dropped the status of the carefree rascal, took on the dignity of the *cheder* boy. I would begin learning Torah next day, the Torah, concerning which my mother had told me so much that was dear and marvellous, the Torah which occurred in the refrain of so many of the songs she hummed in the later afternoon, before evening prayer. The world opened before me, and I saw myself a famous Jewish scholar, a prodigy, a saint: and the gates of the next world opened too: the world to come, Paradise, the golden thrones—all words which were intimately woven into the texture of our homely life, more familiar to me, by the frequency of their repetition, than a thousand physical objects.

CHAPTER THREE: CHEDER YEARS

"Two things it's never too late to do: to die and to become a teacher in a *cheder*." Only the Jew who has known the old life can understand the bitterness of that proverb, for to become a teacher in a *cheder* was the last resort of every failure. If a young husband who, according to the ancient custom, had been living with his in-laws while he studied the Sacred Books, suddenly found himself compelled to earn a living: if a merchant met with disaster, and was thrown on the street: if a decent paterfamilias saw his house burn down, and found himself without a roof over his head—the first thing he would turn to, till fortune changed, would be the job of the *melamed*, the teacher in the *cheder*. It was one of the most melancholy phenomena in our Jewish life of the last century, for it shows clearly how low the concept of child education had fallen among us. Parents sent their children to *cheder* in obedience to tradition, but they paid little attention to the accomplishments or the character of the *melamed*.

There were three kinds of teachers: the first taught the child simply to read Hebrew: the second taught the elements of the Five Books of Moses, and the remainder of the Bible—for with us the Pentateuch occupies a place of special sanctity: it is the first thing taught the child, and it looms largest in our religious life. The third teacher taught Talmud. Children passed through the three grades of *mel-*

amdim (teachers), according to age. But it was very, very seldom that the *melamdim* possessed anything like the necessary qualifications. The tender hopes of a coming generation fell into hands which were frequently ill-chosen, and sometimes downright dangerous.

It should be remembered that the *melamed* was not merely a teacher in the technical sense, but also a mentor and trainer and complete educator. The majority of Jewish homes were wretchedly poor. The father was away from home from early morning till late at night. Either he had a regular occupation, and toiled at it twelve and fourteen and sixteen hours a day, or else he was a *Luftmensch*, living from hand to mouth, petty merchant, broker, commission-man all rolled into one, running from client to client, from shop to shop, like a wild animal hunting for a bite of food. But not the father alone was thus enslaved. The mother too had her share of it. With few exceptions the Jewish mother not only kept her house going, but went out too, took in washing, laboured in the gardens of others. She found work as a berry-gatherer: she went looking for feathers in the meadows where the geese were fed, or plucked the feathers of slaughtered fowl to stuff cushions—the last an occupation which was reserved for the late night, when the little ones were asleep, and the one lamp was trimmed and turned down very low. This was the lot of the average housewife. Still worse was the lot of the shopkeeper, chained to her store from the earliest hour of dawn till late into the night: perspiring in the choking heat of summer, or shivering in the bitter winter cold over the little earthen stove. So poverty stood with lifted whip over Jewish parents, driving them in a blind circle all day, and separating them from their children.

And children were never lacking. They seemed to come

in droves. Every house was a pyramid, with father and mother as foundation and the little ones building it up to the apex. Girls were not so bad; they were quieter at play and more obedient. But when it came to boys, there was only one salvation for the parents: to turn them over, for the length of the whole day, into the hands of a severe *melamed*. And thus the entire point of the *cheder* was lost: it might have served as a salvation for the child from the wretched environment of its home. Its actual purpose was to save the poor parents from their own children. Thus the *melamed* became the lord and master of the Jewish child, and the *cheder*, the narrow one-roomed school, lightless, unclean, laid its stamp on the Jewish child and brought ruin and misery on its tenderest years. In my time the Jewish *cheder* was already an institution rotten in every corner. From a folk-school it had become transformed into a sort of reformatory, in which every inmate was regarded as a young criminal. Only the very few, the chosen ones of fortune, escaped from those years of oppression more or less unharmed, with minds and bodies unruined.

I was one of those happy few. But it was only in later years that I understood how fearful had been the danger from which I had escaped, and to whom I owed gratitude for the escape.

It was a happy Sunday morning in the early spring, soon after the Passover. My body still had on it the taste of the new suit, with the real pockets. That morning my mother woke me early, gave me a bite to eat—I was still considered young enough to eat before prayers—and sent me off with Father to the Shuhl (Synagogue). There I sat down right next to him—a privilege which I seldom enjoyed—and he bade me follow the prayer-leader with the closest attention. Some of the responses I already knew by heart. When prayers were over my father led me to Mottye the *melamed*, and there the formal introduction took place: "Mottye, this is your youngest pupil. Schmerel, this is your *melamed*."

Of course I already knew Mottye, the terror of the small boys of Swislowitz. For though that ancient proverb, "Never tell tales out of school," is as current in Jewish life as elsewhere, it availed there as little as everywhere else. And in that youthful world of ours the day's news bulletins never omitted to mention which boy had been laid across the bench; and we knew also who had yelled during the punishment, and who had borne his stripes in grim silence, like a hero, refusing to give the *Rebbi* (teacher) the satisfaction of a single yell. And Mottye the *melamed* was accounted the cruelest of all when it came to whipping or to pinching. But I also knew Mottye in his rôle of baker of big corn loaves (the gentler art of baking rolls and similar delicacies was beyond him). As a matter of fact it was his wife, who was twice his size, who did the baking. He merely helped her, and then delivered the loaves to the few important householders. But the townlet was not much interested in the division of labour between man and wife, so that Mottye the *melamed* and Mottye the baker were one and the same person. He had other names, too—Mottye the whipper, and Mottye the pincher, and Mottye the bean, this last both on account of his diminutive size and his habit of rolling when he walked, like a little goblin.

At the bottom of Mottye's face there was a little sparse beard, like that of a goat: and small as he was, the addition of the beard, instead of giving him dignity, only made him look like a boy with a false beard on. He seems to have known that the dignity of his appearance was an insufficient source of discipline; so what his goat-beard could not do he entrusted with more certainty to the leathern thongs of his cat-o'-three-tails. It would be quite wrong to imagine that every poor *melamed* had a leathern lash. Most of them had to be content with the straws of a broom. But those who had acquired a larger school could indulge in the luxury of a leathern lash.

Immediately after *melamed* and pupil had been officially introduced, the entire company, relatives and friends, with Grandfather Solomon at the head, repaired to our house. There a fine table had been prepared, with sweetmeats and drinks. I was seated in the place of honour, and a toast was drunk. My mother herself served the guests. To me was handed a prayer-book. Two of the pages had been smeared with honey, and I was told to lick the honey off. And when I bent my head to obey, a rain of copper and silver coins descended about me. They had been thrown down, so my grandfather told me, by the angels. For the angels, he said, already believed in me, knew that I would be a diligent pupil, and were therefore prepared to pay me something in advance. I was immensely pleased to hear that my credit with the angels was good, and I stole a look at my mother. A sweet, tender smile played on her lips, and I could not make out whether it was my credit with the angels which pleased her so, or whether she was keeping back some happy secret of her own.

When the ceremony was over, my father lifted me up, wrapped me from head to foot in a silken Talith, or praying-shawl, and carried me in his arms all the way to the *cheder*. My mother could not come along—this was man's business. Such was the custom among us. The child was carried in the arms of the father all the way to the *cheder*. It was as if some dark idea stirred in their minds that this child was a sacrifice, delivered over to the *cheder*—and a sacrifice must be carried all the way.

Mottye the *melamed* had his own house, standing on a little hill. The house seems to have been patterned after Mottye, and not after his wife: it was small, dilapidated and overgrown with moss: the moss was the counterpart of his sparse goat-beard. The door was small, but Mottye went through without bending. My father had to stoop. Inside, he sat me down without further ceremony, gathered up the prayer-shawl, and left the *cheder*. There I was, on a small, hard wooden bench, with nine other children, two of them my first cousins—Gershon, the son of Uncle Meyer, and Areh the son of Uncle Schmerel—both of them a year older, but also beginners, like myself. There and then, without preliminaries, I was plunged into the work.

The table in front of the bench consisted of rough, unplaned planks, and the heads of the big nails which fastened them together stuck out, so that it was easy to get caught on them. The children sat on two benches, five on each side of the table, and Mottye the *melamed* sat at one end. He had taken off his topcoat, and had replaced his hat with a pointed skull-cap: thus his face lay between two points, the upper point of the skull-cap, the lower point of his goat-beard. In one hand he held a wooden pointer. He did not sit still, but swayed back and forth as he taught. He bade us keep our hands above the table, look out for the nails, and sit respectfully.

In the same room stood the large oven for baking, and above the oven was the usual alcove where one might sleep on frosty winter nights. An odour of fresh-baked bread filled the room. On one wall hung the leathern thongs, and toward one side was a small bench, just large enough for the boy whom evil fortune should befall. Then the Rebbi made the round of the table, administered a friendly pinch to the cheek of every boy, seated himself in his place, and began the singsong lesson. And this was our induction into the immortal temple of the Jewish Torah, which is wider than all the earth and deeper than the sea. . . .

The children had to be broken in, for it was impossible to drag them away abruptly from their play. So during the beginning we were in *cheder* for only half days; that is to say, from nine in the morning until four in the afternoon. But later, when the class was divided into groups, we would get only brief intervals of liberty during the day, taking turn and turn about for play.

But I remember that in spite of that love of study which my mother, by the songs she sang and the stories she told, had instilled in me, I was happy when Mottye dismissed the class, and I could get away from the "bean," from the face with its pointed skull-cap above and its pointed beard below. On that first day the ten of us burst out of *cheder* in the afternoon, filled with joy, singing the crooning melodies which enfolded our first lessons.

Ten young "mighty men of Israel" ran out into the street, and ten powerful young throats filled the air of Swislowitz with music:

"Kametz Aleph A-a, Kametz Beth Ba-a, Kametz Gimel
    Ga-a,
A-a, Ba-a, Ga-a, here we all are."

Even before I became a *cheder* boy—I think it was from the age of three on—not a day went by but I went to Synagogue regularly, for early morning prayer, for afternoon prayer, and for evening prayer. I went either in the company of my father, or in that of my brother Meyer, five years older than myself, who was already, when .I began *cheder*, a Gemara boy; that is, a student of the Talmud. My mother, who never once missed her prayers, made it her special duty to see that we should not miss ours—though the truth of the matter was that we, the very youngest, were not really there to pray. We were merely in attendance. There were only two responses which we were required to make like the grown-ups, and the rest of the time we played outside. We played nuts, ducks and drakes, prisoner's base, and heaven knows what else. One of us, however, was stationed at the door of the Shuhl. It was his business to sniff the air, as it were, and get the feeling of the approaching moment when we would have to be present for the responses. Since we were too young to follow the long prayers in detail, we had to rely not on knowledge but on instinct. And the moment the guardian at the door called out, "Hey! The response!" we left our play on the instant—though the game might be at its most passionate climax—and tumbled into the Synagogue.

And now came my first conflict with Mottye the bean. I am not quite sure whether it happened on the first day after my induction, or on the second, but it happened soon enough. And it came about in this wise. Among my little group, I was the commanding general, issued regular instructions as to the games to be played and the times when they were to be played. Apparently I did not quite realize the extent of the change which had been introduced into my life with my entry into the *cheder*, for on the morning in question I no sooner arrived at the Shuhl for prayers than I gathered my army together, trooped out with it, and decided on the game. I did not even bother to appoint a "sentinel," for it was much too early. The cantor had not even begun. We had been playing for only a few minutes, and the response was still quite a way off, when suddenly there appeared, silently, as if he had shot up out of the earth, Mottye the bean, wrapped in his prayer-shawl, and with phylacteries on arm and forehead. I remember that on one side of the head phylactery the letter *shin* (representing the word Shaddai, or Almighty) had its usual three points, but on the other side there was a letter *shin* which in an ecstasy of piety blossomed into four points. There he was, immobile, silent, suspicious. The little army fell into a panic. Like soldiers caught larking by their officer in an earnest moment, they stood, wordless and trembling, at attention. I was less frightened than astonished. What was Mottye the bean doing here?

And if at least he would say something! What was it he wanted, stealing furtively on us, like this, in the midst of our play?

There he waited, silent as a ghost, looking us over with his green, cat-like eyes, looking us over as a group, then each one of us separately. And we looked back at him. It lasted a whole minute. Meanwhile we saw something kindling in his eyes. He was planning something, choosing some one. And then, sure enough, he picked his victim. Carefully, softly, deliberately, he went up to one of my playmates, seized him by the right ear with two fingers of his left hand, and with all five fingers of his right hand delivered a resounding slap on his left cheek. "*Cheder* boys don't play during prayers! When every one is praying *cheder* boys remain standing near their Rebbi. Back inside, you little heathens!"

Thunderstruck, humiliated, we crawled after him into the Shuhl. Not one of us had the courage to defend himself, to protest at least, to demand an explanation. We followed him as though we had really committed a crime. But within me, I remember, my blood was boiling. First of all, how were we supposed to know? Only yesterday, or the day before, we had been permitted to play during the long prayers, and nobody had said a word. And secondly, if we were to be punished, why had he picked out one of us and thrown all the guilt on him? In brief, the injustice which my Rebbi had committed was great indeed, and the more I brooded on it the greater it became, so that by the time we left Shuhl it was a mountain, a Pelion of evil. I decided there and then that the thing could not be permitted to pass just so. I would lodge complaint against my Rebbi before my father and mother. . . . Let them decide who was in the right and who was in the wrong.

I was on pins and needles during the long morning of prayer. And the last response had not been uttered when, without asking permission of my Rebbi, I flew out of the Shuhl, completely certain that my parents would be on my side. Young as I was I knew that the Rebbi could not be slapped in turn: and I also knew that the slap he had given could never be taken back. But I wanted only one kind of revenge. I wanted grown-up people with a sense of justice to declare clearly that the Rebbi had been wrong. Let Mottye the bean know that there were powers above him, juster than himself.

I got home before my parents, but I could not wait. I told my story to every one, in rehearsal. And then, when my parents arrived, all my pent-up rage burst out of me, so that I could not tell the story of Mottye the bean and my playmate who had been slapped, in proper sequence. I began toward the end, plunged suddenly into the middle, and arrived at the beginning. It took several minutes before I could catch my breath. And then I calmed myself a little, and told the thing more coherently, and there was not the slightest doubt in my mind that sentence could be pronounced only in one way.

But this incident was fated to bring me the first great disillusionment of my life.

My father heard me to the end, and refused to enter into any sort of argument or discussion. "The Rebbi is right, and you are behaving like a fool." Those were his words, sharply uttered, final. I tried to begin all over again, but in vain. My father interrupted me and refused to let me finish.

I turned with imploring eyes toward my mother. She was the last and highest court of appeal. Now, after my signal failure with my father, I was no longer so certain of myself. It was here that the real disillusionment came. For my mother, my own mother, was not on my side. True, she was softer than my father, and her sentence was delivered more mildly. But she too said, "My child, you must know that a Rebbi can do no wrong, a Rebbi can do no wrong." But I repeated my unanswerable complaint: What right had he to choose just one of us, and slap him alone? My mother answered, "But that is the way of the world, my child. You can't slap everybody, so today you slap one, and tomorrow you slap another, and in the meantime all the others are afraid and learn to behave."

I must explain that the slap in and for itself did not astonish me, for I knew that Rebbis slapped. In fact I had already seen boys being slapped by their Rebbi. But those slaps had something remote in them. Here was a slap which had fallen very close to me. And as my mother had put it, "Today you slap one, tomorrow another. . . ." I perceived that the older people had made a conspiracy among themselves, and a hunger for revenge awoke in me. I alone, without any adult to help me, would have to take revenge on

Mottye the bean. . . . I had no plan, but I took counsel with no one, young or old. I buried my rage deep in my heart, and waited for the opportune moment.

That day I sat in *cheder* plunged in sadness. I enjoyed nothing, neither the lessons nor the games outside the house. I had hoped that at least Mottye would not be himself that day. He would be depressed and absent-minded, brooding on the injustice which he had committed. And that, too, would be something of a revenge for me. Nothing of the sort! Mottye sat there, swaying back and forth, collected, as much at his ease as on other days, his little face enclosed between the two points. And not only the Rebbi, but the boys, too, were the same as ever! The entire incident had passed without leaving a mark on any of them. "If that be so," I decided silently, "there is no one to talk to. I too will pretend that I have forgotten." But I could not forget, and for many days my happiness was marred by the protests which I had to choke back.

In the afternoon of that day we came out of *cheder* as usual, but I did not join in the singing. The spring afternoons in Swislowitz were always beautiful, and most beautiful of all was the hour before sunset. Every one comes out then for a breath of fresh air, and the population of the town is seated on the porches and balconies before the houses. Along the broad street the shepherd drives home the flocks: the goats lead, at their head the guide, and after them come the cattle, some with young. The housewives leave their places on the porches, each one to seek out her own goat or cow, to drag it home and get a glass of warm milk for the youngest children. Some of the animals have special names. One of them, a large, quiet cow, slow and stately of motion, is called the Rebbitzin, the rabbi's wife. From the far-off meadows and woods the fresh odour of the springing earth is carried across the town, and a spirit of peace and rest descends upon the houses, upon the watchers on the balconies, upon the shepherd and the flocks.

I cannot remember what became of my plans for revenge on Mottye the bean. I imagine they came to nothing, but my relations with my first Rebbi remained cold and formal. There never awoke in me the faintest spark of love and respect for him. But I do remember that in later years, when I had become a student of Talmud, and was popular in the town, Mottye the bean would often come up to me, stroke my cheek, and declare fondly that he had always liked me and that he had been my best friend. One day he came to our house before evening service, and told us a story.

The story was told *to* the older people, but *at* me. "It is well known," said Mottye, "that one ought to respect one's Rebbi just as much as one's parents—if not more. This is what is written in all the sacred books. But a question arises, does it not, *which* Rebbi? For the child passes in time through the hands of several Rebbis, and a problem therefore arises as to which one has the precedence. Now this question was once brought up in the very highest place, namely before the Divine Tribunal above. And there the answer was given that the place of honour belongs to the Rebbi who taught you the alphabet—simple reading. And the reason is plain enough. The later Rebbis who taught you the Five Books, the Bible, the Mishnah and the Talmud, can have erred. Wittingly or unwittingly they may have misled you. But the Rebbi who taught you the Aleph Beth cannot make mistakes: he will not confuse a *gimmel* with a *nun*, a *shin* with a *samech*. And does not the whole of the Torah consist of letters, single letters in combination? The Rebbi who taught you the letters has laid a sure foundation, but those that come after him build walls which may be straight and may be crooked." The hint was given with a sledgehammer, but it had no effect on me. I remained as cold toward him as I had always been.

Apart from that famous slap, nothing remains of my memories of the first month in the *cheder*. I have a simple way of checking up: I cannot remember the names of the boys who got whipped that month. And a month without some one being whipped is quite impossible. Naturally I did not understand it then, but the picture has since become very clear in my mind. Mottye the bean was an ordinary sadist, with all the symptoms of the sadist. The whippings he administered had no educational purpose: they were an end in themselves. He derived an intense joy from the agonies of the little victim trembling and shivering on the bench. And he used to administer the whippings coldly, slowly, deliberately, in the full consciousness of power, and without ever betraying a spark of rage. This behaviour on the part of the Rebbi only increased the terror and anguish of the child—and thus in turn increased the joy of the Rebbi. All the entreaties in the world, all the frantic promises to behave in the future, were wasted. Mottye the bean did not budge: he asked the boy to let down his clothes, lie across on the bench, and get what was coming to him.

Some of my playmates were weak-natured, and used to submit at once, get their share of stripes, and then go into a corner to weep away the pain rather than the shame: for the truth is, when all of us were in the same boat, no one was ashamed in front of his fellows. But others, stronger and prouder, did not give in so easily. They fought and struggled, defended themselves tooth and nail, until they were exhausted. But in these cases too the Rebbi betrayed no anger. Coldly, silently, he wore the victim out, and when no spark of resistance remained, he put the boy quietly across the bench and pitched in with the leathern thongs.

He used the thongs with the same cruel joy for a slip of memory as for a misdemeanour. He was careful to explain why it was necessary to whip a boy who did not study well. "You must understand," he said, "that in every person there is a Good Spirit and an Evil Spirit. The Good Spirit has its own dwelling-place—which is the head. So has the Evil Spirit—and that is the place where you get the whipping. But the Good Spirit always remains at home, in its own place, whereas the Evil Spirit is forever creeping out of its den and pushing its way into the home of the Good Spirit. Now when both Spirits get into the head, the head gets stuffed up and there is no room for new ideas— the little boy can't learn. There's only one thing to be done: put the little boy across the bench and let him have it. Then the Evil Spirit hears some one knocking at his door, gets frightened, and runs back. That leaves the head free again and the boy can learn. And so, children"—he wound up— "I do you a service when I punish you. Really I do, for my conscience won't let me leave you to run about with your heads stuffed up and overcrowded."

He never got tired of telling the story of the Good Spirit and the Evil Spirit. Two or three times a week he repeated it—every time with unspoiled gusto, as if he had just invented it. In time we learned that he never told the story for nothing: it was the prelude to an invitation. He would finish up the story with the sudden startling question: "Come on, who's going to confess that the Evil Spirit has crawled up into his head?" A terrified murmur went up from the class, a mingling of asseverations and protestations: "Not me—not me—honestly." And Mottye the bean would look grinning round the class, with eyes popping out of his head, as if he could actually see the boy's Evil Spirit crawling out from the nape of his neck. As a matter of fact, his indecision was put on; he had already chosen the victim, but he derived an intense joy from the terror which the uncertainty created. After a dreadful pause, he would quietly address a cowering boy: "What's that you say? The Evil Spirit hasn't left its place? I'll have to look into that, and make sure for myself." And then the usual story of cold-blooded torture would begin.

I do not know whether Mottye the bean was the only sadist among the *melamdim*, but I do know that the elementary teachers had a free hand to whip their pupils—and they used it. The teachers of the Five Books—the Pentateuch—were a trifle more restrained. And the teachers of the Talmud students used the whip very rarely. But whipping was considered an integral part of the educational system. Every one knew the story about my uncle Meyer, the oldest son of my grandfather Solomon. I have already mentioned that this uncle of mine was not a very cultured sort of man. For the sake of appearances—because our family was among the well-to-do—a Rebbi (teacher) was still kept for Meyer after he was married. He went to *cheder* regularly to a certain Ziskind—a man who was quite a scholar. Ziskind was a Jew with a starved, cruel face, reminiscent of those pictures of the apostles which reflect so little credit on their race. When the famous incident took place my uncle Meyer must have been about sixteen years old—probably on the younger side. During *cheder* hours the news was suddenly brought to him that his wife had borne him his first child. But the messenger of the happy tidings found the new father, his nether garments down, lying across the bench, receiving the ministrations of his Rebbi. He was asked to dress himself at once and hurry home to his wife. But Ziskind, the Rebbi, met the situation coolly. He gravely requested the messenger to wait: "Time enough," he said. "I'm not through yet."

The reader may wonder why I consistently avoid my own share of stripes during that first *cheder* term. I am not trying to cover up anything, as it were. I just cannot remember. I am quite certain, of course, that I did not escape unscathed and dry-eyed from under the hands of Mottye the bean. But if I cannot recall the whippings, I do remember clearly my second great clash with him.

On a beautiful, warm summer morning I came home from first prayers and was suddenly seized with the desire to play hooky. And no sooner had I eaten than I ran out of the house, and found a lovely hiding-place in the deep grass behind the Catholic cloister. How my mother got to know, I cannot tell, but within half an hour she found me, and implored me to go to *cheder*. "It's no holiday," she pleaded, "and it is a sin to idle away the day." But I was obstinate. I refused to answer and also refused to budge. She left me— and a few minutes later Mottye the bean appeared. He did not utter a word. He grabbed me, lifted me in his arms, and began to carry me back to *cheder*. I struggled with all my strength, but he was too much for me. He carried me down the length of the broad street, pinching huge bruises in my flesh. But I was not inactive, either. I kicked him as often as I could, and with my hands alternately choked him and tried to pluck handfuls of hair from his goat-beard. A strange procession this, of teacher and pupil, passing before the eyes of the Jews of Swislowitz.

Until this day a shudder runs through my body when I think of the horrible world in which we passed the tenderest

61

years of our childhood. If the famous Joshua ben Gamala, the founder of the *cheder*, could have risen from his grave to see what had become of his idea of the folk-school, he would have hastened back in an agony of shame. I would not be wrong in saying that one-third of the *cheder* hours were taken up by the stupid, ugly squabbles between Rebbi and pupils; the remaining two-thirds poisoned by the first. Who knows how many genuine talents have been brutally done to death by the lash of the Rebbi, how many victims remained buried forever under the ruins of that institution known as the *cheder?* There is a legend which tells that when our forefathers were building Pithom and Raamses under the lash of the Egyptians, they were compelled to build their own living children into the walls of the pyramids and temples. And when the time came for the exodus, all these little ones suddenly sprang out alive from among the shattered walls. The first half of the legend certainly applies to the *cheder*—but of the second half I have my doubts.

The "course" given by Mottye the bean was generally of two years' duration: but sometimes it lasted three years— that is, six terms instead of four. It took all this time to teach the boy how to read Hebrew, and to translate the first few chapters or portions of the Five Books (the Pentateuch). From this the reader can gauge how pitifully meagre was the mental content of the *cheder*—just the mechanical addition of letter to letter, to build up words— planks held together by rusty nails. Not a song to relieve the ear of the unhappy child, not a picture to brighten the oppressed young eyes. The Jewish child was like a sensitive plant abandoned in some old, neglected garden on which neither rain fell, nor dew, and in which no loving hand ever tore out the weeds.

After the first term children were confined to the *cheder* for the entire day. The Rebbi, who thus became the complete master of the child, did not, however, pay any attention to the question of physical cleanliness. When the mother complained that the child came home in the evening altogether too dirty for a single day's play and study, the Rebbi used to retort sarcastically that he was not a wet nurse. He thought it beneath his dignity to worry about such matters.

I cannot stress too often the dominating, the exclusive, rôle which the *cheder* played in the life of the young Jewish boy. He saw his parents only for half an hour in the morning—before first prayers—and then for an hour in the evening, before he went to sleep. So it happened that in the majority of cases there was little intimacy between parents and children, and even between brothers, if they happened to be learning in different *cheders*. As between brother and sister there was even less opportunity for the ripening of friendship and affection. A second factor raised a wall between brother and sister, and alienated them in their earliest years. Girls were not sent to *cheder*, and had nothing to do with studies. The brother looked upon his sister as another kind of creature, belonging to another world. As if God had not created them different enough, the gulf between them was made still wider by differences in education and in duties. When my youngest brother grew old enough to differentiate between those grown-ups whom he might call by the familiar second person singular *du*, and those whom he had to address formally in the plural *Ihr*, he placed in the second class even his older sisters, and it took us quite a time to make him understand that he was entitled to the same familiarity with them as with the other members of the family.

CHAPTER FOUR: THE HOLY DAYS

THE first holiday which I observed as a *cheder* boy was Lag b'Omer ("the thirty-third day of the Omer"—the seven-week period between the Passover and the Pentecost). It celebrates the suspension of the plague among the pupils of Rabbi Akiba in the time of Bar Cochba, the mighty rebel who for three years carried on war against the Emperor Hadrian. They begrudged us a whole day of freedom, so we went to *cheder* for the morning session. But the atmosphere was festive. We used to bring boiled, coloured eggs to *cheder*: the poor boys brought two, one for the Rebbi, one for themselves. The richer boys brought more. The eggs were coloured by being boiled together with onion skins or nettle-leaves, or other plants.

The game of "coloured eggs" we learned from the gentiles who indulged in it round Easter time. It was simple enough. Each of the opponents held his egg at the broad end, and they tapped the narrow ends together. The first egg to crack was the vanquished. At the end of the games one veteran egg, unconquered and unbroken, was master of the field and owner of all the other eggs.

There was a story current in the town that one young peasant knew how to bewitch his eggs, so that they never broke in a contest. There were public tourneys for the peasant boys of the town. When the bells of the churches were pealing to indicate the close of the services, half the population gathered in the middle of the broad street, men, women, and children. And in the centre stood the young peasant, holding aloft the invincible boiled egg, and challenging the world to combat—like Goliath the Philistine standing in helmet and armour before the army and taunting the terrified Israelites. For a whole hour, sometimes for two, the young hero overcame all comers, and the heap of cracked, boiled eggs, the booty of war, grew larger and larger at his feet. The spectators watched the game with breathless interest, and, as boy after boy retreated vanquished and despoiled, they cried out loudly against the victor, not in enmity, but in astonishment.

One other game belonged to Lag b'Omer—bows and arrows, a memory of the struggle between the insurgent Jews and the Roman legions. We made the bows out of bent twigs, and the Rebbi himself taught us this game, because it was part of sacred history. He told us how the pupils of Rabbi Akiba had held war with the enemy. "Who knows," he said, narrowing down his little eyes, "but what some day you might find the art useful?" His ideas of warfare were drawn from sacred history. But he bade us be very careful, and not shoot at each other, for fear we might put out some one's eye. His caution was superfluous. Our bows never carried the arrows more than a couple of feet.

About that time of the year the spring began to ripen into summer—if luck was with us. The opening of summer was marked for us children by one traditional sign: we could no longer go into the woods and tap the birch trees. For in our town we milked not only the cows, but the trees too. As soon as spring began, young and old used to go to the forests, the old with hatchets, the young with small knives, and cut deep into the bark of the birch trees. Then, after a few minutes, a clear, sweet white liquid would come oozing out. The older people gathered the sap in buckets. The young ones used to stick a straw into the wounded tree, and drink the sap on the spot.

There were very few birch trees in town. We had to go either into the forests, or down to the colonnades of Catherine the Great. The only free hours we children had were Friday afternoon and Saturday—and on the Sabbath it was of course forbidden to cut trees. So we used to steal down to the great road when our elders were not watching. We had already begun to build up our own ritual.

The peasants too used to gather birch sap, but they had a way of their own. They used to come down to the forest with ladders, and make the cut in the tree high up. Then they bound a rope round the tree, and fastened a bucket just under the wound. In this way they were protected from young marauders, for the branches did not begin until high up, and it was impossible to climb up. The older people were very severe in these matters: the theft of some one else's bucket of sap was looked on as something specially heinous. What God sent for all, any one could take. But what any man had already appropriated from the hand of God was sacred.

But it was permitted for two people to use one and the same tree. And so trees on the road could be seen standing with double rows of wounds: the upper wounds inflicted by the peasants, the lower wounds inflicted by the Jews. Thus it was that we killed the trees for rafts, and those that we left living we tortured for their sap. And no one thought of their agony. For was not the entire town of Swislowitz, Jew and gentile, dependent on the trees for its very life?

Especially clear and firm in my memory is the first Pentecost of my *cheder* years, and the preparations which led up to it. I remember the clearness and the freshness of those days. I remember how my mother told me for the first time of the giving of the Torah, the Law, to the Children of Israel: of Mount Sinai, wrapped in sheets of fire and clouds of smoke, of the tablets of the Law, engraved with exactly the same letters as I was learning to read in *cheder*, telling the Jews forever and ever what they might do and what they might not do. Her voice was proudest and happiest when she told me of that Rebbi (teacher) of old, the teacher of the whole Jewish people, Moses: how he delivered us from the hands of the gentiles, how he split the sea for us, and how the waters reared on either side like walls, just like the walls of fir trees which made up the royal road on the other side of the town. So dry was the passage left between that the children of Israel did not even have to take their shoes off. Then she told me how Moses led us through a wilderness abounding in scorpions and snakes, with the pillar of fire before us on the march. She explained the incident of the wilderness very simply: Moses wanted to teach us, during those years, all of the Chumesh, or Five Books (the Pentateuch), just the ones I was learning in *cheder*. And the wilderness was good because there were no gentiles there to interrupt the lessons. . . .

Mottye the *melamed* told us the same story, but Mother's way of telling it was better, heartier, tenderer. When the Rebbi told the story I just listened: when Mother told it my heart began to beat, and my imagination to burn with bright fires of its own. I looked in front of me not at the walls of the room, but at scenes so distant that my eyes hurt. I dreamed: perhaps some day the river Swisla would rear into two walls, and sheets of flame and billows of smoke would enfold Castle Hill. There, on the highest point of the five stories of the windmill, Moses would appear, and the letters of the Law would be engraved on the four wings of the mill, telling us again of the things that we might do and the things we might not do.

Three days of preparation—half holidays for us children —preceded the Pentecost. And all the restlessness and curiosity which we had repressed for weeks broke out then. There were a hundred things to do. First of all we used to run off to the banks of the Swisla, behind Castle Hill, to watch the raft-binders at work. Most of the rafts were already gone, and were probably floating near Babrusk, or perhaps even on the broad Dnieper. But some were still left, and the work was pushed swiftly ahead, while the Beresina had plenty of water, and before it became so shallow that the logs stuck in the sand. My father's rafts, that year, were among the late ones, and every day he was on the river bank, urging on the workers. The binders, the willow branches softened in fire and twisted together like rough ropes, were prepared by the peasant workmen under the direction of my uncle Meyer. The actual binding of the rafts was done by the Jewish workers, the Poliessukes. When the day's work was over my father used to invite the workers over to the house. They did not come inside, but gathered on the verandah and around the house. There they received a glass of whisky, and a *beigle*—a sort of doughnut, to go down with it. "Go down with it" is a euphemism. Some of the workers used to settle quietly down to work, and pack away fifteen and twenty *beigles*. But the term "appetizer" was not an exact one in Swislowitz.

What interested us children vastly were the peasant huts —primitive shacks made up of logs which leaned together to form a cone. A hole was left at the top for the smoke to get out. When rain fell, it entered only through the hole, and therefore wetted only a small part of the ground. In the centre of the hut a fire was kept burning night and day: during the day for cooking, during the night to keep the air warm and dry. At night the peasants slept round the fire, on bare earth which had been stamped down.

In these huts lived the gentile binders and builders of the rafts, and they accompanied the floats far down the river, as far as Krementchug and Ekaterinoslav. The principal food of the peasants consisted of rye meal, hempseed oil, and dried, salted *tarane*, a small flat fish which abounded in the river. Twice a week they used to eat salted pork. They slept in their clothes, using their fur overcoats for cushions. Beds, tables, chairs were unknown—Mother Earth was all three. During their travels on the rafts, they were accustomed to even worse. On these, the hovels were smaller than the kennels of the dogs on the Count's estate. More than once a rebellion would break out somewhere down the river between Slobin and Kiev. But the police were on the watch against these incipient revolutions, and the merchant was always protected.

I remember that as a child I would observe closely the lives of these half-serfs. I used to look into their hovels and envy them for the relish with which they ate their rye meal, wielding their huge wooden spoons as they reclined on the earth. And I envied them their happiness and their great bursts of laughter. After visits like these, a group of us would go into the meadows on the other side of the Swisla, out into the forests beyond the gentile cemetery. Around Pentecost the woods still had no gifts for us, but the earth breathed out a marvellous odour, and we gathered green twigs to take home, in preparation for the festival.

The happiest pastime during my free hours was not, however, visiting the peasants in their huts and on the rafts, nor wandering into the woods for green twigs. It was going bathing in the Swisla. Naturally we little ones were not permitted to go alone. Every one of us was attached to an older person, responsible for him. And when the bathing-hour came, just when the *cheder* closed, the entire class rushed for the river like one boy. In our impatience we did not wait till we reached the river brink, but undressed on the way, and arrived naked, carrying our clothes. The joy of the first day when river-bathing was allowed! We flung ourselves into the water like thirsty beasts. Six, seven, and sometimes eight months passed before the river became warm enough for bathing, and with what longing we looked forward to feeling the cool, clean water flowing inexhaustibly over our naked bodies! All the winter we had had to wash in the bath-house, and we were sick of begging Reuben the bathman, an ill-tempered fellow, to allow us another bucket of warm water. Here was clean water for every one, flowing endlessly, without even the asking.

After Pentecost there came long rows of weary, sickening days. Not a single festival to break the monotony of the dull days which followed each other wearily, clung to each other like balls of pitch. I used to complain to my mother that I was tired of everything. My studies no longer interested me, for by Pentecost I was so far ahead of my schoolmates that they were dragging me back. Not that there was anything wonderful in my achievement: I was simply quicker at the art of putting whole words together. But the words themselves had nothing in them for me. They were Hebrew, and I did not yet understand their meaning.

About this time, I remember—that is, round my first

Pentecost as a *cheder* boy—my grandfather took me up one evening for an impromptu examination, and in the presence of a houseful of guests played a trick on me. He asked me whether I could repeat the Hebrew alphabet forward and then "back to front." I answered yes. Forward it went easily enough. But backward was another business. I stammered, found myself stuck, and had to repeat the whole alphabet forward again in order to remember which letter preceded which.

My grandfather did not wait for the end. "I'll show you how simple it is," he said, smiling. He rose from his seat, faced the company, and repeated the alphabet forward. Then he turned his back to the company and repeated the same thing. "That," he said, while everybody laughed at me, "is the way to say the alphabet back to front easily."

At first I failed to catch the point of the joke, and that added to the amusement of the guests. When I did get it I was humiliated, and made up my mind to get even. A few evenings later I came running joyfully into my grandfather's house and, without any sort of preface, stood up in front of the assembled guests, and at the top of my voice repeated the alphabet forward. Then, almost without catching breath, I began at the last letter, *tav*, and ran it backward, as swiftly and as easily as forward, to *aleph*. The guests were tremendously impressed, and if the reader is not, let him try to repeat the English alphabet backward. In the presence of everybody my grandfather took out a silver half-rouble and gave it to me for the performance.

This was my first "appearance" in public, and my grandfather's silver half-rouble was my first honorarium. I was prouder than a Czar. For the achievement had cost me several days of practice. I had learned it in secret, going into corners and mumbling to myself. A half-rouble, by the way, was no insignificant coin, even for grown-ups, and I formed the wildest plans for its investment. I did not look upon this money as a gift; it was fair payment for arduous labour. I ran home with it, clutching it in my fist, afraid to trust it to the recesses of my pocket. Panting, I told my mother that I had made a half-rouble, but it took me some time to explain to her by what productive methods I had earned it. I entrusted the coin to her, to hold it as call money. In the meantime I only asked her for one kopeck as advance, having meanwhile calculated that even if she did give me the kopeck, she would never deduct it later from my capital.

The mercantile atmosphere which reigned in the house was not without its effect on the minds of the young. Fortunately we learned early not only that money must be earned, but that some of it must also be given away. More than any one else, my mother set the example in giving. Still, I cannot deny that we became familiar much too early with the meaning of money and the value of a coin.

At home the hour for rising was very early—almost at sunrise even in the summer. The little ones, too, were not permitted to sleep late, for a lie-a-bed was the symbol of laziness. For myself, I needed little waking. From my earliest childhood I had a hatred of sleep, and envied the big folk who could stay up as late into the night as they liked. And in the morning the first touch brought me tumbling joyously out of bed, happy to look again on God's world.

The first prayer which I—like every other Jewish child— learned to repeat, was the *modi ani* ("I acknowledge . . ."), the words which the Jew must repeat as soon as he regains consciousness and has poured water on his hands. It is the prayer which gives praise to the Almighty for having returned the soul to its body. When we sleep, I understood, we have no souls—only a spirit. The entire business was very clear to me. As soon as a person fell asleep, his soul left him, and flew upward to be received by the angels. The angels strung the souls up systematically on long cords, just like beads. It was true that the soul had no hole in it, so that the process was a trifle complicated. But angels have a way of doing things. When the morning hour arrived, the souls were unstrung, and each one flew back to its own body. I repeated with special fervour the words which thanked God for having returned *my* soul to *my* body. What a ghastly thing it would have been if somebody else's soul had been shoved by mistake into my body! I was afraid not so much for myself as for my mother. What would she do if her boy woke up one morning, and a soul other than his looked out of his eyes at her, uncomprehendingly?

My parents kept open house: that is to say, everybody could come in, at every moment, without invitation. The table was always covered, and the huge samovar, well filled, always stood on it, lit. There were countless glasses, and every one was free to drink as much tea as he liked, with or without milk. The morning hour, just before we proceeded to Shuhl for prayers, was the happiest of the day. My father was in better mood then than at any other time. It was the happy hour for the children too; the house was crowded with guests, neighbours, friends, people who spent their days praying and studying—and chattering—in the Synagogue, "cantors" and "readers" of the various town organizations. They sat around the table and told stories, gave out the day's news, the latest reports brought back the night before by the teamsters from the city of Babrusk, the doings of the great world. I listened entranced, even when I hardly understood what was being talked about.

My father was a stern, silent man. He seldom sat at table without a book open in front of him. I cannot once remember his having spoken evil concerning any one. When the scandal of the town was being repeated, he never took part in it. My mother, on the contrary, did take part, but it was always on the side of the victim. It was in her nature to follow the dictum of the sages, and to "judge all men for the best."

But that morning interlude did not last long enough. Soon it was over, and the company was on its way to the Synagogue, my mother with the rest. My mother always went to the first services, but my father remained home until the second. It was dull, staying alone with Father in the house, for he was always absorbed in his affairs, and seldom had a word for me. And in general he spent little time with his children. When he was free, and in good humour, he used to amuse himself and us by setting us problems in arithmetic. My brother Meyer used to get the hard problems, and the easier ones were for me. Now and again I would burst into my brother's territory, and answer one of his problems before him. Then I saw laughter come into my father's eyes, and that was a rare pleasure for me. My father, endowed as he was with an exceptionally logical mind, used to say that there was nothing better to sharpen the wits than problems in arithmetic. He was always pleased with my progress in this field, and, curiously enough, I cannot remember that he was ever particularly interested in my progress at *cheder*.

My mother used to come home late from Shuhl. Although she went to the first services, she could seldom resist lingering into the second. She had a sort of sweet tooth for religious tidbits, and if she could snatch one or two extra responses from somebody else's prayers she was happy. There were other duties that sometimes kept my mother

74

away from home. She played the rôle of the local wise woman, for in addition to observing the laws concerning the visiting of the sick, she was something of a practitioner. She had not a little knowledge of the names of sicknesses, and I cannot tell where she got them, for she read nothing but Yiddish. She was a great believer, too, in the old, traditional folk remedies, with their mixture of superstition and occasional obscure sense. But she did not administer them herself. Hers was the work of the diagnostician. She would give the name of the disease and leave it to her "assistants" to apply the remedy. Naturally everybody believed in the exorcising of diseases and of evil spirits. But every disease, from the evil eye and toothache to indigestion and a cold, had its specialist in town. There was one old woman, Feige Riveh by name, a tiny, thin old creature, quick in motion like a drop of quicksilver, who was reputed to be able to remove the evil eye as easily as if she had actually laid hands on it. But she was no good for toothache. The specialist in that field was Sossye, the bun-baker. My mother, as diagnostician, was considered a superior person—and with her diagnosis there was no arguing. In fact, the regular doctor (who was not a regular doctor at all) was only sent for after my mother had delivered her decision. And if Elke, daughter of Mendel, said it was typhoid, it had to be typhoid, and if she said it was a cold, a cold it had to be.

As soon as morning prayers were over, my mother used to make the rounds of her patients like a regular practitioner. We children learned early not to wait for her with breakfast. We took it ourselves and hurried off to *cheder*. Only Father waited, and when he became impatient he used to ask, ironically, "I wonder what can be keeping the doctor this morning."

And thus mornings were more or less interesting. But

the days, at that time of the year, were dull. There was nothing for the mind or the body. We were weary of Mottye the bean, with his wooden pointer and his eternal building up of words which had no meaning for us. We were weary of the dingy room and the mechanical lessons. Only now and again a happy break came when a male child was born in the town. On such days we *cheder* boys had the right to go into the room of the mother, and repeat the prayer called Kriath Shema ("The Reading of the Name"), which begins with the affirmation of the unity of God. This prayer was supposed to be potent in keeping away the "Not-Good Ones," the evil spirits, from the bedside of the mother and the newborn child. If the child was born in a poor home, they used to distribute among the youthful prayer-boys boiled chick-peas. In the richer homes, they used to hand out nuts, and, on the evening before the circumcision ceremony, cakes and candies. Every *cheder* boy had a right to go into any house where a newborn son needed his protective spiritual services—but the children of the poorer families went to the poor, and the children of the richer families to the rich. For all its "democratic" character, the community of Swislowitz seems to have woven a class-consciousness into the bone and sinew of its children.

Very slowly, with only rare interruptions of this kind, the summer days dragged along until we reached the "Three Weeks" which precede the Black Fast of the Destruction and the "Nine Days" which close the Three Weeks. The period lies between the seventeenth day of the month of Tammuz and the ninth day of the month of Ab. The time is midsummer.

On the seventeenth day of Tammuz the enemy broke through the walls of Jerusalem, and on the ninth day of Ab, having fought his way through the city, he set fire to the Temple and destroyed it. So the seventeenth day of Tammuz is a minor fast, and the ninth day of Ab is the Black Fast, and in between are the melancholy, grey days of half mourning. During that period it was our *duty* to be mournful. We had to be mournful even in *cheder*, and walk around with heads down and eyes fixed on the ground. We were not permitted to bathe in the Swisla. Only on Friday afternoon we were allowed to take a bath, and that not so much for the body's comfort as for the sake of the Holy Sabbath, which is so sacred that it takes precedence over all mourning. In the last nine days of the Three Weeks our mourning was intensified. We were forbidden then to eat meat—again with the exception of the Holy Sabbath. With regard to this last law—the prohibition of meat— most of the Jews of Swislowitz stood to gain in their heavenly account, for the majority of them never had a piece of meat even to look at during weekdays. Thus a privation which under ordinary circumstances was the result of their poverty could during this period be ascribed in heaven to their piety.

I do not remember whether I was really sad during all the Three Weeks, but I do remember that the last Nine Days did have their effect on me. I lost my usual joyfulness, at least at home. There was little change in my father's dark bearing, but my mother went about the house pale and subdued, and more than once there were on her cheeks the signs of weeping. Round her an atmosphere of real suffering and sadness was formed, and spilled itself through the house.

My mother was the first to recount to us the horrors of the destruction of the Temple, and she laid the colours on thick. She told us about Nebuchadnezzar and Nebuzarodon, and about Nero and Titus the wicked: but it was on the last —perhaps because he was nearest in retrospect—that she poured out all the bitterness of her repressed and tormented

soul. In her telling of the story there was so much freshness, so much passion, and so much personal protest, that
the sense of time was wholly destroyed. It was as though she
had been a participant in the sufferings of our forefathers.
It was not the history of a national destruction, but the re-
cital of a personal disaster. She carried us from Swislowitz
back to Jerusalem, up to the summit of the Hill of the Sacred
House, and she showed us the Temple in its glory, the Ark
and the Cherubim and the Altar of brightest gold, the
High Priest in the splendour of his robes, and the host of
the priests and Levites, with their gorgeous instruments—
viols and harps and trumpets and drums.

Then followed the story of the Destruction. And my
mother always used the words "we," "us," "our," not as a
rhetorical trick, but out of a sense of conviction. *Us* the
cruel enemy cut down, *ours* was the house he brutally destroyed. I felt then as though only yesterday we, our family, our relatives and friends, had been living in Jerusalem
the Marvellous, and only yesterday Titus the wicked had
driven us out to Swislowitz, so that instead of the golden
temple and the High Priest we had the wooden Synagogue
and Mottye the bean. . . .

And just as seriously as she told us of Nebuchadnezzar
and Titus the wicked, she also told us of the hateful rôle
played during the Destruction by the spiders and swallows.
These two creatures were on the side of the enemy. When
the latter laid siege to the city, they poured in from all sides,
carrying fire in their mouths. The sparrows, however, were
on our side, and they came scuttling in, carrying water in
their mouths—but they could not prevail against the spiders
and the swallows. Regarding the swallows she told us, moreover, that until this day they had the sign of their treachery stamped upon them: under their throats there is a speck

of red which commemorates forever their incendiary rôle.

It occurred to none of us to ask Mother how the spiders and swallows could carry fire in their mouths without being burned up. Whatever Mother told us was sacred, so that even if the question had occurred to us, we would have stifled it. Apart from its immediate effect on us, the story resulted in a change of attitude toward the swallows. We had always hated spiders anyway, but until we heard of their unspeakable treachery, we had always had a liking for swallows, because of their black wings, their graceful flight, and the little red mark under their throats. But from now on they were on the list of accursed things. Later on, when we went through our nesting years, we always spared the nests of the sparrows, but we destroyed without mercy the nests and the eggs of the swallows.

I have often wondered where this strange folk legend came from, and why the hatred of a people has been directed against that innocent and charming bird, the swallow. But I have never been able to trace its origin.

Then came Sabbath Chazon (Sabbath of the Vision of Isaiah), the Sabbath before the Black Fast, and it was truly a black Sabbath. On this one occasion the joy and contentment which the Jew is commanded to feel on the day of rest were overshadowed by the huge wings of our unforgettable disaster. A black curtain was drawn that Sabbath across the ark in the Shuhl, and all the worshippers—including even the important citizens who sat in the prominent places by the eastern wall—came in workaday attire. Judah, the president, came almost in rags, with buttons missing on his coat, his shirt visible in front, and his earlocks hanging in neglect over his ears. Judah himself was a symbol of the Destruction. Close to the cantor's desk, apart from the rest, sat his older brother Ziskind (the famous Rebbi of my uncle Meyer), competing with Judah for the palm of desolation. But his thin face, instead of expressing wretchedness and sorrow, bore on it a cruel and angry look: I always thought that he belonged more to the triumphant army of Titus the wicked than to the fleeing hordes of the vanquished and ravaged Jews. In the right-hand corner, under the shadow of the sacred Ark, sat the Rav himself, Rabbi Wolf, an old Jew who was both a scholar and a saint. From his wrinkled face shone piety and learning. He had put on no outward symbols of mourning, but when they called him up to read aloud from the Torah, he walked with slow, quiet steps, like a man sunk deep in thought. And over all of us came the feeling: This is the bearing of a man who remains noble and dignified even in the deepest sorrow. And in later years, when I learned how the Elders of the Sanhedrin had followed in chains the gilded chariot of Titus the wicked, I saw them walking with the same slow pace, the same silent sadness, as old Rabbi Wolf.

The mood in the Synagogue was not only mournful, but eerie. The usual Sabbath chants were replaced by creepy melodies of lamentation, and the portion of the Prophets intoned after the usual weekly reading of the Five Books was taken from the Threnody of Jeremiah. The congregants moved about the Shuhl like shadows. And though I know—and felt even then—that much of this was artificial and forced, yet there were sensitive faces on which was written the reflex of a great sorrow and a great loss.

In the house, too, the Sabbath of Vision was received without the usual happiness of the sacred day. True, the Sabbath was always holy, but it was like a beloved visitor who comes into a house where some bereavement has just occurred. The visitor is too welcome to be ignored, but all the ceremonies are grave and stately—the reception is formal and dignified, without the usual intimacy and affection.

A strange scene would occur that afternoon in the house. There came on their usual visit to my mother her friends and neighbours, all the wives of the well-to-do Jews of Swislowitz. They wore clothes which were neither of the Sabbath nor yet of the week-day, a compromise between duty and pride. On the table, instead of the usual tea, there was nothing but the big leather Yiddish translation of the Pentateuch in use among women. Without greeting, without preliminaries, the women sat down round the table and my mother began to read aloud the translation of the Lamentations of Jeremiah. The original text is oppressive enough, but the Yiddish book was both translation and commentary. On every verse, as on a foundation, was reared a superstructure of gruesome stories and legends taken from the old books of the sages and from commentaries of the Middle Ages. And my mother had not read far before there arose round the table not a weeping, but a sort of wailing, the wailing which goes up from a city given up to the sword. It was as though all the cruelties and miseries of the Destruction were being enacted again in that room.

And I sat next to my mother and mingled my tears with hers. Most of all I was shaken by the story of Hannah and her seven sons, which I heard for the first time in that setting. Even while I sobbed I felt in myself an unconquerable pride in that youngest son, a child perhaps of my age, perhaps a *cheder* boy too, who stood like a hero before the oppressor and under the fiercest threats would not bend the knee to an earthly god. And I swore, too, that never, never would I bend the knee to idols.

It was on the eve of Tisha b'Ab—the dread ninth day of Ab—that I learned for the first time that human beings could eat rolls dipped in ashes. I was astounded by the ceremony. I stared with bulging eyes at the older people who swallowed the horrible mouthfuls—but I did not dare to imitate them.

In the Shuhl we sat in stockinged feet, as one sits in the house of a mourner. The lamps were unlit. Instead, they laid the desks flat, and fastened tallow candles on them. After evening prayer the congregation sat down upon the floor, and the saying of Lamentations began. The darkness in the Shuhl, the desks lying on the floor, the naked Ark stripped of its gilded curtain, the oppressive melody of the Lamentations—all these threw terror into my soul. Every one and everything wept. The stifled sobs of the men were like a bass accompaniment to the shriller sound of weeping which came from the women's section. The naked Ark wept, and a weeping came from the shadowy walls. And the candles fastened into the overthrown stands wept tallow tears which ran over their sides.

In our house, that night, the children were not permitted to swallow anything after the evening meal. Not even a glass of water. And that night, of course, we always felt thirsty.

The next morning the effect was somewhat dissipated. On that first Tisha b'Ab of my *cheder* years, the sun came out bright and clear. It threw its cheerful rays with a prodigal hand into the mourning Shuhl, and disturbed the mood. And besides, we children began to be absorbed in the mechanics of the thing, and we looked with more curiosity into the faces of our elders. We observed that those who were saying the Lamentations with the loudest and most terrifying voices had no tears at all on their cheeks. And the kind of weeping which is not accompanied by tears could not impose on us. For we knew all the degrees of weeping: the weeping that is genuine, and goes with tears; the weeping that is forced, and squeezes out the tears, and the weeping which cannot even get as far as a tear—weeping to order. And then a doubt stole into my mind, and I wondered whether the night before, too, when their faces had been shrouded in darkness, the older people had put upon us. Perhaps their weeping had been tearless then, too. And we noticed also that some of the older people were amusing themselves by throwing burrs into each other's heads and beards: and if the older people were making a game of it, we younger ones were surely permitted to do it.

Thus it came about that for the children the Day of the Destruction, as contrasted with the foregoing eve, was really interesting and pleasant. The visit to the cemetery was full of merriment for us. On the outward journey we went through the woods among the berries and the nuts. We came back through the open fields, ripe with the harvests of corn and wheat and oats. The ears twinkled innumerably in the sunlight, the wind went through the fields and sent shining waves along the summits of the stems, and in this golden sea were the peasant girls in red dresses, with red kerchiefs on their heads; and with their sharp scythes, which flashed silver to the sun, they mowed their way through the harvest. Out of their healthy, powerful throats the harvest songs floated up into the sunlight. And here we went, in Indian file, mourners in the exile, the children of a ruined people. . . . Need I confess that all my heart was drawn from the ruined past to the living fields of the workers?

With the beginning of the month of Elul, which follows the month of Ab (*circa* July-August), Mottye the bean suddenly became a changed man. The stern, bitter Rebbi was

83

transformed, as if overnight, into a mild, loving teacher, and his pupils, without exception, into clever, quick-witted, industrious boys. The reason for this extraordinary transformation was unknown to us. We could not understand why the leathern thongs hung undisturbed on the wall. But young as we were, we knew that something was in the air. The Rebbi was afraid of something, and we could not make out what. But that he was afraid was certain, and the knowledge was a source of joy to us. We only thanked God for having interceded in our behalf, and for having thrown terror into him who had been our terror for so many wretched months.

Poor, miserable Mottye the bean! He was afraid for his little class, and he had to flatter the parents and then cajole the children. The competition in his simple trade was keen, and twice a year he had to make a detour. This was one of the dark patches in his profession. The pay he received was wretched: for his long hours of labour scarcely enough to keep body and soul together, and even this much was uncertain. For his pupils came to him for half a year at a time, and at the end of the term he trembled for his livelihood. Perhaps the next term they would be sent elsewhere.

CHAPTER FIVE: FIELDS AND MESSIAH

WE GOT little joy out of the summer. While the sun was shining outside, and woods and fields were blossoming, we sat imprisoned in the dark narrow *cheder* from morning till night. We seldom saw the happy world, and in our young minds an idea was born and grew stronger from week to week: God had made the town and the houses, the shops and *cheder* for us; and the fields and the woods he had created for the gentiles. So when the end of the term came, round the month of Elul, our liberty fell on us like belated dew, and awoke to open life the suppressed longings toward nature. True, most of the harvest had already been taken in: it stood in sheaves on the shorn fields, or had been carted into the barns. Something of the late summer we still took in. Potatoes, cabbages, and beets were still growing, and the pumpkins lay in the fields and warmed their fat bellies in the sun. As often as the opportunity came, I marshalled my playmates and marched them off to the fields, or the woods. Sometimes we met a peasant of our acquaintance, and he would give us nuts or baked beets. Our conversation with him was limited, for we children knew only a few words of Russian. But we were not afraid. And I was less afraid than any one else, for nearly all the gentiles in the town were employed from time to time by my father. They knew me well, and they treated me with respect.

Without understanding why it was so, I was angered as a

child that none of the earth belonged to the Jews, that God had given the forests to the nobles and the fields to the peasants. I argued the question frequently with my mother, but she had an eternal answer: "Wait, my child. The Messiah will come and we will have both forests and fields." My mother took special pains to implant in me a longing for the coming of the Messiah. . . . She believed greatly in the advent, and she often spoke of it. Her deep faith was in time transferred to us, and as children we helped her to long and to believe, to believe and to long. Our faith in Messiah was born of our faith in our mother.

The week before the New Year we were told not to be terrified if, in the middle of the night, we heard a knocking at the window. These were the wakers to the night prayers which usher in the beginning of the New Year. These night prayers were only for the elders, and we children could sleep on, unless we felt a special urge to come along. Naturally I said that I wanted to come along. I had never attended prayers that were said so early in the morning, before there was any light. And that night I hardly closed my eyes, for fear of sleeping through the call. I heard it, leaped into my clothes, and went into the living-room. The samovar already stood on the table, and my father, my mother, my older brother, and myself took glasses of tea before going to the Synagogue.

The night was cool and clear, and in the deep-blue heavens the stars shone, countless and bright. In my mind, as in the mind of every other Jewish child so brought up, there was not the slightest doubt that there above, behind the stars, God sat: our God, of course, for there was no other god: and from between the stars He looked down and watched the Jews rising so early to go to night prayers. And I was happy that I was there among the older people, passing in review before Him.

The Slichoth, or prayers of forgiveness, made an even deeper impression on me than the lamentations of the ninth day of Ab. There was something too simple about the lamentations. The Temple had been burned, and it was clear enough even to me that after such a fire anybody would lament. There was no mystic idea in it. But here, for prayers which are repeated on the week before the New Year, the prayers which beg forgiveness, I saw a Synagogue packed in the dead of night with the Jews of the town: no Nebuchadnezzar was mentioned, no Titus the wicked. There was only God enthroned above the stars, and toward Him our prayers streamed. And all that was mystic in me woke in response to the midnight prayers.

On Rosh Hashannah, New Year's Day, the Yishuvniks came to town. There is no word for Yishuvnik in English, for the type is unknown to the language. They are Jews who live abandoned in the midst of some village or settlement, alien figures in a world not their own. Months may pass before they see the face of another Jew. Only on the High Holidays they leave their occupations, and flock to the nearest Jewish centre.

On such occasions the Yishuvnik, returning to the family or friends from whom the search for bread has driven him, was received in our town with genuine hospitality. There were familiar faces among these visitors from the remote villages, but many of them were new. We did our best to make them all feel at home, gave up to them our nicest rooms, and in the Synagogue assigned them to the places of honour by the eastern wall. It was not so easy to find room for all of them. Sometimes they had to sit by threes in the chairs of honour by the eastern wall, but the glory was theirs. We children too received the youngsters from the backwoods with all friendliness. Some of them were wild creatures, terrified by the vast crowds, and unable to utter a word. But the elders took special pains with them. My father would take some of them on his knee, caress them, and tell them not to be frightened. And we would give them some of our toys and teach them our games. . . .

And so New Year would have been a very jolly holiday if they had not told us about the Day of Judgment. This *was* the Day of Judgment. God sat enthroned in the midst of the cohorts of angels, and one after another the tremendous account-books were laid before Him, with their debit and credit columns of evil deeds and good deeds. Every Jew, the children as well as the grown-ups, had his special account there, and every account was examined, the balance drawn, the sentence delivered accordingly. With the account-books open before Him, God decided who should live out the next year and who should die, who among the living should be sick and who should remain well; and the prayers went into such detail that my soul trembled. Young as we were, our elders already breathed into us the terror of death, and broke up the pure peace that had been in our minds. We were spiritually careworn in days which should have been utterly carefree: and the Days of Awe, as they are called, became for us Days of Terror. Our parents seem to have been afraid that they could not instill the feeling of fear into us early enough. We were too young for such emotions, and I was scarcely more than a baby when I lay awake the night of the New Year and implored God for mercy on my father and my mother.

The first Taschlich ceremony, when we went down to the river to shake off our sins, is clear in my memory. The place we chose was the spot behind Castle Hill, where the Swisla falls into the Beresina. It seemed to me a first-class idea—this of being able to shake one's sins out into the water, and get rid of them forever. The usual ceremony was to flap the skirts of our garments over the water. But in an excess of piety many of us turned our pockets inside out and shook them over the water, too.

I do not know what my sins were then, and how many of them I had, but I shook my coat-tails and my pockets mightily. And when I left the river brink with my father, I did feel considerably lighter. I had been relieved of a great weight.

The eve of Yom Kippur was the holiday of the Yishuvniks, the backwoodsmen. On New Year's Day—and still more so on the day of Yom Kippur itself, the Day of Atonement, or White Fast—we were all busy with prayers. There was no time for visits. But the eve of Yom Kippur was free, and then the Yishuvniks found a little consolation for the lonely years which they passed in alien worlds far from their own kind.

Little has been written in Jewish literature concerning the life and the spiritual tragedies of the Yishuvnik. And that little has made of the Yishuvnik the butt of our wit: for, sundered from the Jewish world, he came to be gross and earthy, like the peasants, and his children grew up, a cross between Jews and peasants, but having neither the schooling of the first nor the happiness of the second. Nothing has been written of the deep sufferings which must have been theirs, the loneliness, the pain of their uprooting: they were branches which had been cut off from one tree and could never be grafted on to another. They lived forgotten lives among alien fields and could not become part of the environment to which they had to look for their daily bread.

While the father worried about his meagre living, the mother worried about the little ones growing up wild, untutored, taking on, perhaps, the worst habits of the peasants. Those that could afford it would keep a Rebbi (teacher) in the house, cutting down on food and clothes in order that the children might not be utter strangers to Jewishness. But when the children are half grown, the worst time comes: for there is no room for them, and not enough of a living: however few they are, they are too many. It is bad enough with the sons: it is worse with the girls. In the evenings the mother gathers her daughters round her, tries to keep them to the wretched house, trembles for them. . . . And years and decades pass in this kind of life.

Little wonder that the Yishuvniks waited with longing and impatience for the coming of the New Year and the Day of Atonement. Once a year at least they could feel at one again with that world from which the pursuit of a livelihood had sundered them; once a year they felt themselves nearer to their race and their God.

The door of our house never closed once during the eve of the Day of Atonement. There was hardly a Yishuvnik in town who did not come to pay his respects to us. Many of them used to bring their own cakes and sweetmeats to distribute in the Synagogue. There was a curious belief attached to the distribution of this kind of cake. It might be that God had destined you to become a beggar during the coming year: perhaps by the acceptance of this piece of cake, brought in by a stranger, you would fulfil that part of your destiny and be no more troubled by it. For that reason no one refused a piece of the cake offered by a Yishuvnik in the Shuhl. Meanwhile there would be much talk about the marvels of our Jewish laws and commandments: how wonderful it was that feasting on the eve of Yom Kippur should be accounted almost as great a virtue as fasting on the day of Yom Kippur. And the Yishuvniks rejoiced particularly in the first of these virtues and made the best of the occasion.

After we had eaten on the eve of Yom Kippur, Mother told us that this was a day of forgiveness: it was our duty to seek out those of our playmates with whom we had quarrelled, or against whom we had committed evil, and beg forgiveness of them: likewise to forgive them without hesitation for all faults and misdemeanours, and to carry no hatred in our hearts. I immediately began to cast up accounts, and perceived that with regard to most of my playmates I stood about even: but if there were doubtful cases I sought out my friend and asked forgiveness. I liked the ceremony: it made me feel edified and important.

In Shuhl, during afternoon prayers, I was astonished by another ceremony. I saw grown-up Jews stretch themselves out on the floor, while Lazar the psalm-sayer (who was the same as Lazar the bath attendant) stood over them with leathern thongs and lashed them unmercifully. I knew, of course, that this was the ceremony of *malkoth*, or stripes, but the actuality of it was altogether too reminiscent of the *cheder*. The whipping was done systematically: one stripe on that part of the anatomy which we submitted to the lash in *cheder*, then two stripes on the upper part of the back. So once, twice, three times—sometimes up to fifteen times. I was still more astonished when I saw the victim get up from the punishment, and throw a few coins into the plate held out by Lazar. It was surely a marvellous thing to pay for being lashed.

Immediately after the feast at home, my father put on a white robe, and a prayer-shawl over that. My mother too clad herself in white. Then the children were led one by one before them. My father laid his hands on us, and gave us his blessing. Then, steeped in the atmosphere of the Day of Atonement, all of us went to my grandfather's house. There the entire family was assembled, four generations. The ceremony of the blessings was repeated, and we received a double benediction from the grandfather and grandmother.

The floor of the Synagogue was thickly strewn with hay. On all the window sills, as well as on special tables, were ranged the huge white wax candles—the soul-lights—which were to burn for twenty-four hours in memory of the dead. The windows were kept closed, for fear a candle might be blown out, and it was accounted a good omen when the candles burned evenly right down to the socket, without spilling their wax over the sides. There was soon created that special atmosphere which belonged to Yom Kippur. The room became hot, and the mingled odours of the wax candles and hay became thicker and thicker.

When prayers were over most of us went home. But there were some who, in their piety, remained at prayers all night. Among them were a few heroic spirits who vowed that they would remain standing in the Synagogue all night and all next day—and they carried out their vow to the letter. There were even women pietists of this heroic mould. And all through the night the wax candles burned in the Shuhl below, and from the open windows of the galleries the white faces of the women peered down.

The later morning prayers of Yom Kippur were much beloved of us children, for they touched the mystic places in our souls. With regard to mystic ceremonial the Jewish Synagogue stands closer to the Protestant church than to the Catholic or Greek cloister. The Synagogue is dry, formal, and too workaday. But Yom Kippur is an exception.

First, there are the white robes of the congregants, and second, the special melodies of that day. Third, there are the strange genuflections, when the congregants do not simply kneel, but prostrate themselves almost at full length on the floor. There was something intimate and terrible in the sight of these grown-up men humbling themselves in the dust, and a tremor ran through my body when I observed them.

And here I must confess that in my earliest years, even before I went to *cheder*, I used to love to pass by the Orthodox church, and, on the rare occasions when it was in use, the Catholic cloister too, and listen to their services from without. The doors of the churches were kept open. I could look in, and see the golden altar, the pictures framed in gold, and the innumerable candle flames, also set in gold. Above the altar stood the priest, in a mantle which shimmered silver and gold. In vain my mother explained to me that the gentiles worshipped false gods, and that their services were not even worth looking at. In this respect my mother did not show all the caution she should have shown. In order to alienate us from the faith and church of others, she used to tell us of the marvellous raiment, the silver bells and pomegranates, which adorned our priests and Levites in the days of the Temple: and she also told us that the gentiles parodied in their services the vanished glories of our past. . . . She did not understand that in telling us these stories she was not alienating us from the worshippers of "false gods." On the contrary, she made us all the more curious to find out what they looked like. I knew it was a sin to go by and look upon the altar and the forbidden pictures and the false raiment: but in the struggle between duty and curiosity, the latter always won. I used to say to myself,

"I am not looking at the worship of false gods. I am only looking at that part of the service which was stolen from us."

Something mysterious drew me to that alien altar, to the twinkling lights and the gilded images. And in the sweet singing of the choir I heard the invitation, "Do not be afraid. Come to us, little Jewish child, see how beautiful, how pleasant is our service. . . ."

And as often as my mother told me about the Temple and the priest, my childish fantasy was awakened, and I saw pictures. I knew they were the false pictures of the worshippers of idols, and I tried to chase them out of my mind. I tried instead to associate the Temple of ancient days with our Synagogue and the High Priest with our cantor. I tried in vain, for always there returned the images of the Catholic and Greek churches, the "false" priests before the altar, the lights and the singing. I kept these pictures secret, like a sin, for I knew that if I spoke of them my mother would be unhappy. I carried on an internal struggle against the worshippers of idols, but I could not conquer them.

It was only on Yom Kippur that my soul was satisfied, and chiefly it was by the ceremonies of the noon prayer. I too fell prostrate at the signal, just like the older folk. At that moment I could think of our High Priest without evoking the image of the cloister. And I felt that for this moment I had been purified of all evil thought.

After the plain evening prayer of that day the congregation dispersed. The women went home at once, but the men still remained about in order to greet the new moon with prayer before they went home to break their fast.

Many years ago I remember reading in *Hashachar* (*The Dawn*) of Perez Smolenskin, that periodical which opened the *Sturm und Drang* period of our latest history, a poem

94

called "Benediction of the New Moon," by Salman Luria. The poet describes a poverty-stricken Jewish home in a little Russian town. It is winter. The house is unheated. The hungry children lie on beds of straw, dozing and dreaming of food—and the sick mother huddles close to them, for comfort and warmth. But outside, in the clear freezing night, the father stands with anxious eyes fixed on the sinking sickle of the moon, and he prays to God to fill out the missing portion of it. He prays as if no other worry existed for him than this—that God might forget to round out the incompleted moon. And if God will only take pity on the helpless moon, all will be well. . . .

And what, indeed, did the Jews of Swislowitz lack on that night of Yom Kippur, when they issued with purified souls from their day of fasting and prayer? They had forgiven each other their sins against each other, and God had forgiven them all their sins against Him. "He sprinkled them with clean water and they were purified of their sins." And that was all they needed. So, with clear eyes they looked up into the heavens: and a feeling of pity for the incompleted moon overcame them: so they lifted their hands toward the moon and begged God to take pity on that too.

But the Benediction of the New Moon did not close the day. No sooner had Father come home than he took off his white robe, found a hammer and two nails, went out of the house again, and drove the nails into that part of the wall against which the Tabernacle would rest on the ensuing festival. It is a sin to hurry over sacred duties. Let not the Evil Advocate be able to plead against the Jews that after their day of prayer and fasting they rushed home like gluttons to gulp down—a glass of tea. Slowly then: fast all day, pray all day: when it is over, first pray for the welfare of the moon: then go home and take your time: doff your white garment, drive in a couple of nails for the Tabernacle, and then sit down to a glass of tea. There'll be time enough for the good things of the flesh. . . .

During the four days between Yom Kippur and the Feast of Tabernacles the Jews of Swislowitz were preoccupied with the building of the Tabernacles. There were only a few householders in Swislowitz who could boast the luxury of a permanent Tabernacle or booth standing the whole year round. Others put up their booths only for the Festival—insecure structures patched up of thin planks, old doors, old windows, and the like. It was not worth while wasting too much effort on a structure which had to stand only for eight days, and would then be pulled down again. The permanent Succah, or booth, had a great many virtues, of course. In the first place it was so strongly built that it did not fear storm and wind, frequent visitors at that time of the year. Second, it had a roof with two wings that could be lifted and lowered with a rope—so that it did not fear the rain. And third—not less important than the first two—it had firm doors which could be closed against thieves, and Swislowitz had its share of these.

But against the advantages of the permanent booth you had to set off the rather obvious spiritual superiority of the man who, every year, built his booth afresh, rejoicing in the labour. And indeed, the very insecurity of it, the dependence on the will of God, gave it a special touch of fineness. You had to show faith in God, and be ready to believe that "He would not empty His beaker into the face of His important guests."

Within the Succah I felt altogether wonderful. The light of the Festival Candle drew itself upward, toward the roof of branches, which was not a roof but a portion of the sky let down over our heads. And among the branches of fir the stars peeped out, crystal clear, as if they too had been purified and washed for the festival. Thus the candlelight streamed upward, and the starlight came down, and at the meeting-place of the two a warmth and tenderness was born which is known only to him who has dreamed the evenings away in the Tabernacle.

Here the Jew, symbol of man uprooted from his mother earth, alienated from the magic contact of nature, touched reality again. Condemned by the miseries of his history to a withered, colourless existence, he suddenly felt the richness of the old life which flows from the inexhaustible soil. Above him was laid a roof of fresh, odorous branches of fir: in a corner of the booth, in an earthen pitcher, stood the slender palm, brought a thousand miles from the Orient, while round it stood the willow withes from the fields outside. At no moment of the year did the suppressed nostalgia of these descendants of shepherds and Bedouins and peasants waken more poignantly, or come nearer to a sense of satisfaction.

The half-sanctity of the four days which break up the holiday of Tabernacles (first come two days of high festival, then the four less sacred days, and then two more days of high festival) were not without their charm for the youngsters. The Shuhl was illuminated during that week as never during any other festival. Tabernacles is a jolly festival. The older people were merrier, more lighthearted, than at other times of the year: and not an evening passed without the distribution of candies and cakes among the children, after service. We were allowed to stay up as long as the older people, and during the day there was no *cheder*—or next to none.

And of course the highwater mark of jollity was reached

on Simchath Torah, the day of the Rejoicing of the Law. On that day the last portion of the Pentateuch has been ended, and the round of readings is begun again for the year. Should we not rejoice? On that day Judah, son of the preacher and president of the Synagogue, used to run from house to house, followed by an army of children. He wore a topcoat turned inside out and a silk hat battered and wrinkled beyond recognition. On his back he carried a sack, and every housewife had to pour her contribution into it—cakes, apples, pears, berries. . . . These were provisions for his army. Every five minutes he would turn round to us, and call out, "Sacred flock of Israel!" And we would answer in chorus, "Ba-a-a, ba-a-a."

As provider of goodies for the youngsters of Swislowitz on the Day of the Rejoicing of the Law, Judah, the preacher's son, had a rival in the person of Eliakum Yoshes, a peddler, a Jew who lived mostly out among the villages, a man low in the social scale. Once a year, on the Day of the Rejoicing of the Law, Eliakum Yoshes achieved public recognition—his one moment of personal satisfaction, when every one admitted that he too played a rôle in the scheme of things. Though the prerogative belonged exclusively to Judah—who was both president and chief reader in the Synagogue—Eliakum Yoshes organized an army of his own, by promising the mercenaries richer booty: he also put on a topcoat inside out, found a battered silk hat, and led his cohorts to the conquest of the cupboards of the town.

Between the two field-marshals there was enmity of many years' standing. Judah resented the impudence of Eliakum, the ignorant peddler: Eliakum hated the hereditary insolence of Judah. And the mercenary troops—with the paradoxical capacity of mercenary troops for fierce and transient loyalties—took sides as if they had been separate tribes led by respective chiefs of many years' standing. When the two hordes passed each other on a street in the course of their forays, looks of enmity would dart from one camp to the other, and sometimes the unconcealed rage of the troops would break into open hostilities: then knots of youngsters would be seen pummelling each other vigorously until the by-standers interfered and restored at least a semblance of peace.

The evenings were gayer still. On this one occasion, the women were permitted to come down from the enclosed galleries into the men's division of the Synagogue: and this was the signal to the youngsters that all regular laws had been suspended. For on this one day in the year the Torah, the Law, that stern mistress which for the other three hundred odd days is an unrelenting ruler, bends a little toward her followers, and shows them her gentler, tenderer side. Six hundred and thirteen commandments, precepts, and prohibitions she imposes on her followers, and the breaking of any one of them is a great sin: she has put a fence round every action, every moment, of her followers, and not a daily act, from the most important to the most trivial, is outside the scope of the Torah. All this is true enough. But she does this for the sake of her followers, as a mother imposes commands on her children for their own good. But like a mother, she knows her moments of sweetness and relaxation, and then her children dance around her, wild with joy.

On the eve of the Day of Rejoicing every burgher in the town, from the Rav himself down to the humble water-carrier, has this privilege: he may join in the procession round the pulpit, carrying in his turn the great parchment scrolls in their mantles of velvet, with their ornaments of bells and pomegranates. And the youngsters follow noisily, carrying banners, on which are painted lions and hares: "Be swift as a hare and strong as a lion to carry out the commandments of the Torah." Among the youngsters the girls too dance and sing: they seem to be keener than the boys on one traditional symbolic rite: bestowing quick kisses on the silk and velvet mantles of the scrolls, as they pass in procession. But the boys, in whose instincts the foretaste of a girl's kiss has already half awakened, have a trick of their own. They watch closely: and when a pair of girlish lips darts toward the mantle of the scroll, a boyish hand darts even more swiftly between the lips and the velvet: and instead of the sacred scroll, the girl kisses the hand of an impudent boy. Then a great shout of laughter goes up through the Synagogue, and the face of the little girl turns fiery red with shame. Sometimes she spits out the kiss again: and sometimes she swallows it in her embarrassment. . . .

A Day of Rejoicing preceded by an evening of rejoicing, for the bridegroom is dancing with the bride, the Chosen People with the Law. For so it is written in the books: the Torah is the bride, and the Congregation of Israel is the bridegroom, and God Himself is the marriage broker, sometimes leading the bride and sometimes the bridegroom to the altar. The bride wears a crown of silver and a robe of silk and velvet, and the bridegroom puts his arms around her and leads her in a dance around the pulpit. And the divine Marriage Broker laughs, and asks the bystanders, "A wonderful match, is it not? Twin souls, affinities . . ."

The Day of Rejoicing which followed was not as merry as the evening before, for the daylight took away the intimacy and softness of the ceremonies, and shed too garish a light on the secrecy of our emotions. The night is Delilah and the day is Mephistopheles. The night is tender, the day is brutal. And though the ceremonies of the night before were repeated, in every detail, during the afternoon of the Day of Rejoicing, the effect was not the same. The same processions round the pulpit, the same girls kissing the mantles of the scrolls or the hands of impudent boys, but not the same tempo, nor the same high spirits. Hour by hour the mood died down, so that by the time we had reached the interval between afternoon and evening prayers, the merriment was forced and artificial. The mood changed at last into that old melancholy of the Jews; the melodies went over into minor keys, and instead of the jolly songs of the night before, ancient chants, filled with undefined longings and immemorial loneliness, stole through the Synagogue and echoed from its walls.

On the Day of Rejoicing it is meritorious to drink; and the Jews of Swislowitz obeyed the law and drank. But I cannot remember a single instance of a Jew getting drunk. There were many who pretended to be drunk, and went clowning through the congregation. Judah the preacher's son loved to play this rôle, but the joke of it was that, like some others, he never swallowed a drop of liquor. The fact is that when the cantor gave the signal for the evening prayers—three heavy blows on the reading desk—the congregation suddenly collapsed into seriousness, and the regular prayers were resumed as drily, as evenly, as if this were any other day in the year. The merriment died off the faces instantaneously, and the old wrinkles, the old worries, appeared on them as if by magic. The Day of Rejoicing was over. The weary course of the days was resumed.

On the evening of that day a large company gathered in our house. Among the guests was Mottye the bean. I was not particularly overjoyed by his appearance. He spoiled the evening for me by his mere presence: and he made it a thoroughly miserable one for me when he came over to me, and, beaming, confided in me that I was to remain in his *cheder* for the coming term, that is, through the winter until Passover.

CHAPTER SIX: THE TORAH AND LEVIATHAN

Early in the first term the *cheder* had been divided into groups according to the abilities of the pupils. I was placed in the advanced group, together with two of my cousins. We could already read Hebrew text fluently, and Mottye the bean now carried us as far as lay within his scope as an elementary teacher: he began to translate the Five Books with us, the Chumesh, the most sacred of the Holy Writings. Thus, in my second term, I already became a Chumesh boy, and I, together with my companions, bore myself with more dignity. We were proud—perhaps a trifle haughty, and assumed toward the other children the attitude which the Rav assumes toward the assistant and the ritual chicken-slaughterer. That term new children were added to the *cheder*, beginners. We, the advanced pupils, were placed among those who still remained from previous terms, the backward children, so that all in all we were the *crème de la crème* of the *cheder*. The position had its advantages. Mottye the bean treated us with a little more consideration. Or, to be more correct, he used the newcomers as scapegoats, and automatically vented his bad moods on them rather than on us.

Before we were allowed to peep officially into the Five Books the Rebbi thought it necessary to make a formal introduction via a few stories intended to impress us with the awful sanctity of our new studies. Even Mottye the bean understood that it was not fitting to pass without ceremony from the plain reading of senseless words to the privileges of the Five Books. Some of the stories he told us have passed out of my mind. A few remain.

We were not to believe, he told us, that the Torah was something new. God gave it to His people Israel through his servant Moses, on Sinai—but He had created it two thousand years before the creation of the world. There was no hurry about it, for there were not any Jews to give it to. But God Himself wanted to play with the Torah. It was His toy. God Himself needs something to amuse Him.

At the bottom of the sea, Mottye went on, lies Leviathan, the monster fish, who encircles the world and holds his own tail in his jaws. God plays daily with Leviathan, as He plays with the Torah. When the end of the world will come God will slay Leviathan and roast him, and those who have been careful to observe all the laws of the Torah will eat roast Leviathan in the world to come. "Nothing for nothing," said Mottye the bean. "Everything must be earned. If you want to eat first-class fish in the world to come, you must study Torah in this world."

Mottye the bean had a materialistic outlook on life. As a teacher, he should have been a trifle more idealistic, but his secondary occupation, that of baker, was not without its influence. Thus his stories were always opposed, in their tone, to the stories which Mother used to tell us at home. In substance the stories were the same, but Mother made them more idealistic in purpose. Mother never used to tell us about rewards for studying the Torah. It was her point of view that we ought to study the Torah because there was nothing nobler and finer in the world.

Another story which Mottye the bean told us—and I still do not see the point of it—was about the argument between two Tanaim (Teachers) in the Talmud. One Tana said that God created the world in the month of Nisan, which is in the spring. The other said that He created it in the month of Tishri, which is in the autumn. The details of the argument escape me. I can only remember that it served to confuse me completely. For it did not fit in with the facts. There was no question about it to me that Adam, the first man, was a Jew, for it was unbelievable that God would first produce a gentile. Now: if the world was created in the month of Nisan, in the springtime, where on earth did Adam get his Matzoth for Passover? And if the world was created in the month of Tishri, in the autumn, where did Adam find a *baal tekiah*—a man to blow the ram's horn on the Day of Atonement, which falls in that month?

In a word, every story that Mottye the bean told us awakened a thousand questions in my mind, and I pelted Mottye with questions from morning to evening. For I was quick by nature, both in thought and in word, and no sooner did a doubt occur to me than I expressed it. Mottye, on the contrary, was cool and phlegmatic. A duel rose between Rebbi and pupil. I hardly gave him time to collect material for one answer before another question was on the tip of my tongue. Until in the end, exhausted, he gave me the stereotyped answer: "That's enough: if you learn too fast you will grow old too soon. Take it easy, and learn slowly, and the answers to your questions will come of themselves." After I had heard this from him several times, my questions died out. Not that I was satisfied with his explanation, but that I knew my questions to be useless. But all the more did my imagination play within: the material for my phantasies came from my studies. I swam in other worlds, the upper worlds; I dreamed of God, the Torah, Leviathan, angels, Adam, the first man, the first Passover, and the first New

Year: a fearful mixture of reflections, inspirations, and doubts which ran riot in my mind, so that I went about, frequently, like a child bereft of its senses.

For some weeks we learned the first portions of the Book of Genesis, translating it word for word into Yiddish. *Bereshith*, in the beginning; *boroh*, created; *Elohim*, God; *eth*, and; *hashomayim*, the heavens; *v'eth*, and; *ho-oretz*, the earth; and so on till we came to the first close: "And the evening and the morning were the first day." And we were not permitted to go any further until we knew this first section of the first chapter by heart. And here something very extraordinary occurred. I learned the few verses by heart easily enough, but not the Hebrew alone: the Hebrew and the Yiddish translation were organically bound together into a single text. I could not repeat the Hebrew without the Yiddish. And no sooner did I begin to recite the Bible, than I automatically lapsed into "*Bereshith*, in the beginning; *boroh*, created; *Elohim*, God . . ." Every word was really a double word, Hebrew and Yiddish together, like a coat and its lining. So that the two languages were worked into me with equal strength, each language cleaving to the other. They had their separate points, their particular appeal: if Hebrew was nobler and more dignified—the exterior of the coat—Yiddish was warmer and more comfortable—the lining of the coat. And even Hebrew was warmer to me because of the Yiddish lining. Just so, Yiddish also acquired more dignity and importance because of its association with Hebrew. For Yiddish had already ceased to be the street language, the language of daily intercourse. It was a language necessary to the learning and understanding of the Torah, and it suddenly rose to a higher level.

So we learned, verse by verse, the first chapters of the Five

Books, till we had acquired three of them by heart: and the evening and the morning were the third day.

I remember well that as I learned the first portion of the Pentateuch, with its description of God's creation of Heaven and earth, of the plants and animals and beasts, a sense of peace and satisfaction grew in me, and the restlessness of my childish mind began to subside. I seemed to have found an anchor in the tumult of questions which assailed me, a foundation of rock in the midst of a sea. For even as a very young child, I was inordinately curious. I could not accept things as they were, and either in the street or in the fields, I could not be content with appearances. The "why" and "how" which work in the minds of all children seemed to work with special fury in mine. Of course the old stock answer was given me: "God made it, and God made it just as it is." But of course to this answer came that old question which has danced in a million childish minds: "Yes, but who made God?" The mind of a child is simple, and is moved by straightforward, primitive logic. The child is not aware of any prohibitions: it pushes its questions right to the logical conclusion.

And it is therefore amazing to me that the first portion of the Bible should have had this calming effect on me. For it tells only the "what." And to that question of questions, the "how," there is not even a shadow of an answer. I can think only of one explanation, and that lies in the supreme artistic form of the first chapters of the Bible. The story is told with such simplicity, such elementary power and conviction, so harmoniously, that it carried me along, overwhelming my mind and filling me with a marvellous satisfaction. The telling of the story was enough. "And the earth was void and without form, and the spirit of God moved upon the surface of the waters." So thrilled was I by this description that all questions of accuracy, historicity, simply disappeared. It was the mood of the story which conquered me, and that was enough.

In the town of Swislowitz electric lighting was of course a thing unknown, and we children had never seen any one press a button and flood a room with light, instantaneously. But I remember that when I first saw this marvel—it was years later, in the city of Minsk—my mind flew back, and to my lips rose the words: "*Vayomer*, and said; *Elohim*, God; *yehi*, let there be; *or*, light; *vaihi*, and there was; *or*, light." The foundations of Genesis were laid in my mind like six gigantic stones, one stone for each day of the creation. I still see them concretely. But the Sabbath day never produced a concrete image in my mind. It remained abstract and nebulous, thin and translucent, hanging like a vague cloud over the six vast stones. So it happens that, until this day, when I think of a week, I picture only six days, and the Sabbath is a sort of addition to the six and not an integral part of the week. It is still the effect of those first lessons: "*Vayecholo*, and He finished; *hashomayim*, the heavens . . ."

As soon as I knew the first portion of Genesis, most of it by heart, and all of it with the translation, Mottye the bean persuaded my father to hold the first official examination at home. The ceremony took place on the Sabbath afternoon, immediately after my father rose from his nap. The table was decked with the Sabbath cloth: on it stood the big-bellied copper samovar, the oven-warmed tea in it—no fire, of course, on the Sabbath—and all of us drank. My father sat at my side, and Mottye the bean opposite me. Then my father gave the signal, and told me I could start. I stood up for the recitation, but my father told me I could sit down this time. I began—and got stuck at the second verse. I began again, and fared no better. I became nervous, and everything went out of my head. Mottye the bean turned as red as a beet: the truth was that these examinations were aimed no less at the Rebbi than at the pupil. Suddenly an instinct told me to stand up in spite of the permission to sit down. And no sooner was I on my feet than everything rolled back on me like a flood. The Hebrew words and their translations came flowing out of me so smoothly, so easily, that Mottye's face began to shine with joy and pride. My father looked proudly at me, and I, with confidence restored, carried on without one mistake and without one stop, right to the very end.

The slow autumn days grew darker, greyer, dragging their length across the skies under a covering of clouds. The sun rarely broke through. The Russian autumn wind began to blow, first in gusts, and then more frequently, till it blew continuously, bringing down with it now and again fierce bursts of rain. The melody of the winds, and the drum accompaniment of the rain on the window-panes, was like the minor-key chants in the Synagogue. The days became shorter, dimmer, and winter was in the air.

How different the house was now! Only a few months ago we had opened the doors and windows wide, to welcome in the summer. Now we locked and double locked them to keep the winter out. It was not an easy task to keep the Russian winter on the other side of the walls. We stuffed the cracks in the house with felt and lined the windows with tufts of cotton wool. The poorer folk did the same, using paper and straw. But it was not enough. We put in an extra set of windows, and those too we lined with cotton wool. Farewell, fresh air, until spring and Passover come.

However, the Jews of Swislowitz were not fresh-air fiends. True, you couldn't keep away from fresh air in the summer, and at that time of the year it probably did you little harm. As to the winter, you would have been thought crazy if you had opened a window to let out some of the warmth, which cost so much money, just for the sake of a little fresh air. There was only one way of looking at it. Either you don't waste your money on heating the house, or else, having heated it up, you keep it warm. It is a simple, literal fact that no house in Swislowitz ever opened a window from the beginning to the end of winter.

The children, who were kept indoors from morning till night, and saw the outside world only through the small, frozen windows, breathed for months the stuffy, thrice-used air of the closed rooms. The result was a good deal of sickness among the children—sometimes in the form of epidemics. In cases like these the old traditional methods were invoked. The old Rav decreed a fast for the Jewish inhabitants of Swislowitz, and the mothers went to the cemetery to "tear open" the graves and to obtain the intercession of their dead ones at the throne of Mercy. They thought it safer to try and open the windows of heaven than those of their homes.

I remember well that now and again one of my playmates would fall into a faint, right in the middle of the lessons in *cheder*. Rebbi and pupils were astonished, and could not account for it. There we were, the Rebbi, his wife, and ten or eleven pupils all crammed into one room—the wife, I think, counted at least for two—and no one understood that under these circumstances it would have been miraculous if one or another of the children had not felt sick from time to time.

The picture is still clear in my mind. A day in winter: outside the frost stabs and burns the wayfarer. A door opens, and a heavy cloud, so thick you could have cut it, forms there—the warm, thrice-breathed air from the lungs of the children congealing when the cold touches it. Instinctively one of the little ones makes for the door, panting for a breath of fresh air. And then there is an outcry from the mother: "Close that door! Don't you know that a wagon of wood costs five gulden?"

At home, in addition to the regular preparations to keep out the cold, there was also much to-do round the laying in of the winter stock of provisions. My mother was busy from morn till night pickling beets, salting cucumbers, boiling cranberries, and chopping cabbage. The cabbage heads were laid out on long tables, and round the table stood women, hired for this purpose, cutting the cabbage into thin strips. They worked swiftly, neatly, pressing the cabbage down with one hand, and slicing with the other. Watching them, I thought that at any moment one of the big, sharp knives would cut off somebody's finger. We used to linger round the tables, not only to watch, but also to get the hard cabbage cores. They were good to eat raw. The children of poor families used to bring cabbage cores to *cheder*, and eat them with bread for their second breakfast.

The poor boys in the *cheder* seldom used to go home for the midday meal. They brought their food along with them, and most of the time it consisted of a piece of unbuttered bread, a tail of salt herring, and a *beigle*—a sort of doughnut—for dessert. If the bread was buttered, or smeared with chicken fat, the herring or the doughnut was "off." The Jewish children of Swislowitz were never spoiled in the matter of food—or of fresh air. From earliest childhood they learned the lesson of renunciation, the war against the Evil Inclination. Parents seemed to be afraid that their children would grow up into gluttons and winebibbers.

I remember well that during the whole week none of my

poorer playmates ever brought to *cheder* a piece of meat or of fish other than herring. Nor did they ever have milk to drink. Milk was either for the very little ones, or else to be sold. Of dairy food they knew only sour milk and an occasional piece of soft cheese. An egg was a very rare luxury. And when we remember that in those days food was ridiculously cheap by comparison with modern prices, we can get some idea of the poverty which reigned among the Jews of Swislowitz. The modern man can hardly get a notion of it—unless he has studied the infinitesimal calculus.

A little world, little people with little ideas. Their needs were little; so were their sins and their virtues. But their worries were great, and so were their sufferings, for even their little demands could not be satisfied.

Even the children of the well-to-do were brought up on a Spartan régime. Our clothes were less patched, our food was a little better, but we knew nothing of luxuries. As far as my own home was concerned, I know that this did not arise from a spirit of frugality, for our budget was a generous one, even on modern standards. But our parents were afraid of spoiling us. My mother was surely good-hearted and kindly, but whenever I asked her for something which she thought a little out of the way, she would counsel me, "Don't look up, but down. See how your poorer playmates live." And the argument was unanswerable.

The severity of our early upbringing was reflected in other matters besides food and clothing. It affected our entire bearing. My poorer playmates had to become "independent" at an early age, for the simple reason that there was no one who could spare the time to look after them. At the age of five or six they were already little men. They went to Shuhl alone, with their prayer-book clutched under their arm. They went alone to *cheder*, through the darkness, the

111

rain, and the frost. They had to look out for the dogs, for the horses wandering on the footpaths. I too was brought up to look after myself at a tender age, and to be "independent" at the same age as they.

Our *cheder* studies ended with the evening—we had not yet reached the stage of night studies. As a rule we were confined to *cheder* from nine in the morning till about four in the afternoon, and then it was time to go to the Synagogue for afternoon prayer. But if the snow lay too deep, or the cold was unbearable, we were permitted to remain in the *cheder* until the time for evening prayer. Even then no one would come to lead us home. In larger, wealthier communities, there are *cheders* which have an usher for that purpose. In Swislowitz the usher was unknown. The only thing we had to help us was a lamp made of writing-paper, and fashioned after the Chinese hanging lantern.

During the long autumn evenings our house was always filled with people. The woods for which my father had contracts lay on both sides of the town, beyond the Beresina and beyond the Swisla. Our agents, or employés, used to spend the whole day in the forests, and in the evening they returned to the town. The elder among the employés, Pesach Mareina, lived in Choloi, a townlet not far from Swislowitz, but during the week he slept in our house. Both Jews and gentiles used to come to us, twenty and more at a time, and mostly for the purpose of settling their business affairs. When this was done the greater part would disperse, but a few would remain to chat of things in general—and most of all they loved to talk about the doings of the great world.

In those days Russia was preparing for the war with Turkey, impelled to it by the quarrels in the Balkans. And even the autocratic Russian government found it necessary to prepare public opinion for this step, and to explain to the Russian people that this war was not a war like all others, but that it was to be a Holy War, conducted for the sake of the Orthodox Church, which was being trodden underfoot by the infidel Turk. It was not going to be a selfish war; Russia had no other motive than the protection of her weaker brothers in the Balkan countries. And the war might eventually enable Russia to take down the Crescent from the Mosque of Sophia and to restore the Holy Cross in its place. Russia—so the government declared—was not so much interested in the Bosporus and in Constantinople, as in the Moslem mosque of San Sophia, which had originally been built as a Christian church by the immortal Constantine, and had then been defiled, changed into a mosque, by the infidel Turk. It would therefore be a war for God and for His holy name.

Every Sunday the priests would gather their flocks outside the church, and read articles from the papers, describing the fearful sufferings of the faithful under the domination of the Turk. Reading out the articles, they would add their own stories and interpretations, till the reading became a bitter harangue. The idea of a war with Turkey became popular in Russia several years before hostilities began.

And the chief subject of conversation, in the church, the Synagogue, the inn, and the home—when conversation turned from personal affairs to those of the world—was the impending war with Turkey. Many of the peasants used to work themselves up into a rage talking about the infidel Turk, and about the insolence of the British. By the latter they meant chiefly Queen Victoria and her ministers, whose policy was a thorn in the side of the Russian government.

Even we, the little ones, had some notion of the tremendous quarrel which was brewing in the outside world. I remember that the rage of the peasants infected me, too, and I could not get over the "insolence" of the Queen of England, a mere woman who interfered in such high matters, and that on the side of the Turk, too.

The biggest talker among the gentiles was a neighbour of ours by the name of Stepan Harnai. He was the chief trustee of Matzkevitch's congregation, and for that reason the Jews called him the gentile Synagogue President. Stepan Harnai was regarded as a man of knowledge—almost a scholar. He knew all the commandments of the Greek Orthodox Church, and all of the long prayers by heart. He also knew a great many stories out of the Bible. The gentiles of Swislowitz were proud of him, and used to say to us Jews, "You're not the only scholars. We have our Stepan Harnai." But the Jews, too, treated him with respect as a fine type of gentile, a man who was learned in the details of the faith of the gentiles. Our respect was increased by the fact that Stepan was a pious man, fond of religious discussions. The words "So God commands," "So the angels command," were frequently on his lips. This same Stepan used to spend long evenings in my father's house. They had no sort of business relations, so that the visits were devoted to higher purposes, to the discussion of "the worth-while things of life." Above all he liked to talk with my mother, who was greatly loved among the gentiles both for her piety and for the goodness of her heart. Slowly, carefully, he used to steer the conversation toward his religion, praise it to the skies, and tell marvellous stories out of the New Testament and later sacred books. With these he used to mingle stories from the Old Testament, to show how tolerant he was and with what respect he treated the faith of others. "The main thing is," he used to wind up, "you have to believe in God and in His

114

angels. If you do that, you are certain of your place in the next world, Jews, Christians, and even Tartars. But not the Turks and the Bashi-Bazouks." The Turks and Bashi-Bazouks he excluded categorically from heaven, in deference to the national politics of the times. The concession to the Tartars he made on the ground of local politics, the District Commissioner being a Tartar by blood. And faith in God and angels went hand in hand with a proper respect for the representatives of the government.

Stepan Harnai used to speak slowly, carefully, counting his words like coins. He always remained cool: his face was calm, his bearing restrained. He never became excited. And yet there was something of the eternal missionary in the man. We used to feel that we were listening to one who had secret motives which he would not reveal to any one, but which he never relinquished. His religious faith was deep, and he sought to infect others with it. He chose for his experiments the pious Jews, feeling that where piety of one sort or another existed, he would succeed soonest. The hardest part of the task was the laying of the foundation, but once that was done, the sacred building could be reared easily enough. The truth was—I recognized it in later years—that Stepan Harnai was not an ordinary man. He had a life-philosophy of his own, and in that philosophy there was no room for doubts. He was one of those types which haunt the pages of Dostoievsky and Gorki, types which belonged to old Russia, and which were to be found among the simple folk of that land in greater numbers than elsewhere. Stepan Harnai was a true seeker after God.

My mother's nature was stormy and passionate. With her, faith was deeper than conviction. She wanted to do more than believe: she wanted to be of the defenders of God and the faith. But what was the good of arguing with Stepan

Harnai? First, she could not keep pace with him, quote chapter and verse for every assertion, as he did. Second, it was a dangerous matter: we, the Jews, were the people in exile, and not the Russians. An unwary word might fall from her lips, and she would never be able to take it back. So my mother would remain silent most of the time, and only now and again venture a cautious word. But it could be seen that she suffered under this restraint. Her resentment grew in her, gathered because it found no outlet, and always tormented her.

But when the company had dispersed, and we, the family, remained among ourselves, the dam was swept away, and the floods of resentment were unloosed. "God in heaven! Why hast Thou given so little sense to the gentiles that they cannot see how vain their faith is, how foolishly they bend the knee before idols and images!" And then, turning to me, she told me the story of Abraham and his father Terah: how Abraham the child, left in charge of the shopful of idols, destroyed all but one with an ax, and placed the ax in the hand of the one that remained—so that when his father returned he could say that the one remaining idol had slaughtered all the others, thereby forcing from his foolish father the admission that it was impossible, because the idol could not stir a finger. She told me also the story of Nimrod and Abraham, and the fiery furnace. "Let *them* show us miracles like these," she wound up, angrily. "With their wooden images and their gilded pictures and all their rubbish. Never!"

My mother told *me* the story—but she was talking at the absent Stepan. She was pouring out her heart, strengthening herself in her faith, and carrying on a one-sided debate with the adversary who had gone home. She was defending her offended God.

My father would never interfere in these discussions. During the evening he would either be talking with his employés or going over his accounts. He was a severely practical man, with no use for idle talk. And when my mother became excited, he would interrupt her with, "Elke, aren't you ashamed of yourself to let such a silly business upset you? Who is Stepan Harnai? And why do you take his words to heart?"

But—how beautiful my mother was in those moments! She became in my eyes a saint. She surely loved her husband, Samuel Chaim, and her children—but she carried in her heart a love toward God that was incomparably greater. She was of the stuff of martyrs.

All evening long the samovar stood on the table. When the water ran low, we filled it again—it was never allowed to run dry. And when the fire at the bottom began to grow faint, and the samovar began to sing a hoarse chant, like the cantor at the end of a long day, we piled on the coal at the bottom. Tea was not regarded as a special delicacy: any one who wanted it was entitled to it.

This was the atmosphere in which I passed the winters of my childhood. Toys of the kind which might enable a child to find amusement alone were quite unknown. Little girls were allowed their dolls, but boys, belonging to the sterner sex, had nothing to correspond. I could not go to bed early, because my inmost nature revolted against it, and all the threats and blandishments of my parents were of no avail. In the end it was tacitly understood that I was permitted to stay up with the others. I sat there, breathing in a psychic atmosphere in which mingled the talk of forests and logs, business accounts, stories of God and the angels, and the rumblings of war among the nations.

CHAPTER SEVEN: WINTER

A FEW weeks after Chanukkah (the Feast of the Maccabees) the winter "fastened on us." We used to make a distinction between summer and winter; we said, "Summer has
come," and "Winter has fastened on us." The latter phrase
is easy to explain, for we took it that winter had not arrived
until he had fastened up the waters of the Beresina and the
Swisla. The snow might be lying on the streets and roofs of
the town, but it was not winter until the rivers were tied up.
For the snow was uncertain: it might come earlier or later, it
might stay for a day or a month. But once the river was
"fastened" it remained that way until the coming of spring.

The freezing over of the river was awaited impatiently
by the inhabitants of Swislowitz. In the interval between
autumn and winter the town was sometimes cut off from the
rest of the world, for just before the waters froze they often
overflowed the banks, and spread out beyond the meadows
into the wheatfields. And then, when the freezing set in, huge
ice-floes would go careening down the rivers, crashing into
each other with a tremendous, riotous noise. They were
heavy enough to endanger the supports of the wooden bridge
thrown across the Swisla. And more than one autumn the
attacks of the ice-floes removed support after support, and
the bridge began to totter and to tremble like a pious old
Jew in the ecstasy of prayer.

When the bridge was so dangerously close to collapse,

nobody dared cross it. The teamsters in the town refused to go out to the villages, and the peasants from the villages did not bring their produce into town. So Swislowitz was cut off from the world, and a dark, terrified atmosphere descended on its inhabitants. It should be borne in mind that for its knowledge of the outside world, for its "cultural" activities, no less than for its supplies, Swislowitz was dependent on the city of Babrusk: and the teamsters used to bring, together with their merchandise, the news of the world's affairs. And when the teamsters refused to cross the bridge, Swislowitz was abandoned, marooned in the midst of an ocean.

That alone would have sufficed to plunge the town into gloom. But there was also the economic factor. The peasants did not bring their produce in, and something like a famine was created. The shopkeepers at once raised their prices, and refused to sell quantities: they came down from the *pud* (forty pounds) to the one-pound measure, from the dozen to the unit. They had the impudence to charge a kopeck (half a cent) for one egg, when the usual price was eight kopecks a dozen—with one thrown in extra. The prices on milk, meat, beets, potatoes, cabbage, also went up. But the bitterest blow was the increase in the price of wood. This fell heaviest on the Jewish population. Little wonder then that they waited impatiently for the coming of winter and the freezing over of the rivers. Between afternoon and evening prayer they used to go down to the river and watch the ice-floes. The early ice-floes looked soft, vague. The peasants used to call them "lard-floes," and the Jews, to avoid the mention of swine-meat, called them "chicken-fat" floes. Later followed the real ice-floes, large, heavy, clear-cut, with the glint of steel on them. These meant business: within two or three days the waters would stop running, and there was rejoicing in the town. The news was carried from house to house: "The river is frozen: you can cross to the villages, you can go to Babrusk."

The first Festival of the Maccabees which I remember fell in the midst of a furious winter, which had "fastened" the rivers in a silent rage, and laid an invisible, bitter hand on the town. The cold burned intensely, the houses dripped icicles throughout the winter months. The chief preparation for the Festival of the Maccabees—at least, as far as the youngsters were concerned—consisted in the making of the tiny leaden tops, four-sided, with a grip protruding at the upper end—the traditional game for this festival. The making of leaden tops was no easy enterprise, and it belonged to the older boys. My brother Meyer was one of the principal manufacturers. The mould was made of four pieces of wood, one for each side, and within the mould had to be cut out—in reverse, of course—the four Hebrew letters which appeared in rotation on the sides of the top: *shin, nun, gimel, he—Shom nes godol hoyo,* "A great miracle was performed there," an allusion to the drops of oil in the "Eternal Light" of the Temple which burned for eight days while the Maccabees were driving the enemy before them. Above and below the mould tapered off into thin lines, to make the grip and the base of the top: then the mould was tied together with cord, and molten lead was poured in from above. It had to be done quickly, because the spoon was of some alloy which melted easily. It had to be done skilfully, too, or else some of the lead would be poured out over the fingers which were holding the mould. And more than one boy would be seen round the Festival, carrying a bandaged hand as evidence of his clumsiness. With these tops we played a special game which resembles American put-and-take. As a rule we played for the fun of it: but sometimes we played for money. And this was our introduction to gambling games, later concentrated in cards, of which more anon.

The most moving ceremony of the Festival of Maccabees is the lighting of the candles. On the first night one candle is lit, on the second two, on the third three—and so on till the end of the eight days which commemorate the period during which the unfed lamp continued burning miraculously in the Temple. The candles were short, grooved, and prettily coloured. But the first few nights the ceremony made no impression on me. The fact was that Channukah was not then regarded as one of the important festivals in the Jewish calendar. The miracle of the inexhaustible oil in the Eternal Light did not seem to grip the imagination of the Jews, who had become accustomed to miracles on a larger and more imposing scale. And for some reason or other they told us little about the heroic wars of the Maccabees—little or nothing at all. The Rabbis were not interested in wars, and pious Jews had the same tastes. It was only years later, with the rise of the forerunner of the Zionist movement—the Chibath Zion, or Love of Zion—that the wheel made a half turn, and Channukah became one of the great and important nationalist festivals of the Jewish people. It was then that the lighting of the candles became a significant and moving ceremony.

That first winter in my memory was famous for its cold and for the great snows which fell. The waters were invisible under the uniform sheet of snow which levelled rivers, meadows, and wheatfields into one blinding white plain. On the broad street the snow lay "just as when it was born"—that is, in a vast drift along the centre. But along the sides of the street, and from door to door of opposite houses, paths were cut through the snow. The hand of winter lay dead and even on town and river and field and forest. Only the summits of the evergreens, the firs, and the yews peeped through, unconquered. They were like stubborn fingers, thrust upward by the gnarled old forest, to show the world that the winter had not bludgeoned it out of existence.

The sunsets of those winter days were indescribably beautiful. The sun went slowly down among strata of colours, light blue, deep blue, yellow, rose, crimson, and blood-red, hot like the horseshoe which the smith laid on the anvil after he had blown for ten minutes with the bellows. And so it happened that when a furious wind swept through the heavens, I used to think that a piece of that fiery sky would be broken off and laid somewhere on an anvil to be hammered, and storms of sparks would be beaten out of it, to stream like falling stars to every corner of the sky.

Among these days came also the Krischenye, the Pravaslavna christening of Jesus, the holiest day in the calendar of the Church.

Two broad paths were cut through the snow from the portals of each church—Yuremitch's and Matzkevitch's—down to the bank of the frozen Beresina. When the snow had been swept off these paths, yellow sand was strewn on them, to make sure no one would slip. Then, on the ice which covered the Beresina, a large circle was cleared of snow, and marked off with young fir trees. Right in the centre of the circle a cross was cut into the ice, and in the geometric centre of the cross a hole was bored through to the dark waters underneath. These were the preparations of the festival.

In the early morning the frozen air was bluish as if a breath of steel had gone through it, translucent, biting. The bells of both churches rang out, the big bells and the small

bells, the big ones stately and golden, the little ones hurried
and silvery. And in the air gold and silver and steel were
mingled in a cold, clear harmony, penetrating all the senses.

Along the centre of the broad street came the sleds, dozens
and scores of them, bringing the peasants of surrounding
hamlets. These were the Yishuvniks of the gentiles. The
men wore brand-new leggings, and on their heads were new
bearskins, covering their ears. Round the middle they wore
many-coloured girdles. The women were dressed in gay and
brilliant holiday attire, throat and bosom were brilliant with
beads, the head was covered with a nun's wimple of white
linen slashed with red. Instead of leggings the wealthier
peasants wore long, polished boots, and instead of felt
mantles, sheepskin coats.

The churches were packed to overflowing. As in all Greek
Orthodox cloisters, there were no seats for the congregants,
so that the peasants crowded in until every inch of space
was filled. Even so there was not room enough; crowds of
young peasants remained standing outside during the services, and a wooden fence, encircling them, made them part
of the congregation. The numbers of those who could not
find admission ran into several hundred. They pressed together closely, to ward off the bitter cold, and while they
listened to the chants from within the church, they stamped
their feet and clapped their hands in rhythm, to keep their
limbs from freezing. The men stood with heads bared, but
the women kept their white and red wimples on. Outside of
that crowd, stamping rhythmically, not a soul was to be seen
in the streets. Every now and again the heads were bent in
prayer, and then were raised again: it was as if a wind
had swept over a field of poppies, bowing the stalks and
lifting them again.

When the prayers were over, the congregations streamed

simultaneously out of both churches. First came the bearers of the holy banners—brilliant pictures painted on silk, and borne aloft on gilded standards. The edges of the banners were rich with silver and gold fringes. There were pictures of the Father, the Son, the Mother and Son, pictures of the later saints, in which the Orthodox Church is particularly rich, and pictures of the apostles. Some of the banners carried whole groups of figures, and scenes that told the stories of the Church.

After the banner-bearers came a group of very young peasant girls, carrying a heavy image in a gold frame. This was the image of the Virgin Mother of God, the symbol of purity and sweetness. Not every one was permitted to touch the frame around the image. Only the fingers of unstained girls were allowed to come in contact with it. And so, in order to be certain, the carriers of the image were chosen from among very young peasant girls, such as could not have had even a foretaste of sin.

After the image of the stainless Mother came the priest Yuremitch. He was dressed in his finest raiment, old gold, velvet, and sky-blue silk. Over his robes he wore an "imitation" ephod, worked in gold and silver, and decorated with countless crosses and images of flowers. A velvet mitre towered on his head, and on either side of him walked the deacon and the reader. In one hand Yuremitch carried a prayer-book, and from the other a silver censer swung on silver chains. And while the censer swung free, and sent out its incense into the air, he read the prayers in his deep, ringing voice. The red-hot coals which lay in the censer sent out a cloud of steam and incense, and the crowd breathed in the prayers and the odours of the incense. And Yuremitch, with his majestic figure, his long black and silver beard, his pigtail and his robes, looked like the figure of an ancient elder of the Church who had stepped out of the framework of one of the banners in front of him.

At the top of the hills, where the cleared road went down toward the Beresina, the two congregations met, two processions alike in all respects, the same banners and the same order—except that the procession from Matzkevitch's church looked poorer. Matzkevitch went, like the members of his flock, bareheaded—he had not the rank which entitled Yuremitch to a mitre. Step by step the two processions went down to the Beresina, and on the ice the priests, the banner-bearers, the bearers of the images, entered the cleared circle, while the crowd of worshippers formed in ranks around them.

Those of us—the Jews—who had watched the processions from far off, never went down to the river with them. We knew that "down there" they were baptizing some of the images in the cold waters, through the hole which had been bored through the centre of the cross on the ice. So that this intimate ceremony remained a secret to us. None of the older Jews ever went out even on the street—only a few of the younger ones were tempted by the colours and the numbers of the procession, and could not resist the appeal. There was many a quarrel in Jewish homes before the more obstinate youngsters were permitted to go out and watch. Our elders told us contemptuously that there was nothing to see, but not all their arguments—not even their warnings that some of the younger peasants might drive us away with stones—could prevail. We had a powerful counter-argument. "Don't some of them sometimes come to watch our processions round the pulpit on the Day of the Rejoicing of the Law? And if they can look at us, why can't we look at them?"

So as a child I already looked upon their God, and upon

the Mother of their God, and even then I knew that between us, between the gentiles and the Jews, ran a deep stream which divided two worlds. No bridge or ferry could carry us across the waters. I knew that, and yet, like a child which breaks its toy in order to see how it works, I lingered round their church and their procession, driven by a painful hunger to penetrate the secret of their faith. Was our God indeed common to them and to us, as Stepan Harnai used to argue, or were they really idol-worshippers, worshippers of images and false gods, as my mother said?

The ceremony ended, the congregations streamed back quickly to the churches, the images were replaced, and the bells rang out the close of the services. Then the crowds scattered over the town, the Jews opened their shops, and breathed a sigh of relief: "Thank God, another Krischenye over."

Swislowitz, on the top of its "mountain," was always safe from the danger which threatened so many villages in our vicinity—the overflowing of the rivers. It was uncomfortable to be cut off from the rest of the world when the Swisla and Beresina rose over their banks and flooded the countryside, but at least we were safe. When the other villages were inundated, we felt like Noah in his ark, saved from the floods which covered the rest of the world.

But this source of relief was also a source of another danger: lifted up as we were, we were exposed completely to the fury of the winds. There was nothing to break the impact. The lighter winds, though they brought much discomfort, were not an unmixed blessing: they were the only street-cleaning department we knew anything about, and when one of them had blown through the town and carried off the rubbish accumulated in the streets, the place looked astonishingly neat. But the real storm winds—and they came not infrequently—were another matter. The houses, or rather hovels, of the poor were not firmly built, and the roofs sat on them like a cap slipped over the head. I use this figure advisedly: most of the Jews of Swislowitz used to wear skull-caps under their hats, to be safe from the sin of ever being bareheaded, even for an instant. And under the flimsy roofs of their houses some of them used to build "skull-caps"—a defence against the storm winds which might slip the regular hats off the heads of the houses. But some of them had not this reserve, and a strong wind would leave their houses uncovered, just like a booth in the feast of Tabernacles, but without the covering of branches.

The hot summer winds brought a great deal of discomfort, but they were tolerable compared with the mad rage of the winter blasts. When one of these storms descended on the town, the doors were sealed, and no one dared venture into the street. On such days life was suspended, congealed. Then Swislowitz looked like a town of the dead, half buried under the snow, with the wind howling a furious dirge over it. Within the howling of the wind we also heard the howling of hungry wolves, and the covered city was half hidden from the heavens in the whirl of the millions of snowflakes. Within the house we sat huddled close to each other. No work was done. All we could do was wait for the storm to die down. And if the reader bears in mind the sanitary arrangements in the houses of Swislowitz, he can form some idea of the kind of life we were reduced to during those winter storms.

Storms like these came several times in the winter. Sometimes they raged for twenty-four hours, and sometimes for days at a stretch. The little ones trembled in every limb. In order to comfort us and remove our fears, the older folk told us that the wild dance outside was the dance of witches and evil spirits, who could not hold out very long. Another purpose of this explanation was to give us some insight into the nature of things, so that we should not be altogether ignorant of the laws which governed the world. As to its first purpose, at least, the explanation was quite unsuccessful, because to the terror which the winds inspired in us was added the terror of the witches and the evil spirits. They haunted me in the night and entered my dreams. While I lay awake I used to repeat the Kriath Shema, a prayer which drives evil spirits away: and I used to pack myself close into my covers. But I was still afraid.

On one of these stormy days, I remember well, a singular incident occurred which shook up the whole community of Swislowitz.

Dave "the ascetic," a poor teacher blessed with a big family, supported in his house a younger brother, a lad of eight, an "all-round orphan," that is, an orphan with neither father nor mother. I can no longer remember the name of this boy; I will therefore call him the orphan. There were quite a number of orphans, but this little fellow had, for one reason or another, become a public character. He was *the* orphan of the town, and every one was interested in his welfare—particularly on the spiritual side. Every one was anxious that, though he had not the guidance of either father or mother, he should grow up into a good, God-fearing Jew. And every one took it upon himself to correct him, sometimes with a harsh word and sometimes with a slap. The latter he would get in Synagogue, during services, for omitting an Amen or failing to bow at the right moment. The slap was given out of collective affection for the poor little fellow. The pity of it—he had not even a father to slap him when he needed it!

Then something happened. On one of the stormiest days of my first year as a *cheder* boy, Dave the ascetic insisted on sending the little fellow to morning services in the Synagogue—and to first services at that. Dave and his sons did not turn up until the second service. The roads were only half cleared, and the frost was unusually severe even for Swislowitz. When Dave arrived at the Synagogue the orphan was not there. Nor had any one seen him during the first services. At once a hue and cry was raised, and angry accusing fingers were pointed at Dave for having sent the orphan out alone. The older people organized a search. They looked for the child on every street of Swislowitz. They beat the snow on the sides of the roads, believing that the boy had fallen by the way. But not a sign of him was found. There was not even a trace of his footsteps. And before long a rumour spread through the town that evil spirits had carried off the orphan. Characteristically enough, no one thought of looking for him in the houses of the peasants.

It is hard to say how this tragedy would have ended for Dave the ascetic if the next morning the orphan had not returned all alone and unharmed to the house of his brother. It transpired that the boy had actually lost his way the morning before and had fallen exhausted in the snow. A peasant saw the little body and carried it off to the District Commissioner's headquarters. There they rubbed him with snow and towels until he came to. The child could not speak a word of Russian, and therefore was unable to give any account of himself. The peasants, for their part, were not unduly exercised by the fact that somewhere a family might be worrying itself to death over the missing child, so they kept him for twenty-four hours, and then, the storm having abated, they let him out. Their intentions were not unfriendly: they were only playing what they thought was something of a joke on their Jewish neighbours.

And here begins the second act of the tragedy.

On the third morning the orphan came as usual to services in the Synagogue. When services were over, the congregation surrounded him and began to ask him for details of his adventure. The child naïvely told everything. He said that the gentiles had treated him ever so nicely, much better, in fact, than at home. He was kept comfortably warm, and they fed him bread and "white herring."

"White herring!" There is no such thing! Like a lightning flash the truth broke on the assembled congregants. The child had been fed bacon! A universal horror was expressed on the faces of the crowd—horror and indescribable pain. At once the centre of the tragedy was shifted to the "white herring," and the rage of the older people against Dave the ascetic rose now not from his cruelty in exposing a child to death in the snowstorm, not from the near-murder he had committed, but from the abomination which was now to be recorded forever against the Jewish community of Swislowitz. A Jew had partaken of swine-meat! In the person of the helpless orphan the entire community was touched with uncleanness. On the orphan they looked with genuine commiseration. They only questioned him more closely: they only tried to make him admit with his own lips that he had eaten the meat of the swine. But the child looked back out of innocent eyes, and repeated that he had only eaten "white herring."

When the big ones were done with the child, the youngsters got their turn. We surrounded him, and submitted him to a minute and merciless cross-examination. He had to tell us ten times over what the "white herring" tasted like. And at last he found a description for it. "It tasted like fat stewed meat dipped in salt." In our subconscious we envied the orphan. The horrible sin would not be laid to his account, but to that of Dave the ascetic. And there you were: he had had this extraordinary adventure, and yet was as untainted as if it had not taken place!

The Jewish community of Swislowitz was not destined to have much joy of its orphan—or its orphan of the community. Soon after Passover of that year the orphan disappeared a second time, and now, it seemed, for good. It was taken for granted that gipsies had spirited him away. But years later it transpired that a group of Jewish tumblers had tempted him to join them, and had taught him their trade. In time, feeling certain that the child had been forgotten, they even came to Swislowitz to offer a performance. The orphan happened by then to be their star actor, their best drawing-card. But right in the middle of the performance Moses the shoemaker rose up and cried, "It's the orphan!" The band of tumblers denied everything, and when the young acrobat was questioned he remained stubbornly silent. When he was made to speak, he tried to play the idiot, and made his answers unintelligible. Finally Moses the cobbler mentioned the story of the "white herring," and in spite of himself the boy laughed outright.

A great battle ensued between the community and the actors, and the community won. Swislowitz had its orphan again.

Whatever illusions the world may have about the wealth of the Jews one thing is certain, as I learned from the Talmud in later years: we are the richest people in the world as far as sacred festivals go. I found out that even in the matter of New Years there were no less than four on our calendar: the Jewish year was a monster with four heads. There was the New Year which was held in highest esteem because it belonged to our God, the New Year of the day of reckoning and of judgment. There was a second New Year, which we had set apart for our kings, whom we also held in esteem. The third New Year was the day of purely earthly accounts, the day when all notes and bills fell due. The gentile economists who believe that the Jews are the inventors of the promissory note would have found great support for their theory in this third New Year. But there was a fourth New Year, the New Year of the Trees.

He who would understand the significance of that fourth New Year must turn to the Orient. It is only in the Orient that the tree plays so overwhelming a rôle: it gives food and casts a shadow, and the second is not less important than the first in lands which are exposed to the burning sun, day in, day out, for nine months of the year. Out of gratitude to the trees was born this fourth New Year, concerning which I learned only during my first year as a *cheder* boy.

One fine morning Mottye informed us that another holiday was approaching, and we would get an afternoon of freedom. He also informed us that on this holiday it was accounted a merit to eat fruit—as much of it as possible: and we should all come to *cheder* that day well provided with fruits of all sorts. It happens that this holiday falls in the dead of the Russian winter, when the landscape is covered with snow, when the trees are mantled in white and the long icicles hang like inverted candles from the roofs of the houses. And the stories which the Rebbi told us about the rebirth of the trees were unconvincing: they sank, lost, into the snow that surrounded us, and died of exposure to the frosty air. And I pitied a holiday born in the midst of winter.

This holiday is seldom called by its right name, which is the New Year of the Trees. Somehow the name is too noble for such a wilted festival. So they call it, popularly,

Chamisho Osor Be-Shevat—which means simply the Fifteenth Day of the Month of Shevat, or, briefly, the Fifteenth. On that day the trees have their resurrection. Not *our* trees, the trees in the forest round Swislowitz, but the trees of our forefathers, in Palestine. There, the Rebbi told us, is neither winter nor cold nor snow. The land lies close to the gates of Paradise, and in the warm winds which blow from within the gates, the land blossoms into all sorts of marvellous fruits, figs, dates, locust, oranges, and pomegranates. He repeated: "Don't forget to bring plenty of fruit to *cheder* on that day." We got the impression that he was more interested in the fruits than in the holiday. Figs, dates, and locust we knew: but oranges and pomegranates were strangers to us. We had no idea what they looked like, but the sonorous names—oranges and pomegranates—worked in our minds, and produced a rich, golden effect.

I did not let the Rebbi carry off his holiday too easily. I plied him with a thousand questions, not so much for the sake of the answers—which I knew could never satisfy me— but because I was outraged by a sense of discord. What had golden fruits to do with the harsh winter landscape and the howling winds? On days like these I could not lift my fancy into a land of eternal summer. I tried hard, but the distance was too great. And being angry with myself, I expressed my anger by the stubborn, sceptical questions which I heaped on the head of Mottye the bean.

"How is it with the lakes in Palestine?" I asked. "Do they never freeze over?"

"Never!" he answered sternly. "Haven't I taught you that the rivers of Palestine flow out of Paradise, four rivers, Gihon and Pishon and Tigris and Euphrates? How can rivers freeze which have their sources in Paradise? Of course there is a fifth river, called Sambatyon, but that river, far from freezing, throws up hot stones all the year round. Only on the Sabbath day it rests, because it is a Jewish river."

Mottye the bean was weak on geography. He took it that the four rivers which flowed out of Paradise were Jewish rivers for the simple reason that Paradise was a Jewish place. As children we were therefore imbued with imperialistic notions that ours was Paradise, ours was Aram Naharaim—which is Mesopotamia—where Terah and his children lived, and ours too were Hermon and the forests of Lebanon. I was made part possessor of these and many other places. At this point I became confused. I learned in *cheder* that Paradise was located right on this earth: I had some notion of its location, and I also knew that four earthly rivers flowed out of it. But my mother always spoke of a Paradise where the saints and sages sat after their death, eternally absorbed in the study of sacred Jewish lore. My mind alternated between the two Paradises, the Paradise which is on earth, and that which is in Heaven. In the latter I saw the sages seated at their studies, and in the former I saw Adam and Eve wandering among the trees and plucking the full, soft fruits. The earthly paradise was a clear picture, but the Paradise which is in Heaven, with its golden thrones, its bearded students, its volumes of lore, was covered with a mist.

And no sooner did Mottye touch on the subject of Paradise than my tongue was loosened and I began to fire my questions at him. Was it not written in the Pentateuch that God made both Heaven and earth? Why then did the Sacred Book mention only the earthly paradise, and not the Paradise which is above? And without waiting for the answer, I asked him something even more difficult. If there were two Paradises, one for earth and one for Heaven, did it not follow that there had to be two Gehinoms, two Hells, one for earth and one for Heaven? And why was there no mention of *either* in the Sacred Book? Did not the Sacred Book contain everything?

Poor Mottye the bean bowed before the storm of questions. It was obvious that I had confused him, and he did not know where to begin. The questions resolved into a sort of debate between Rebbi and pupil, with the other pupils as audience. None of them interfered, but it was clear that they were all on my side. I was regarded as the most learned among them. They knew I would not let Mottye fool me, and that he would have to give a halfway satisfactory answer or acknowledge defeat. I saw the joyous, expectant look on the faces of my schoolmates, and I brought up the heavy artillery. "If in Palestine there is summer all year round, what do the trees need a New Year for? Can't they continue growing all the time?" The shell landed and exploded! For this was a simple question within the reach of every child in the room. They knew that trees die in the winter; therefore they must be reborn. But if there is no winter, there is no rebirth. And immediately a rebellious murmur spread through the *cheder*. There *was* no such thing as a New Year of the trees! The whole thing was a lie!

All this was not much to the liking of Mottye the bean. I was too sharp-tongued and too obstinate. Himself a simple man, he had never debated these questions with himself, and I was exposing him to the derision of the *cheder*. And then, all his stories about the Fifteenth had only one point: he wanted us to bring plenty of fruit to the *cheder*. He perspired under the cannonade of questions, afraid that the exposure would leave him without his gift of fruits. He answered my first questions evasively enough: but to that last and most puzzling question he told us something too obviously thought up on the spur of the moment. "In Palestine," he said, uncertainly, "the trees are so lovely, and so

135

delicate, that even in that marvellous climate they cannot grow all year round, and there has to be a special New Year for their resurrection." And again there swam up the fabulous oranges and pomegranates, which we had never looked upon, but which had bewitched us by their names.

On the holiday of the Fifteenth—the Arbor Day of Palestine—the house remained prosaic and unadorned. All that happened was that my mother gave me dried figs, dates, and locust to take to *cheder*. While she made up the bundle for me, she told me of the glories of Palestine—a land flowing with milk and honey, and set with trees which bore wonderful fruits. The fruits we ate in the exile were of no account there. Even the locust was fed to goats, or the goats came and nibbled them right off the trees.

In the *cheder* every boy poured out his fruits on the table, and a common stock was made. We ate what we could and the rest remained for Mottye. We did little studying that day. Mottye went over a few verses with us, for form's sake, and then told us more stories of Palestine. It was a withered holiday for me. Figs and locust and dates we could buy all the year round in the shops of Swislowitz. What was the point of it? The fruits were dried, hard—old stock with the softness long since pressed out of them. And with these withered fruits they sought to awaken in us soft green memories of a far-off land, and delicate trees which fail even in eternal summer and must be reawakened by the soft breath of the New Year.

CHAPTER EIGHT: CHERNEH THE WIDOW

Soon after the fifteenth day of Shevat the town began to liven up—Purim was coming—the festival which commemorates the triumph of the Jews of Persia over Haman the persecutor in the days of Ahasuerus, Esther, and Mordecai. Now Purim itself is certainly not among the major festivals, but it is the merriest and most jovial of them all. And the Jews of Swislowitz looked forward to it less on its own account than for the sake of the Purim players, the only approach to a theatre known to us.

The Purim players of Swislowitz were preparing that year to give two grand performances: "The Story of Esther" and "The Selling of Joseph." The first of these was the authentic play of the festival, a sort of mystery or miracle play, given every year. It already had its trained actors, some of whom conserved their rôles for several years in succession. But for "The Selling of Joseph" new forces had to be trained, and a tremendous hubbub arose in the town concerning the distribution of the rôles. There were three candidates for every rôle, and it was impossible to satisfy even the successful candidates. And the quarrels spread from the candidates to their families, and from the families to their friends, and the whole town seethed with claims and counter-claims, ambitions and artist's passions.

The general organizer of the plays was Benche, son of Cherneh the widow. He was régisseur, stage-manager, and promoter rolled into one. He had a heart-breaking task in front of him, for no matter whom he chose, he alienated more than he won over. But to the honour of his memory be it said, he was an honest man. He chose his actors without fear or favour, solely on their merits, and without regard to their influence and family connections. He was an artist in search of artists. He put all the candidates through their paces, tested their elocution and their memory. Perhaps he would not have been so stern and masterly if he had not had behind him his mother—Cherneh the widow. And Cherneh the widow was an important factor in the life of Swislowitz. She deserves more than passing mention.

This tall, middle-aged woman was possessed of a waist-line which had no rival in the town of Swislowitz. But a second possession made her dangerous—a restless and poisonous tongue. She talked inexhaustibly—and woe to the listener who fell into her clutches, for without something approaching physical violence it was impossible to escape from the torrent of words. They poured out like peas from a hole in the bottom of a barrel. And her arguments were clear, sharp, and irresistible. She had a finger in every pie in the town. Private affairs not less than the affairs of the community engaged her attention closely. When questions like those of the Rabbi's salary, the hiring of a second slaughterer, the fixing of the ritual baths or of the public lodging-house, came up for discussion, Cherneh the widow had much to say, and she said it. She went from house to house making propaganda for her views, and preparing public opinion for her special solution of all questions. Within her inexhaustible general interests she also had a special field, the protection of the widows and orphans of Swislowitz. And if there was in Swislowitz a heavier tax on the wax candles of the rich than on the tallow candles of the poor, it was the work of Cherneh the widow. "If," she argued passionately, "there are luxurious homes which cannot do without wax candles, let them pay. Let not the poor, the widow and the orphan, be burdened with all the costs of the community."

And Cherneh the widow was a force to be reckoned with in Swislowitz; not because of the power of conviction which lay in her words, but because of the fear which she inspired. She was the most daring person in the town in the matter of interrupting the reading of the Torah during the Sabbath services in the Synagogue.

This immemorial privilege of the poor and the powerless was an extraordinary institution. The interruption of the reading occupied the same place in the life of the small town as the strike does in the modern industrial world. The scene must be recalled in its fulness if we are to understand the force of the action. It is a Sabbath morning in the Synagogue. The congregation is deeply absorbed in its prayers; the sanctity of the day rests on all the worshippers, and in their minds there is a mingling of holy thoughts and a foretaste of the dainty Sabbath dishes which wait for them at home. They come to services early, and on empty stomachs. And at home waits, as *hors d'œuvre*, a dainty appetizing piece of herring, surrounded by onion parings, all swimming in a sea of sharp vinegar. After it will come the sweet, stewed fruit, with a succulent morsel of meat in it—perhaps the only meat tasted during the week. And, most luscious of all, the warmed dishes kept in the oven since the last day, because it is prohibited to touch fire on the Sabbath. Thereafter comes the crown of the meal, the *kugel*, the Sabbath pudding, majestic, satisfying, somniferous. There will be leisure, ease, forgetfulness of the sordid week-days, when the midday meal is only a tasteless, hurried interlude between morning and afternoon slavery. And, after the meal, the Sabbath siesta. The mouth of the worshipper waters, and expectancy gives a sharp edge to his religious joy. Who would not happily pay the price of the morning prayers for so joyous and kingly an afternoon? He prays with double reverence, secure in the knowledge of immediate as well as of heavenly reward.

The last of the regular prayers is said: the last roulade of the cantor dies away, and the high officials of the Synagogue make ready to bring out of the Ark the Scrolls of the Torah, the vast parchment copy of the Pentateuch, in order that the week's portion may be read. And suddenly . . .

Suddenly a Jew appears in the pulpit, where the Scrolls are to be laid down, delivers a resounding blow with one of the heavier prayer-books, and cries out at the top of his voice:

"I forbid the Reading!"

The effect is electrical. First there is a gasp of astonishment: then a mutter of angry and astonished voices—and then silence. The Jew in the pulpit waits, and when the silence is complete, he voices his complaint. He knows that he is secure. He is exercising an ancient privilege which it would be blasphemy to challenge. Yet it needed a certain degree of daring. Not every challenger had a case that would carry the day: nor was every challenger strong enough even if his case was good. The congregation listens for a moment, and if the man falters, or if his words have no appeal, some one steps out of the mass of worshippers, approaches the Ark, flings open its doors, and cries out the first words of the ceremony of the Reading. The real test of character then begins. If the complainant is strong, or if he is inspired to strength by a sense of deep outrage, he will continue crying out. He may even guard the way to the doors of the Ark, and either by his threat of opposition, or by the strength of his indignation, prevent the resumption of the ceremonies.

Now the right of interruption was common to women as well as to men. And as often as not the pulpit would suddenly be occupied by a woman who had come rushing down from the women's gallery. She herself would strike the pulpit, or, if she was weak, she had a right to demand from the beadle that he do it for her.

Cherneh the widow was the most effective "interrupter" in the whole of our town. She seldom exploited the privilege on her own behalf. She spoke for others—and the congregation knew that Cherneh was *not* a person to be intimidated, interrupted, or overridden. Once she had broken up the services she would keep them suspended until she had obtained satisfaction.

In such cases Cherneh would make full use of all her gifts —her bitter tongue and her physical bulk. She had developed a high technique in the interruption of the reading— for she had little faith in the power of abstract justice. No sooner had she attracted the attention of the congregation by a mighty thump on the pulpit than she would retire at once to the foot of the steps which led up to the Ark, where the Scrolls are kept, and block the approach effectively with her massive, immovable figure. There was no way of slipping by her, for her huge girth left not an inch of room. The attempt to push by her would have been both difficult and ugly. And then there was the lash of her tongue, and any one who might have been ready to expose himself to an act which was in itself both mean and ludicrous, shrank from the verbal counter-assault of Cherneh. In abuse she was utterly fearless, sparing no one, from the Rav himself down to the bathman. If, in addition to all these advantages, she was armed with a just cause, she was terrific: she did not content herself with pleading the case, but would pour out the venom of her resentment against all the evils ever perpetrated by the Jews of Swislowitz. Nor would she step down until the elders of the city had given their solemn assurance that the wrong would be righted on the very next day.

By profession Cherneh was a baker of pancakes. But she really had many professions. She knitted socks to order, she plucked feathers for cushions, chopped cabbages, kneaded and spread the dough for Matzoth, served at weddings, and watched the dead. But pancakes were her specialty. Whosoever wanted pancakes, fresh, crisp, right off the pan, had to go to Cherneh, early in the morning. Later she was distributing them from house to house. The pancakes were big enough to cover a whole plate—and the price was two for a kopeck.

It was a difficult and thankless profession, but Cherneh could not raise the price for fear of competition on the part of the bakers of *beigle*, or doughnuts. It was generally conceded that though the pancake was heavier and more satisfying, the *beigle* was daintier and sweeter: it was therefore impossible to give either of them the advantage of price. And Cherneh used to complain bitterly: "Would to God I had begun with *beigle* instead of with pancakes. But too late now. I am known as Cherneh the pancake maker, and I daren't experiment." And the truth was that her pancakes were famed all over the town for their peerless crispness and flavour.

If I remember rightly Cherneh was the enterprising soul who first introduced a credit system in Swislowitz. She used to sell pancakes to the *cheder* boys on credit. And many a quarrel arose from her inability to keep books: she had to remember every one of her sales during the week. I must admit, to my shame, that not all of my schoolmates were honest customers, and on one occasion Cherneh issued an ultimatum that she would close the credit department of her business. "There is no hope in credit," she complained; "the only way you can make money is on a cash basis." But under pressure she gave way again: she had to meet formidable competition.

Such was Cherneh the widow, mother of Bencheh the *régisseur*, who undertook, that Purim of my first *cheder* year, to present the community of Swislowitz with two full performances in honour of the festival.

Bencheh was an old bachelor in the neighbourhood of thirty—old bachelor being the designation for any Jew who had not taken a wife unto himself before he had passed the early twenties. Physically he presented a strange contrast to his mother, for he was short and lean. He wore a beard *à la* Napoleon III. He must have inherited his build from his father, a teacher and—if Cherneh's memory and story were to be trusted—a scholar. From his mother he inherited his quick and skilful tongue. Like his mother's, his untrained elocution was swift and clear-cut. His mother's speech reminded one of a large barrel of peas emptying through a hole at the bottom: his reminded one of a thin paper bag of rice, also with a hole at the bottom. And when he became excited, his words beat on your ear with the rattling impact of bird-shot.

Bencheh was by instinct a vagabond, a hobo. Swislowitz was too narrow for him, and from childhood on he was tormented by the *Wanderlust* of the gipsies. He brought his mother little joy, and long and bitter were the plaints which she poured out to the housewives of Swislowitz. When he was nine years old she apprenticed him to a tailor, but at the age of twelve he ran away, dreaming of the great outside world. He thought of going down the river, down to Kiev, to Krementchug, and perhaps even farther. But he stopped short in Choloi, finding his adventures unpleasant. He came home, tailored another year, and ran away again.

All his youth passed this way, intervals of respectability alternating with intervals of unsuccessful vagabondage.

For the Purim I am now speaking of, he had returned from Kiev, after an absence of some months. In that metropolis he had picked up another, more modish pronunciation of Yiddish, and he made fun of our peasant thickness of speech. He expressed his superior culture in other ways, too: he was the only one in the town to wear a short coat instead of the usual long capote: he wore a derby instead of a cap, and his trousers had cuffs at the bottom—the only trouser-cuffs in Swislowitz. He walked apart, like an aristocrat whom evil fate had cast among boors and savages. But in spite of his contempt for us, he loved to gather crowds around him and recount the marvels of the vast world he had sojourned in.

Life in Kiev, he said, was glorious. You lived there like *Gott in Frankreich*. The poorest eats rolls and butter every day in Kiev. In the evening every one goes out to stroll on the Krestchatik. The houses are built of a kind of crystal, and the streets are paved with coloured stones. A district commissioner, such as made us tremble in Swislowitz, was of no account in Kiev. As for the police sergeant—he was just dirt. No one below a general counted for anything. The commissioner's clerk was a general! And then, the theatres! "But what's the good of telling you: you'd never understand me. The actors wear coats of real gold and silver, crowns on their heads, with real diamonds in them. On their feet they have full-length boots of red morocco leather, with silver

144

spurs at the heels. And in their hands they carry little whips with golden bells. When they walk about the stage the silver spurs ring, the golden bells tinkle, the crowns flash on their heads, and you see a million rainbows of diamonds and emeralds. And the curtain is a million times lovelier than the curtain on our ark, and big enough to cover all the eastern wall of the Shuhl. And when the curtain rises, there they all stand, in their crowns and their spurs and their diamonds, and the audience applauds like mad. That's what Kiev is! And that's what real life is!"

Whenever I think back on Bencheh, with his lean figure, his gestures, his wild tricks, I am reminded of Charlie Chaplin. I am convinced till this day that Bencheh was a man of real gifts, a born artist. His *Wanderlust* was only the expression of his thwarted hunger to live himself out. And he had to satisfy his artistic longings by organizing the Purim plays of the town. He wanted to show us what he knew: for this once he would lift the inhabitants of Swislowitz to the level of the happy inhabitants of Kiev.

No easy task, this. Where were the men, the means, the interest, to come from? But Bencheh was not only an artist, but a man of restless, enterprising spirit. The first thing he did was to create a fund. He asked nothing for himself; his gifts and his labours he gave away, like a true artist. But there were many things to be bought, and neither he nor his mother—who supported him in this enterprise with all her moral force—could spend money of their own. The first thing that Bencheh did, then, was to tax each one of the actors. After all, they were not real artists, and they were actually getting instructions in the art from the incomparable Bencheh. The levy was graduated according to the importance of the rôle and the number of lines assigned to it.

The heaviest taxes were laid on Pharaoh and Ahasuerus: next came Haman and Joseph, and after them Jacob and Mordecai. Vaisoso, the clown of the Esther stories, got off scot-free. A second factor in the levying of taxes was the expense tied up with every rôle. The kings were ruinously costly, and their ministers were only slightly less so. Jacob and Mordecai were only two old Jews, and clothes for the former might be borrowed from the Rav, while clothes for the latter—who had to appear in the tattered raiment of a beggar—could be obtained from the water-carrier. Toward the end of the play, of course, Mordecai did become an important figure: he was elevated to Haman's place. But Haman having been hanged, his clothes could be used for Mordecai—an economic stroke and a fine symbolic act in one. The levies raised from the actors could not cover the costs: and here Cherneh the widow threw herself into the struggle. She advanced her own money on the basis of the income of the two performances: it was at least as good an investment as selling pancakes on credit to hungry *cheder* boys.

The largest item of expenditure was paper. Much gold and silver paper was needed to cover the crowns and the robes of the kings and ministers. Gold and silver paper was not on sale in Swislowitz; so it was ordered from Babrusk through one of the draymen. Then there were needed swords: and Bencheh insisted that they look like *swords*, and not like the wooden imitations which the children wore on the Black Fast. The blades had to be covered with silver paper, the hilts with gold. Then we needed flax and hemp, the first for Jacob's beard, the second for Mordecai's. Flax is smooth and gracious, and looks well combed, as is fitting for Jacob the Patriarch: hemp is rough and knotted, and is more suitable for Mordecai the beggar.

Having attended to all of these details with loving care, Bencheh next set about the training of the actors. For himself he reserved the rôle of Haman the wicked. True, the rôle of the tyrant and Jew-hater—the greatest Jew-hater the world has ever known—is not a grateful one. But Bencheh was an artist, and he chose a rôle that had plenty of action. Besides, the more hateful the rôle, the more room there was for skill and subtlety.

The severest test of his managerial ability came in the choosing of Vashti and Esther. If it had been up to Bencheh, he would have stopped at nothing, and actually invited girls into the drama. But modern realism was beyond the taste— and the morals—of the Jews of Swislowitz, and neither the Rav nor the elders of the community would have tolerated it. Bencheh, brought up short by this iron wall, gave in, and found boys for the rôles. Of the two, Esther was the easier to satisfy. He needed a good-looking boy and some women's clothes. But in the case of Vashti a fearful historical complication arose.

The rôle of the rejected and humiliated queen was a short one. She appeared on the stage just once. But when she did appear, she had to satisfy the traditional history of Vashti. And tradition says that the incident which set in motion the drama of Purim, and the saving of the Jews of Persia from the enmity of Haman the wicked, namely, the refusal of Vashti to appear in all her beauty before the assembled guests of the tipsy monarch, had a most ludicrous and pitiful explanation. Far from being a woman of innate modesty and good taste, Vashti the queen was as wicked as her husband was foolish: *but* on the day when she was summoned to display herself to the banqueters, something exceedingly ugly and exceedingly immodest grew out on her forehead. And the modesty which prevents me from saying exactly what it was that grew out on her forehead, also prevented the historic presentation of the rôle of Vashti the queen. And yet how could all allusion to this providential if shocking accident be entirely omitted? For if Vashti had been as good-looking on that day as on others, she would have been proud to show herself: and if she had showed herself, the king would not have divorced her: and if the king had not divorced her, he would never have married Esther: and if he had never married Esther, the plot of Haman would have succeeded, and the Jews of Persia would have been massacred down to the last child.

As is to be expected, every boy in Swislowitz knew what had happened to Vashti the queen, and what the biblical account does not mention. Who told me, I cannot remember, but it was certainly neither the Rebbi nor my mother. We just knew. And we asked each other, "Do you know what grew on the forehead of Vashti the queen?" Therefore neither historical accuracy nor public curiosity would have been satisfied unless Vashti was in one way or another properly represented. Of course Bencheh could have wriggled out of it—as most Purim players did—by putting a few allusive words into the mouth of another character. But Bencheh was made of sterner stuff. He could not bring himself to such intellectual dishonesty. After fearful inner tortures, he found a way out. Vashti would appear on the stage. But besides her crown she would wear a veil covering half her face. What was under the veil could be left to the imagination. The town applauded Bencheh's ingenuity—and the arrangements continued.

Other inspirations came to Bencheh in the course of the preparations. He felt that his talents and his dignity entitled him to a special mark of distinction on the stage. He who had looked upon the actors of Kiev in all their glory could not appear on the stage in the same pitiful village make-up as the amateurs of Swislowitz, with their paper crowns, their imitation robes, and their wooden swords covered with gilt.

He felt, moreover, that the king's first minister, the actual overlord of one hundred and twenty-seven provinces stretching from Ethiopia to India, could not appear in the makeshift rags of a silly *cheder* boy. And Bencheh found a way out. By devious ways, through backstairs influence and perhaps with the use of a bribe, he obtained a cast-off uniform of the district commissioner himself. The coat lacked epaulettes, but these he supplied. By the same obscure and circuitous routes he obtained an ancient sword discarded by the town sergeant, unbent it, and polished it up. And he had a regular crown made for himself by the cooper, so that he towered above his fellow actors not only by virtue of his superior talents, but by virtue of accoutrements never before seen among Purim players of Swislowitz.

In the second play, "The Selling of Joseph," he took the rôle of the hero, and had his brother-in-law, Mottye, the best ladies' tailor in Swislowitz, make him the famous coat of many colours. But "The Selling of Joseph" was only dessert to the banquet. It was in the real Purim play that Bencheh took the town by storm.

The preparations for the Great Show lasted about a month. The actors—most of them apprentices to various trades—were occupied during the day, and Bencheh himself had been driven by need to take up again the despised needle. So only the evenings were free. The training therefore had to be intensive. Cherneh's home—a two-room cottage— became for that one month a dramatic school with Bencheh as the director.

During that one month Bencheh, snobbish enough during the rest of the year, became so inflated with importance that it was impossible to hold sensible converse with him. The ordinary pride of his adventures was mitigated by a certain feeling of helplessness. He had seen the marvels of Kiev, he had tasted the joys of the metropolis, and he had a right to despise the yokels of Swislowitz. But the yokels of Swislowitz were free to believe or to doubt. Now, on Purim, Bencheh delivered the goods in person under the noses of the Swislowitzers. "I take dolts, village idiots, and I make actors of them. Say what you like about Kiev—but what can you say about my talents?"

Bencheh's family took on, for that brief period, some of the haughtiness which radiated from the central figure. Cherneh had more than once bewailed her fate in the possession of Bencheh. "An old bachelor, a dead loss . . . a fine head on him, could have been a great scholar, and there he sits—when he does sit—with the needle in his fingers. What can I hope for from him?" But during the time of the Purim plays Cherneh forgot her blasted hopes; instead she shone with happiness. "You'll see him in the rôle of Haman. I tell you not a hundred district commissioners and not a thousand police sergeants are a patch on him. I tell you, not the governor himself could be half as terrifying. When he opens his mouth the walls and the windows tremble."

Poor Cherneh! It didn't need much of a voice to make the walls and windows of her hovel tremble. And who would have cared to contradict Cherneh the widow when she sought consolation for the woes of her life in the talents of her wayward son? A grain of happiness was all she got to console her for a lifetime of sorrows. And for the time being the grain was enough, so that during the month which preceded Purim she resembled one of her own hot, crisp pancakes, fresh from the oven.

No spectators were permitted at the rehearsals. To begin with, Bencheh's home was hardly large enough even for the actors. But more than this, his instincts revolted against a display of talent in the making. Close relatives of Cherneh, and one or two chosen friends, were excepted. But it was impossible to keep away the crowds which gathered at the windows and looked on from outside. The winter having relaxed its grip, the boys and girls used to gather eagerly outside Bencheh's home on the evenings before Purim, and get their first glimpses of the preparations for a play. I, because of the close friendship between Cherneh and my mother, was once admitted to the sanctum, and great was my pride and the envy of my playmates.

Parallel with these formidable preparations, the Jewish community went about the minor tasks which preceded the unimportant festival. And among these the most important was the preparation of the rattler for the young people. The rattler is a simple instrument for the production of noises whereby, during the Synagogue services of the Purim festival, the children express their contempt whenever the name of Haman is mentioned. It consists of a toothed wooden disk, circular in shape, attached to a handle. A rotating framework brings against the teeth of the disk an elastic wooden prong, with ear-splitting results. This was the sole weapon allowed us in our war against the memory of "Haman, son of Hamidatha, the persecutor of the Jews."

On the eve of Purim there is a fast which commemorates the fast of Esther the queen before she went to visit the uxorious king. The gorgeous three-cornered little cakes, stuffed with nuts and poppyseed, which are called Haman's ears,

had been prepared in vast numbers for us. Their shape alone
was joy. They were neither round, like rolls, nor long like
the loaf: they were like nothing else that we ate during the
year: queer, characteristic, three-cornered dainties, with a
name as queer as their shapes. The poppyseeds used for
stuffing the cake had been fried in honey. The stuffing was
inadequate, but we used to eat the cake systematically, so
that with every mouthful of cake there came at least a nibble
of honeyed poppyseed.

The older people fasted on that day. It was not one of the
important fasts of the calendar. We had several classes of
fasts: the Black Fast and the White Fast, the Big Fast, the
Small Fast, the Short Fast, the Long Fast. The Black Fast
is the ninth day of the month of Ab, for the Destruction;
the White Fast is the Day of Atonement: the Long Fast is
the seventeenth day of the month of Tammuz, when the walls
of the city were breached; the Short Fast is the tenth day of
the month of Tebeth, when Gedaliah, the last ruler of the
House of David, was murdered. The fast of Gedaliah being
masculine and the fast of Esther feminine, the Jews made a
match between them and paired them off. It was the Jewish
matrimonial instinct at work. My mother fasted with special
pleasure before Purim, for here was a fast-day in honour of
a woman. But while she fasted, she was occupied from morning until evening with the preparation of the Purim dishes.
And I lingered around to catch the drippings and the waste
from her preparations.

The joyous reading of the scroll of Esther, during the
Purim service, was by tradition the right of Judah, the
president of the Synagogue, a man whose stern appearance
belied his jovial nature. On the Day of the Rejoicing of the
Law he organized the army of the children for the pickings
of the town pantries. On Purim he organized no army, but

he knew that during the reading of the Scroll the youth of
the city would be there to see to it that Haman did not
escape alive. We waited, breathless with impatience, for the
third chapter of the Scroll, where the name of Haman is
mentioned for the first time. During the first two chapters
we sat like soldiers awaiting the call, our rattlers gripped
tight, our muscles tense. And then, when the word "Haman"
rolled off Judah's tongue, a deafening roar broke through
the Synagogue, a tumult of several hundred rattlers whirled
vigorously by as many youthful hands. Some of the older
people, too dignified for rattlers, but too human to be kept
out of the fun, brought along sticks, and contributed to the
uproar by beating the floor and the desks. For several
minutes the reader was unable to proceed. But this was not
enough. The whole name reads "Haman, the son of Hamidatha, the Gagite." When the reader resumed and gave the
genealogy of Haman, the same wild tumult broke out again.
And Judah, who loved children, and loved to play with
them, tolerated the noise good-humouredly, and made no
sign of impatience.

But the lean and bitter Ziskind, his elder brother, had no
patience with us. He stood near the pulpit and protested
against our abuse of the time-honoured privilege of booing
the name of Haman. Two or three twirls of the rattler were,
in his opinion, a sufficient demonstration of dislike: he begrudged us the pleasure of a longer and fuller expression
of opinion. We ignored the protests of Ziskind. We had the
encouragement of Judah, our commander, who, while he read
the Scroll, used to pause an instant every time he came to
the name of Haman—paused, hung in the air for a moment, and then flung the syllables at us, an open signal,
in defiance of his brother and our ancient enemy alike.

Children as we were, we knew well that Haman was not in

our Synagogue, for he could not be in our Synagogue and in those throughout the world at the same time. But we understood the symbolism instinctively. There were Hamans everywhere, great enemies and little enemies of the Jews. And we took revenge for the evil they had done us and the evil they contemplated. If noise could kill, the Hamans of the world would never rise for the resurrection. We felt that these blows of ours, delivered in the air, were not without effect. In one way or another the Hamans of the world felt the noisy onslaught in their bones. And we were filled with contentment. We had done something to get even with the enemies of the Jewish people.

And in the special melody which is attached to the Scroll of Esther—a lilting melody, a melody of mockery and triumph—we felt the character of the holiday. Neither the melody nor the holiday was serious. We were poking fun at somebody, laughing at a discomfited enemy, rejoicing in his downfall. Judah the preacher's son understood us, and he added a tang of his own to the droll story. He read with relish, pointedly, as if Haman in person were before him. A high point in his performance was reached when he came to the names of the ten sons of Haman: these he rolled off neatly, rapidly—hot morsels to be swallowed at once for fear of burning his tongue. Or as if he were stringing the names with incredible swiftness on a single rope, and hanging them up by the side of their father. Only the last name, the name of the youngest son of Haman, Vaizoso—which has acquired a comical and disreputable significance in the Jewish folk mind—he paused over. And we children were astonished. We knew the ugly word: and we were astonished that Judah, the president of the Shuhl, should permit himself to linger over it in such a holy place.

The eve of Purim was no sort of holiday. It was distinguished from all other evenings only by the Haman cakes. In other respects it was quite profane. There was the same crowd at our house, the same employés come up from the river to talk business, the same meals, the same occupations. There is an old folk saying: "A muzhik is no brother, a rouble is no coin, malaria is no sickness, and Purim is no holiday." It applies, however, only to the eve of Purim, for the Purim night which follows the next day is the happiest in the year.

On Purim day we read the Scroll a second time in the Synagogue. And we accompanied it again with hostile demonstrations against the name of Haman. But like the second reading of Jeremiah's Lamentations on the Black Fast, the repeat performance was a failure. It is hard to weep to order a second time with the same intensity and the same passion as the first time. It is just as hard to triumph over a fallen enemy more than once. On Purim day, too, we twirled our rattlers and beat the desks, and despised Haman: but we did it now out of a sense of duty. And when the second reading of the Scroll was over, we did not feel, as we had done the night before, that we had just achieved a signal victory over the implacable enemy of the Jews. When we left the Synagogue, we were further disarmed of our holiday feeling by the fact that all the shops were open. And it was only in the afternoon, when the shops began to close, and when the final preparations for the Purim banquet were being made, that the mood was restored.

Between the closing of the shops and the opening of the celebrations occurred the Sending of the Gifts, an ancient tradition of this festival. For several hours the carriers of the gifts were seen hurrying from house to house, bearing plates covered with a white napkin. Carrier after carrier came into our house, an interminable succession of messengers with the gifts of friends and relatives. There were two kinds of gifts. The gifts of individuals and official gifts from the cantor, the beadles, the bathman, the water-carrier . . . Others were "officials" by tacit understanding—certain widows, the Sabbath *goy* (the gentile hired to make fire on the Sabbath and perform other duties forbidden us on that day), and the "ascetics," the anchoretic souls who studied day and night in the Shuhl. Only the Rav of the community, though he received gifts, never sent any. He did not believe in the practice. The gifts of the "officials" had a significance of their own. We did not examine them: we took nothing, we added nothing. We only put a few coins on the plate, and returned it with our compliments to the sender. And the messenger, too, had to get his little fee. Far different was the *social* or *personal* ritual of the Sending of Gifts. In this case the gift was not only examined, but weighed in the balance of social values, counted, scrutinized, appraised from every angle. And it was a point of honour to make the return gift, in this case, a little finer and more distinguished than the original. There was infinite care and forethought, infinite calculation, to make the gift expressive of the exact degree of affection or esteem which the receiver was to deduce from it. My mother took the whole business very seriously. So, for that matter, did every one else. But when my mother had gone through the entire list and when, just before we sat down to the Purim banquet, she despatched the last of the messengers or carriers, she sat down with a sigh of relief, the anxious look died off her face, and she sighed, "Thank God: the last plate sent out. I only hope I've offended nobody, and that everybody will feel satisfied."

And what was all the worry and the excitement about? Another piece of cake, another piece of candy, another little package of honeyed poppyseed . . . But against the background of that small, pitiful life of Swislowitz these trifles assumed vast importance. There was a sort of gift-language for Purim, with subtle shades of meaning, a language as expressive as the language of flowers in Spain; for every degree of respect and love there was a different combination of goodies, a larger plate or a smaller plate. And on more than one occasion a gift which seemed—to the recipient—to fall short of the respect it should have conveyed, occasioned a minor feud which lasted for months.

The children, too, used to have their own Sending of Gifts, and they imitated the elders in the choice of things—cakes, cookies, and poppyseed. But there was a children's specialty which was the language reserved for *their* use—candies of many colours and many shapes. A week before Purim, Sosheh the widow imported from a real candy-store in Babrusk a collection of fancy candies, birds and animals and soldiers in gorgeous uniforms. We used to buy the candies at the beginning of the week in order to play with them: and we used them at the end of the week for the Sending of the Gifts. But the flesh being weak and the candies tempting, the birds and animals and soldiers which were ultimately packed into the plate lacked not only their original lustre, but occasionally wings and limbs as well. Of course the children did not use "carriers," like the grown-ups, but made their own deliveries. In my first *cheder* year the following incident—a childish mirror of the life of the grown-ups—occurred. Being the youngest in the *cheder*, I had delivered all my gifts first. By the time we sat down at home to the banquet every one of my friends, with the exception of Gershon, the son of my uncle Meyer, had made a more or less satisfactory return. I waited and waited for Meyer's return until my patience gave out. I rose from the table, rushed over to my uncle's house, and demanded my return. To which Gershon replied, austerely, "The gifts you sent me were no good. The animals and soldiers were all broken. I won't send you a return." Whereupon a quarrel ensued, followed by a fight, and we did not speak to each other for a whole month, that is, until the Passover.

After a brief family reunion at the house of my grandfather we came home to the grand Purim banquet. The table was more richly prepared than for any other meal in the year—foods and drinks of all kinds, twisted loaves that shone yellow, a huge baked fish touched up with saffron, golden colours that harmonized with the light of the candles stuck in the big Menorahs or seven-branched candlesticks that burned brilliantly, one at each end of the table. But in the centre of the table, and near each Menorah, had been placed three piles of plain boiled chick-peas. I asked my mother why these plebeian dishes had been permitted in the midst of this glorious company. And she explained that they were commemorative of the extreme piety of Esther the queen. For Esther was a good Jewish daughter, and though she lived in the luxurious and profligate palace of the great king, she would touch none of their food. Haman the wicked, knowing of the laws of the Jews, had forbidden the presence of a Schochet or ritual slaughterer in the palace. And Esther therefore contented herself, at all the feasts, with plain peas and beans: yet on this diet she was as well fed, and as beautiful, as those that gorged themselves on the most tempting dishes.

And then, after the banquet, came the sublime moment for the youngsters. The door was flung wide open and the Purim players, accompanied by a host of children and grown-ups, poured into the house. Our dining-room was probably the largest in Swislowitz, but on this occasion it was too small, and protesting voices began to rise: "Let me in, I'm Haman's brother. Let me in, I'm the queen's first cousin. . . ." And when order of a kind had been established in the pent room, the players began. Of course I knew every one of the players personally, and could have told you to a man who was hidden behind that flaxen beard or within those girlish clothes. But the hunger for illusion was strong, and I felt that these boys were the same, and yet not the same.

And when Vashti, a young Yeshivah student, dressed in women's clothes, with a little crown on his head and a veil half covering his face, piped the first lines: "Would that I were a little bird, would that I were a little flower, nay even a little worm," my heart melted toward the unhappy queen. Ahasuerus sat in glory, sullen, gross, almost wordless, as befitted the stupid monarch. And then the word of the chamberlain Mehuman was heard: "Come forth, come forth, O Haman the prince," and Bencheh himself strode into the centre of the room, magnificently caparisoned, and taking up a haughty pose, glared upon the players and spectators with the look of an outraged general—nay, a field marshal. The Jews of Swislowitz had never seen the inside of a theatre, but instinct told them that here was no ordinary village Purim player: here was a man who understood both make-up and histrionics. Before Bencheh had spoken a word, a shudder ran through the audience: here was Haman himself, an enemy implacable and resourceful. His furious gestures, his bitter glances, his intolerant bearing, said, "There stands before you the Persecutor, the Eternal Persecutor, who will pursue you to the gates of Destruction."

The play took up half an hour, and was followed at once by the presentation of the second play, "The Selling of Joseph." But the addition to the programme was not a success. For Vashti the queen suddenly became Joseph the victim, and Haman became Reuben, and Mordecai became Joseph. And in the centre of the room a barrel was placed, end up, to represent the pit into which the older brothers threw the spoiled darling of their father.

A second banquet followed the close of the performance, and for the remainder of the evening Bencheh was the hero of Swislowitz. He told again the stories of his wanderings, the marvels of Kiev, and the glories of the theatre. We sat up very late that night. The older people were sleepy, and I could hardly keep my eyes open. My thoughts became confused; Haman ears, the Scroll of Esther, rattlers, drama, banquet, beards, everything flowed into everything else, and the entire tumult moved slowly, dimly, into the darker spaces of my mind. At last everything sank into a dream, the misty and eternal dream of a people forever at war with an invisible enemy.

CHAPTER NINE: SPRINGTIME IN SWISLOWITZ

THE first *cheder* year, which had given me a definite human status, had also awakened in me a special sensitiveness to everything that happened around me, had made me observant and self-conscious, so that my memories date clearly from that epoch. For that reason the coming of the spring that year has left a clear mark in my memory. I saw around me the enactment of the Resurrection: I saw the trees discard their white winter cerements, I saw the first green things break out on the sullen landscape, I saw men and women take on another aspect, and in myself a deep well of joy was unportalled, and I danced and sang at home and in the streets, a new thing, as fresh and happy as the re-awakening grass which lay, thin and almost misty, on the meadows. For the winter term at *cheder*, with its dark days, its imprisonment, its suffocation, was over. The long nights were dying away. Life and freedom were in the air, and I wandered over the streets in a happy daze, seeking nothing, desiring nothing, but filled with unutterable content. I wandered over to Castle Hill, and stroked the bark of the old birch-trees. I watched them thawing, regaining their graciousness and softness, yielding to the spring winds and swaying as a Jew sways in prayer, grateful for the soul which has been returned to his body.

The first signs of the spring were on the rivers too, the

Swisla and the Beresina. Till now the ice had covered as with a single sheet of dark, lustrous steel the stretches of the river and beyond. Now dark lines and patches suddenly showed on the cruel, level surface, like wrinkles on the face of an old woman. The lines deepened and widened, till they became cracks and gulfs, and the imprisoned water began to break through, to spread over the ice. A few days pass: the sun shines steadily, the rays bore quietly, persistently, and the waters rise slowly from the darkness beneath. And at last, under this soft, unyielding attack, the ice gives: it breaks in a hundred places; and again the floes are rushing down the river, just as in the autumn days before the winter sets in.

But what a difference! In those last autumn days the floes looked grim, like cold grave-stones carried on heavy waters in the funeral procession of a victim. And they rushed along the waters tumultuously, crashing into each other and against the banks, heralds of storm. Now they were lighter, softer, and they were the heralds of warmth and sunlight. And they seemed contented, too, to appear in the new rôle: they were melting as if with joy into the rolling waters. And I, standing on the bridge and watching them pass under me, melted into them, and rejoiced with them.

The snow was almost all gone. Only here and there a tiny patch of it clung to the roof of a house, but it looked so tender, so gentle, that I thought one of the fleecy spring clouds had floated down out of the warming blue sky, and was resting below. The air was still chilly, but there was no more mist in it: clear, crystalline, it gave new colour to the whole world. The fields, too, were uncovered, and the winter wheat and winter corn already covered them—a marvel I could not understand. How could those sweet, tender green

162

blossoms stand up under the covering of snow and not freeze to death?

And the trees! They were naked, of course, but not with the hard nakedness of winter. They were awake. You could almost look through the bark, and see the stirring of the sap in their veins, and feel the thrill which passed along the awakening branches. A few days will pass, and you will feel the inward press of life in every twig, feel the fibres stretching farther and farther, till overnight they break out in a million fresh buds. And under the buds the folded leaves strain to get into the free air: they thrust unceasingly at the enclosure, like chicks pecking from the inside at the covering of eggshell.

Day by day the feeling of spring grows stronger in the air. One by one the stalls and stables are opened, the young colts rush out, tasting freedom for the first time. An old hen ventures out, followed by her new brood: the farther out she gets, the more proudly she ruffles her feathers, conscious of leading her little ones out for the first time into the great outside world. She teaches them to peck at the earth, to find their own food. But her little ones are still too young, their covering of down and feathers is not heavy enough, so every now and then she gathers them under wings again, and warms them.

Soon the first swallows appeared, first singly and then in flocks. They looked for the old nests under the shadows of the roofs and in the tangles of the branches. I watched them and marvelled at their inexhaustible energy. I loved their speed, their restlessness, their grace—and I forgot that they were our enemies, and that they had carried fire in their mouths and helped to burn down the Temple. I greeted them affectionately, like old friends.

But of all the wonders of the spring, the greatest was within me. For I knew that with the ending of the second or winter term I was going to leave Mottye the bean forever. I would not have to look on him again, and never have to set foot in his *cheder*. I did not know yet who would be my new Rebbi, and I did not care. Anybody rather than Mottye. I hated his *cheder*: it was suffocating, mentally as well as physically. Even as a child I was a restless spirit, and I agonized when I was chained to others, forced to keep slow step with them. By the middle of the winter term I had left my schoolmates behind, and while they were laboriously working their way through the week's portion of the Pentateuch, I ran ahead and struggled with the next portion. But I was chained to a group, and the speed of the group was that of its slowest member. The chains galled, and I could not break them. I was discontented both with the meagre portions of the Pentateuch he gave us for each week, and with the manner of his teaching. His translations were simple, dull; his uninteresting stories only whetted my appetite for something keener, harder, and livelier. It was in spite of him that I broke through to the wonder of the biblical stories. They took a direct hold on me and made me their prisoner, so that the translations and explanations were a hindrance. I began to learn without him; I studied nights at home, and did the best I could. Before my second term was over I knew the whole of Genesis almost by heart, and understood all of it, with the exception of the obscure passages toward the end. But even in those dark places I felt the power of the narrative, and yielded myself to it. Mottye the bean was proud of me, and foretold great things for me. He openly admitted that I had outstripped him, that he could guide me no longer in my studies, and that I would have to have a greater scholar than he.

The two weeks between the Purim festival and the first day of the month of Nisan (which begins the civil New Year, and contains the Passover) we learned nothing new in cheder. We attempted no new portions, but simply revised what we had learned during the winter. To me the revision was so dull that I rebelled and told my mother that I would not go to cheder even for the half days. And neither my mother nor Mottye protested. I won two weeks of freedom, the happiest of that year and among the happiest of my childhood.

There was enough, and more than enough, to occupy mind and body from morning to night. The weeks preceding the Passover were the busiest in the life of Swislowitz. Behind Castle Hill hundreds of men stood from morning to night, twisting willow withes over slow fires, preparing the ropes to hold the rafts. The logs were already on the Swisla. They were thrown in at a point higher up, allowed to float down as far as the bend where the Swisla joined the Beresina, and held fast there by a huge barrier stretched from bank to bank. Down at that point a raft would assemble, the logs would be bound together, the huts would be built on them. And of course all this was vastly interesting. Every day I had to run three or four times to watch the workers twisting the strands into tremendous circles which looked like doughnuts prepared for the table of the mighty Og, king of Bashan. Or else I watched with amazement the family of the Poliessukes leaping from log to log before these were bound, without ever tumbling into the water. The logs rolled under their nimble feet, yielded, and slid: but they were as swift and as light-footed as birds.

And then—Passover was coming, the greatest and most splendid of the festivals. New clothes for everybody, everything brand new, from head to foot. So there were visits to Hershel the tailor, who spent one half of his time working and the other half running down his rival, Yenkel the tailor. There were visits to Isar the shoemaker, Isar with the red nose whom everybody in the town, from the president of the Shuhl to the water-carrier, feared because of his fiery advocacy of the cause of absolute justice. First were the necessary visits—for measurement. Then came the unnecessary visits—at least, so they were regarded by Hershel and Isar. But how was it possible for Hershel to sew pockets in my suit, or for Isar to put a stiff strip of raw leather in my shoes, to make them creak with newness when I put them on, unless I was present to watch? My visits to Hershel took place in the daytime, and to Isar I went in the evening. I had a friend in Isar's best apprentice, a certain Shaikin who taught me how to twist a waxed shoemaker's thread, and even let me hammer a few nails into the sole of a shoe. But he would not permit me to handle the awl which made the holes for the nails. And when I hammered straight, and the nail did not bend or break, I was a happy boy: I knew a trade already! But Shaikin exploited my friendship. He made me bring him a pound of sugar and a quart of whiskey. Not in payment for these privileges, but because he needed them, he told me, to make the leather strip without which the new shoes would not creak. And how could I wear a pair of new shoes if they did not creak?

Last, but certainly not least, there was the Matzoth bakery. There were really several bakeries for Matzoth, but the most distinguished belonged to Mottye Kailes. His product was delicate, thin as paper and neatly holed in lines, as if with the best machine. I used to go from one bakery to the other and watch them punch the holes in the Matzoth. I had pull with Mottye Kailes, for we had our own Matzoth made there; and the chief "holer" was a Talmud student who ate Fridays and Saturdays in our house. Cherneh the widow was the chief dough-kneader at Mottye Kailes's bakery, and she instructed me in all the details of the work, the pouring out of the dough in equal quantities and the flattening of it into Matzoth cakes. My greatest joy was when the Talmud student let me take the holer in my hand, roll it across the dough, and produce the line of neat punctures.

What a pity it is that the vast majority of grown-ups have never learned to understand the powers of direct and honest observation which belong to the child before the ways of life have distorted its intelligence! The child not only observes every detail in the behaviour of the grown-up, but is quick to sift the false from the genuine, pretence from unaffected truth. And in my own childhood I learned that older people, careless in this respect, can do much damage to the pure souls of the young.

On a moonlit evening not long before the Passover, I sat with my mother at the window of the living-room, and watched at a distance the procession of the Greek Orthodox worshippers round the church. They were carrying images and banners, chanting as they walked. And suddenly my mother broke into laughter and said, "See; they are making preparations for their Pascal festival. They take their god and hide him in a certain place, and then they pretend that they have found him again."

On the night preceding the Passover eve, my father went through the ritual of removing from the house the last traces of leaven. With a lighted candle in one hand, and with a goose-feather and wooden spoon in the other, he searched from room to room. This was the preparation to *our* Passover. But I knew that he was only pretending to search. Those little crumbs and fragments which he "found" he had himself hidden away. And I noted that my mother did not laugh at the pretence, and I was hurt.

There was something which hurt me even deeper. The next morning my father made a fire in the yard at the back of the house, and burned the last fragments of leaven together with the feather and the wooden spoon in which he had gathered them up. The fire was lit not far from the barn which was crammed full of leavened food for the peasants who worked on the rafts.

Then I asked my father, "But why don't you burn the barn, too? It is full of leaven." And my father replied, "No need to, for it no longer belongs to us. We have sold it to the gentile water-carrier."

Then I asked a second question. "The water-carrier is very poor, isn't he? I know, because he goes from house to house and begs pieces of bread. So how can he buy that big barn from you?"

My father answered me again. "We sold it to him for one rouble."

But my mind would not rest. I began again, "But what are we going to do without all that food? How are we going to feed all the peasants who work on our rafts?" Whereupon the answer came that we had sold the barn to the water-carrier under a special arrangement: as soon as the Passover was ended, and Jews were again permitted to possess leavened food, he would return the barn to us.

I asked no more questions after that. But I remember that a feeling of shame stole over me. I thought to myself, "They're fooling me; they're fooling the water-carrier, too." On the evening of that day, when the family was assembled round the shining table, and I, as the youngest, had to ask the "four questions" of the Passover ritual, there were seven questions on the tip of my tongue. Four came out of the prayer-book, where they always are: they had to do with the story of Passover. And three came out of my own brain, and they had to do with the selling of the barn.

By ten o'clock of that day the house had been wholly purified of its leaven, and the only food given us was Passover food. But not Matzoth, for it is forbidden to taste these up to the moment the festival begins, on the evening of that day. So we waited for the first bite of Matzoth as the bridegroom waits for the bride. Even the mention of bread was forbidden; it had to be alluded to as "leaven." The sole food, apart from meat, therefore consisted of potatoes in various forms, and the students who ate at our house complained to each other that, with neither bread nor meat, there was no filling the stomach.

There were, I remember, three or four of these students. On the day which ushered in the Passover they stayed in, and made themselves useful. This habit of putting the students to work in the house for that particular day had been introduced by my grandfather, and he explained it in the following fashion: "Passover is the festival of freedom, and during the Passover every man must feel himself free. Now these Talmud students eat in your house without payment. How, then, can they feel free men? There is only one way: let them work for their meals on that day, and not be beholden to you for their food." But the work they were put to was of the lightest; they carried small parcels, they ran errands, and they went to Hershel the tailor and Isar the shoemaker to bid them hurry with the new clothes and shoes, lest we might be compelled to sit down to the Seder ceremonies unbefittingly clad. They also prepared the bitter herbs for the ceremonies, checked up on the number of Passover prayer-books, and so on.

The evening draws close, and the last sunlight is spilled

on the town of Swislowitz. Every Jewish home shines that evening, renewed and purified, and on every table the biggest and richest and whitest cloth is spread. The children are dressed in new clothes, and even the street has been swept, and the entrance to the house covered with clean, yellow sand. Along those quiet streets, with their trees in first blossom, we go, young and old, to the Synagogue. There is contentment in the air, peace and the feeling of plenty. For at what other season of the year can every Jewish family in Swislowitz boast that it is provided with food for every bit of eight days ahead—the duration of the festival? The poorest household, haunted by hunger fifty-one weeks in the year, is stocked up till the last day of Passover: such is the Law. And when else, in the course of the year, can they lay aside their pitiful cares and rejoice in the festival and in the spring? What wonder that Passover is the most beloved of the festivals? On the eve of that day the poorest man in Swislowitz could repeat with generous sincerity the prayer which opens the home ceremonies, "Let every man that is hungry enter and eat, let every man that is thirsty enter and drink." It is forbidden for any one to be hungry. And the sages of the town argued, knowingly, "Could God have chosen a lovelier festival than Passover on which to liberate the Jews from Egypt?"

We have returned from the Shuhl. We are at home. Nothing, in the memories of my childhood years, shines so clearly and so lovingly as this evening of the Passover. The luminous shadows of it have been cast forever across my life, and the magic does not decrease with the years. For on that evening the house was a palace, my father was a king, and all of us were members of a royal family, queen and princes and princesses. Even the poorest guest that sat at table with us was an ambassador. My joy was too full to be contained; it spilled over, and poured itself through the room and over the people in it. I wanted the older people to tell me wonderful stories, and I wanted to tell others in return. I was full of the glorious exodus from the land of Egypt, and I lived, in my own way, through all the acts of that greatest of world-dramas.

The table had been stretched for that evening, filled in with extra boards to accommodate the guests. At the head my father sat, leaning upon cushions at his right hand—a symbol of his freedom, majesty, and rule. My mother sat by his side. After them, in places of honour, were the guests, and then the members of the family. Countless beakers and glasses of wine sparkled on the table, and they were flanked by glowing carafes. My father conducted the/Seder ceremonies with royal dignity, without haste, without impatience. My younger brother being still too young to ask the "four questions," that part of the ceremony fell to me. But I was almost ashamed to take so simple a part, for I understood nearly the whole of the ritual. And I repeated the four questions in Hebrew, with their Yiddish translations, like one who obeys a command. After the questions came the reading of the answers. Great was my glee when we reached the counting of the plagues which were inflicted on the Egyptians: greater still was it when we repeated the complicated calculations of certain sages who proved by a logic of their own that the Egyptians were smitten not with ten, but with every bit of two hundred and fifty plagues. Serves them right, I thought: that'll teach them to leave the Jews alone.

There is a certain tradition attached to the Seder ceremony, the stealing of the Afikomon (a specially dedicated Matzoh) from under the cushion of the father. Of course it must be stolen between the time it is tucked away, near the beginning of the service, and the end, when it is drawn out to be divided and eaten. My brother wanted to aid me in the theft, on condition that we divided the reward which must be paid by the father. But an excellent idea came to me. I went up to my father and asked him what reward he would give me if I did *not* steal the Afikomon. The idea pleased him mightily, and he promised me more than I would have expected in payment for a successful theft. I got my reward and remained honest into the bargain. Not only did I make no attempt to steal the Afikomon, but I even watched my brothers to prevent them from stealing it.

In the centre of the table stood the beaker of wine which is set apart for Elijah the prophet. None may drink from it but he, when he appears invisibly at the right moment. And I watched it closely for a sign of diminution in its brimming contents. Of course none of us doubted that Elijah appeared that evening in every Jewish home. But we also knew that it was quite impossible for him to drink up those thousands and thousands of beakers of wine set apart for him. A tiny drop he *might* have taken from every cup, and I watched, fascinated, for the slight shrinkage. When the moment came we stood up, my father flung open the door and repeated the tremendous words, "Pour forth Thy wrath on the nations that know Thee not . . ." I held my breath and looked and listened. Oh, I knew well that Elijah would not enter like a common mortal, grossly visible and audible! But I waited for a shadow, a ghost of a sound, a whisper of footsteps. The invocation ended, the door was closed, and I could not tell. Had I heard something? Had I felt something pass? I looked back at the table, and scrutinized the beaker of the Prophet. But again my own intensity had defeated me, and I could not remember exactly where the wine had stood before. Perhaps the lips of the prophet had touched the wine, invisibly, faintly. And all that evening I wondered, and, wondering, slipped into a half sleep, till my father woke me up and bade me sing with every one else the last of the songs of that evening, "*Chad gadya, chad gadya*, a little kid, a little kid, which my father bought for two *zuzim, chad gadya, chad gadya.*"

We children were not the only ones who believed that Elijah the prophet was going to appear, and that he was compelled, by elementary considerations of courtesy, at least to touch the wine-glass with his lips: for millions of Jews had prepared it for him, and millions of Jews had shown their faith in him. There were adults, bearded Jews, who expected his momentary appearance, who would not have been at all surprised if the stern Tishbite had suddenly swept in through the open door. Far from regarding it as supernatural, they would have said that even a prophet should not let himself be asked too often. And after all, it would not have put the prophet much out of the way. Saints less illustrious than he had achieved the magic "conquest of distance," and could fly over hundreds of miles in the twinkling of an eye. There were faithful believers who were bitterly disappointed when, year after year, Elijah the prophet failed to put in an appearance when the door was thrown open on the Passover night.

There was only one man in our town, the most illiterate among the Jews of Swislowitz—none other than Asher Pakess, keeper of the free lodging-house and public watercarrier—who had been honoured by a glimpse of the prophet, and that not only once, but fully twice. He was a man of extreme simplicity; that is, he had carried over into his manhood the naïveté of his childhood, and understood all things literally. And he was as honest as a child; his mind did not bend to the right or the left by the breadth of a hair. No one ever had to watch Asher Pakess: and in this he differed greatly from Palahei, the peasant woman, another water-carrier, who could not be trusted in the kitchen if a wooden spoon were lying around. Asher Pakess could be trusted alone in the kitchen with a fistful of gold coins on the table. Often enough householders, not having change, would run up a debt with Asher Pakess, to as much as four and five buckets of water. And then they would give him a ten-kopeck piece and trust him for the change. And Asher Pakess could not rest until he had returned the last kopeck.

He would not even accept the change as an advance on future deliveries of water. "Tomorrow," he would answer, "I'm going to forget. Tomorrow I don't remember." He spoke like a child, too, short phrases, six or seven words at a time and no more. At the seventh word he stopped and panted, as if the full load of a completed sentence tried him more than the full buckets he dragged uphill from the Beresina.

In the Shuhl, Asher Pakess's place was the bare bench behind the pulpit—always reserved for beggars. But he never sat down. He stood there through all the Sabbath service, in his tattered and greasy praying-shawl, a look of wonderment and abstraction on his face, as though he were not a part of the world that surrounded him. During weekdays I never saw him in the Shuhl. He used to say his prayers with the first morning service.

"Say his prayers" is a euphemism—for he never did any praying: unless his attentive silence, while others prayed, might be considered a prayer. Once Asher Pakess got a bad fright. An ordinance was issued from headquarters to our district commissioner, instructing him to compel all Jewish

merchants and shopkeepers in Swislowitz to report to Babrusk and to bring their trading permits with them. It was
suspected at headquarters that many shopkeepers had not
paid the full tax for their permits; they had misrepresented
the volume of their business. Some one in the town—every
one believed it was a Jew—had "squealed." And there were
many who believed that they knew the culprit, a shopkeeper
who had found this method for getting even with some of his
competitors. Asher Pakess was too simple to understand what
it was all about. He only heard, everywhere, the frightening
word *pramisel*, licence, and he confused it with *karamisel*—
the shoulder-frame on which he carried his buckets of water.
It looked to him as though he, too, would have to go to
Babrusk, carrying his frame with him, to get some one to
put a new signature on it. And he was nonplussed, for he had
two frames, an old one and a new one, and he did not know
which one he would have to drag along. And it was a difficult
task to make him understand that though *pramisel* and
karamisel sounded slightly alike, they had nothing to do with
each other, and he could carry on his trade in Swislowitz
without bothering police headquarters in Babrusk.

To this same Asher Pakess the privilege was granted of
looking twice on Elijah the prophet in person. During the
Passover, the free lodging-house was empty, for even the
beggars found some sort of home during that festival. So
Asher and his wife remained there alone, and the two of them
went through the ritual. Asher's wife, somewhat more intelligent than he, knew all the details of the ceremony. She
knew, therefore, that among the beakers on the table the
largest and handsomest was set aside for Elijah the prophet.
She also knew that when that passage, "Pour forth Thy
wrath," was reached, the door had to be opened wide. Right
enough, when the moment came, Pakicha flung open the
door—and a goat entered at once. Neither Asher nor his

wife thought of driving the goat out. They knew who the goat was. This was Elijah the prophet himself, in one of those disguises that are spoken of in the folk stories. The goat, finding this friendly welcome, advanced to the centre of the room, leaped with its two forefeet on to the table, mouthed one of the Matzoth as if saying a prayer over it, and upset the beaker of Elijah the prophet.

And at this point Asher Pakess could not contain himself. "Rabbi, prophet," he exclaimed breathlessly. "Don't be angry, please. Eat as much as you like. Drink as much as you like. But oh, please, don't break anything."

On the second evening of the Passover, when the same ceremony is repeated in detail, a second visitor appeared at this point. A man, dressed in a long white gown, his face covered by his hat, appeared at the door, entered and strode up to the table. Asher was much more terrified by this visitor than by the goat. He cried out in his terror. But the visitor only lifted the cup of the prophet, drained it, and disappeared. Among the Jews of Swislowitz it was known that the visitor had been Israel, the son of Joseph Bear, the cantor. But Asher Pakess was convinced that none other than Elijah the prophet had appeared again, in another disguise, to empty the beaker of wine.

These two stories were very popular in Swislowitz, and Asher was always ready to repeat them on request, to the vast amusement of his auditors. He told them simply, straightforwardly, as a child recounts something. But there were some who did not laugh. They asked themselves: Who knew who the goat was? Who knew who the visitor in the gown was—despite the claim of Israel, son of Joseph Bear? And above all, who knew who Asher Pakess the simpleton was? Had it not often turned out that the woodchopper was no woodchopper, the water-carrier no water-carrier? And what of the Thirty-Six Hidden Saints, the modest, silent spirits who haunt the earth in humble guise, and whose merits keep the world going? Who could tell when he had met, under the guise of some pious, honest simpleton, one of these?

In between the first two high festival days of Passover, and the last two days, are four days of half festival. It is still Passover. All leavened things are forbidden. But you may work, you may carry on. And during the full festival days at the beginning and the end, we lived a happy life. Nothing to do after Synagogue services but to visit and be received in style. Cakes, cookies, ginger candies, special delicacies made of Matzoth flour and filled with the baked parings of beets and carrots . . . And then chicken necks and chicken guts, roasted and stuffed, and jams and fruits of all kinds. And on top of all these they gave us wine and mead to sip—as much as we wanted. And we could drink a great deal of it, for it was a home-made raisin wine on which it was difficult to get drunk.

The traditional game for the Passover is with nuts— little Brazil nuts and big walnuts. With the walnuts the game was difficult. Five or six of them were placed in a row; the challenger stood at a distance of twenty paces and tried to hit them with a small steel pellet. The girls played at Pots and Pans. Among the boys the favourite game was Odds and Evens. All you had to do was guess whether your opponent held an odd or an even number of nuts in his hand. But there were sharks and swindlers among us, too. Jakey, the son of Reuben the bathman, introduced us once to a new game. He took up a fistful of nuts and held his hand over the table. Any one who wanted to gamble with him had to place one nut on the table for the privilege of guessing odd, two nuts on the table for guessing even. And then the nuts would be counted. If Jakey won, he kept the one or the two nuts. If he lost, his opponent would get the entire fistful. It looked like a marvellous and attractive gamble. We played with Jakey and lost. We played again and lost. We played with him all day, and all the next day, and Jakey never lost a fistful of nuts. We were stripped of our hoard, with never a single pause in the process.

I was amazed and baffled. How could a man be so lucky, never lose once to an opponent, always hold even when his opponent said odd, odd when he said even? I complained to my father. My father heard the description of the game carefully, then smiled and said, "Stupid! Don't you see that Jakey always puts an odd number of nuts in his hand? When you guess odd, and pay one nut for guessing, he adds the nut to the odd number and that makes it even. When you guess even and pay two nuts for guessing, he adds the two nuts to the odd number in his hand, and that leaves it odd."

Burning with rage, I ran out to my playmates and explained the swindle to all of them. We did not speak to Jakey for nearly a year.

On the afternoon of the eighth day of Passover they gave us Matzoth doubled and bent—a symbol of the fact that Passover was closing. And with it was closing also my first *cheder* year. I was still a child, but with something of the adult. I already knew much about our people and the lore of our people. I understood something of the meaning of that dark word *golus*, exile, which recurs so frequently in our talk, and I also understood why the Jews pray so often for the coming of the Messiah. The child in me was still happy, carefree, merry—but now and again a sigh escaped from my lips—a sigh which I could not account for, and could not explain.

CHAPTER TEN: RESCUE

THE second Rebbi to whom I was turned over—I was then a little over five years of age—was called Abraham Berchifond. How a Jew of Swislowitz came by such a sonorous name I do not know. Berchifond smacks of the old Balt aristocracy: it seems to beg for a *von;* or perhaps it ought to be de Berchifonda. One look at my new Rebbi opened up a fearful gulf between the name and the owner of it. The fact was that few of the Jews of Swislowitz thought of him by his family name, and a stranger who came looking for Abraham Berchifond would not have found him very easily. Only the élite among the residents of our town were called by their family name—and there were perhaps five who had attained to this status. Every one else was known either by his occupation, or by the name of his father or mother, according to their relative prominence. Otherwise they were referred to by some nickname.

There were also exceptions. We had three Jews in Swislowitz by the name of Areh. One was Areh the drayman. The second was Areh the grocer. The third Areh had neither an occupation nor yet any personal peculiarity by which he could be named, and he constituted a problem. In his case we had to fall back on his family name, although he was far, far below that social level where a family name is the proper thing. He was therefore called Areh Barshai. A certain Benjamin was lifted by a similar coincidence to equally un-

179

merited social dignity. We had Benjamin the drayman, and Benjamin the grocer, and Benjamin the scribe. But the fourth Benjamin was also a drayman, so we were reluctantly compelled to call him by his real name, Benjamin Singer. The curious nickname of Kazar by which my second Rebbi was known is the only one of its kind that I have ever met. It came from the contraction of the Russian words for Kazyonni Rabin, the crown or state Rabbi. But the real state Rabbi lived in Babrusk. In small towns like Swislowitz there were only underlings, but for some unknown reason the greater title had been conferred on my Rebbi by the local Jews. It was his duty to keep the register of the Jewish population for births, deaths, marriages, and divorces— and the manner in which he performed this duty baffles description. The forms were sent him from district headquarters in Babrusk, every form numbered and bound into a small volume. But Abraham had a wild system of his own. In the first place he ignored completely the Russian rubrics at the head of each column, and made all his entries in Hebrew. He also made it a principle to ignore marriages and divorces, and the births of girls. He concentrated on funerals and the births of boys. But even in this respect he was shockingly careless, so that dates, names, births, and deaths were jotted down at random in the wildest confusion. The register should, according to law, have been locked up in the Synagogue, under the keep of the high officials. But the volumes lay around in Abraham Kazar's home, among pots and pans and food supplies.

The register kept by Abraham Kazar was the only one recognized by the courts in all disputes regarding inheritance laws, military duties, etc., and the miseries which frequently resulted from the stupid and disorganized entries can hardly be imagined. In thousands of townlets the same disorder prevailed, and the Jews of Russia, disfranchised and half-outlawed as they were, saw their few recognized rights swept away through their own negligence and incompetence. One instance will suffice. It often happened that a state Rabbi of the type of Abraham Kazar would, through sheer ignorance, enter the birth of a girl under the rubric headed "Males." Having done so, he would go on to a complete description of the child, and add the date when the circumcision took place. Twenty years later the government would turn up and demand a conscript, and failing the appearance of the conscript, would impose a fine of three hundred roubles. And there was no getting out of it. It was widely contended among the Jews that many a Russian church had been built with the moneys collected for the "disappearance" of the young men who had originally been young women.

I shall have occasion to write at some length on this entire subject of the state Rabbis appointed by the Russian government in those days. It has been treated frequently in stories and annals of Russian Jewish life, but seldom, I believe, from the proper psychological point of view. In my opinion this institution was the perfect mirror and symbol of the political bondage and the general degradation of the Jews of Russia. I know that from my earliest childhood I learned to hate this institution with a deep and burning hatred, and in my manhood I dedicated a great deal of myself to the struggle for its eradication. So bitter was my hatred of it that I did not hesitate before the most painful sacrifices. I myself became a Kazyonni Rabin and I took upon myself the name and the title which I had always regarded as the sign manual of our shame and slavery. It was my dream then to fight against the evils of the institution from *within*. I believe that the fight which I waged was not without success—but I could not endure it for long. During my years in Vilna I was no longer Kazyonni Rabin: I was lecturer and preacher. And when I did throw off the ugly governmental title, I felt as though the yellow badge of the Middle Ages had been taken off my cloak.

Now, as I look back closely on the course of my life and try to locate the first origins of my lifelong hatred toward the institution of the state Rabbinate, I find it in my memories of Abraham Kazar. And the strange irresponsibilities of human destiny overwhelm me. We seem to choose the paths of our life; we declare ourselves vehemently for this course, for that course. And none of us knows the true, inner reason for the choice or understands the driving forces which work in the secret places of his heart. The wind bloweth where it listeth: without plan or intention it lifts a seed from the earth, carries it into unexpected places, and the seed takes root and grows into a tree. In my soul, too, a seed was planted by accident, and roots were driven into strange underground places, into the dark labyrinths of my being. And much of my future life was determined by the accident of my contact with this man.

Abraham Kazar was in my eyes—even then—a meaningless and contemptible person. I did not develop the faintest feeling of affection or respect for him—and yet he was, beyond doubt, a deep influence in my life. From him I derive that hatred of the Kazyonni Rabbinate which in later years gave me no rest. The very name Kazyonni (state, crown) became a negative symbol to me. I knew that by law a Kazyonni forest or field or even dog was passed on, by inheritance, from one district commissioner to the next. Could the same thing hold true for a Kazyonni Rabbi? I was of course too young to understand the profound irony which lies in the yoking of those two words Kazyonni and Rabbi. But instinct told me that I had touched on something base and false, and my uncorrupted child mind protested against it. More than once I had seen Abraham Kazar trembling like a leaf not only in the presence of the district commissioner, but even before the sergeant or the village policeman, the humblest official in Swislowitz. What kind of government or state did *he* represent? And on the other hand I perceived that he was just an ordinary *melamed* or teacher of the lower grade, to whom no student of the Talmud would be entrusted for instruction. What kind of Rabbi was he, then?

In appearance Abraham Kazar reminded me of my first Rebbi, Mottye the bean. He had the same lean, hungry frame, the same sparse goat-beard. But he was much taller than Mottye the bean and his beard was reddish in colour. He differed from Mottye in another respect. He used his hands instead of leathern thongs: he slapped his pupils instead of whipping them. He did this out of laziness, finding that it was easier to hand out a few slaps right and left than to go through the formalities of a regular whipping. And it was all the easier for him because he was tall, while his arms were long and elastic. He just had to stand up where he was, bend over the table, and make the complete round of his little class with his merciless hands. His fingers were bony, hard as nails, and every slap left its mark, sometimes in five distinct red patches. If fewer than five fingers left their mark, this was due less to his want of skill than to the want of area in a young cheek. Some of the pupils complained bitterly that the slaps of Abraham Kazar were worse than the whippings of Mottye the bean. First, they hurt more. And second, they left visible signs, whereas the signs left by Mottye's whippings could be covered up, and nobody at home needed to know. They were miserable that they could not wear a pair of pants over their faces to hide

their disgrace. But disgrace was not the only unpleasant con-
sequence. No sooner did the child show up at home with the
marks of his Rebbi's displeasure blazoned on his cheek than
there began an inquisition on the part of the parents: "What
have *you* been up to now? If the Rebbi slapped you, it
must have been for something. Rebbis don't slap for nothing." And so the homecoming was frequently more miserable than the original punishment.

Abraham's place in Shuhl was among the most distinguished next to that of my father along the eastern wall.
This place, I am certain, he must have received by inheritance, for neither his merits nor his own social standing entitled him to it. The truth was that beside his official name
of Kazar, he was also known as the Kazyonni jackass—a
tribute to the man and to his official status.

This is about all that I can remember of my second Rebbi.
Not a thing of what he taught me remains in my memory.
I cannot even recall whether I stayed with him one term or
two terms. I can see now that the time I passed with him
was a blank in my life, a lacuna between two written
passages, like a sandy strip unsown and uncovered along
a planted field.

When I examine my past carefully, and trace the devious
and accidental paths along which I wandered blindly before
I found my contact with the culture of Europe, I am compelled to admit that mine was not among those powerful
spirits—powerful either in talents or in impulse—which
could break their own way through the walls of the dark
labyrinth which the old *cheder* represented, and without
assistance find a fruitful field for the exercise of their crea-
tive faculties. Not modesty, but a simple regard for the
truth, compels me to make this statement. I might easily

have gone down with the rest of my schoolmates—and their name is legion—who were drowned in that ocean of ignorance, or asphyxiated in that ugly, pent atmosphere. A miracle was needed to save me: some unexpected outside force which might lift me out of the tangles of my *cheder* life, and set me upon a clear path.

And the miracle took place. I look upon my life as one in which many miracles have occurred, but I believe the greatest was the one which came to my rescue when I was a child of six. And the angel who came to my rescue was my uncle Meyer—but not the one whom the Rebbi Ziskind had laid across the bench even after he was married. My grandfather Solomon had an only daughter, by the name of Liube Henye, and her husband was my second uncle Meyer. His family name—Wendrow—had a lofty and heroic ring about it.

Meyer Wendrow came from somewhere around Slutzk. He had received his education in the city of Slutzk itself, that is, in the very cradle of the secular Hebrew renaissance of that time. He was generally regarded as the handsomest man in Swislowitz, and it is as such that he has remained in my memory. He was a man of middle height, well proportioned, with a handsome, black beard. In later years, when I saw Theodor Herzl for the first time, his beard reminded me vividly of my uncle Meyer Wendrow. But my uncle was respected for something more than his handsome beard. He was considered the foremost Hebrew scholar in Swislowitz. His Hebrew letters were the wonder of the town, and were carried around by their recipients and displayed to every one who had the slightest understanding of such matters. He was extraordinarily skilful in the art of piecing together half verses and fragments of verses out of the Bible in order to reproduce a complete thought of his own—an art which was considered the supreme form of expression among the "stylists" of that time. He knew the entire Bible by heart, and was a great believer in the commentaries of Moses Mendelssohn and his followers. Moreover he could speak, read, and write Russian well. His character, in contrast to that of the Levins, was gentle and dispassionate. He was slow and careful of speech, always finding the right word in the right place.

His outward appearance corresponded with his character: he was always well dressed—sometimes to the point of foppishness. He affected the mode, but with a slight compromise; that is to say, his coat was short—in contrast with our long capotes—but not quite as short as the coat of a city fop. His vest was cut out at the throat, but not too deeply. Had any other man in Swislowitz concentrated on Bible study, understood the modern commentators and even the profanities of grammar, worn a short coat and a cut-out vest, and—on top of all—spoken Russian, he would have been regarded as next door to an atheist. But Meyer Wendrow was deeply respected. Even the Rav of the town, a great scholar and a greater saint, treated him with respect, frequently drew him into conversation after prayers and went for walks with him under the colonnades. Their conversation revolved round the affairs of the world, for in Talmudic studies—the specialty, of course, of our Rav—my uncle was not beyond the stage of the decently educated Jew of the middle classes. In Bible studies, as well as in grammar, our Rav was a comparative novice: he did not have much use for them. The Talmud was his element. And if he happened to need a biblical verse he would look for it not in the original sources, but in a quotation in one of the Talmudic tractates which he knew by heart.

In the field of learning, therefore, there was little to

draw them together; yet it was the Rav who made the first friendly advances toward my uncle. There were two reasons, I think, for this attraction. My uncle was elegant not only in his appearance, but in his spirit and in his behaviour. He conducted himself with all the carefulness of a fine, religious Jewish householder. The second reason was perhaps equally cogent; my uncle had the merit of not living in Swislowitz. Only his family lived there; he himself passed almost his entire life in Dinaburg, where he was one of the foremost agents of the famous firm of Meir and Leib Friendland, the great building contractors. Any agent of the Friendlands was looked upon with respect. And if a man who occupies such an exalted position, builds armories and forts for the Russian government, deals daily with generals and even with ministers of state—if such a man remains a good religious Jew, and comports himself in all details as a good Jew should, then the respect due him is almost without limit. And my grandfather, like the rest of our family, was proud of Uncle Meyer, who, against the dull life of Swislowitz, shone like a stripe of silk in a plain woollen garment.

As I have already said, my uncle passed most of his life in Dinaburg, a city far, far away, a city with a German name. He used to come home once, or at most twice, a year, and I cannot say that he had too much joy of his homecomings. My aunt Liube Henye presented a painful contrast to him. Her looks, and particularly her huge, masculine nose, were very much against her. She paid no attention to dress. To these virtues she added a quarrelsome nature. All year she would boast about her Meyer, her husband, who was as handsome as a count and as clever as a minister of state. I do not know where she could ever have seen a count or a minister for purposes of comparison, but she never forgot to mention them in connection with her brilliant husband. But when the great visitor came home, trouble began. On the one hand, she would never leave him out of sight, and would not take her eyes off him for a moment. On the other hand she was perpetually tormenting him with foolish questions. She worked at it until my uncle was exhausted and irritated; a strained atmosphere was created between them, and there ensued the usual connubial quarrels.

I was present more than once during these quarrels, and I was always on my uncle's side. My aesthetic instincts were stronger than my family patriotism, and even as a child I wondered how on earth this Adam had chosen himself such an Eve. I did not like the match. And I do not believe that my poor uncle liked it, either. But among "decent" families divorces hardly ever took place in those days. If a man had made a bad bargain, he would stagger along silently under his load, doubled up and resigned. As I now see it, my poor aunt Liube Henye was terribly jealous, and she suffered a great deal from the fact that she saw her husband only once or twice a year. It is true that the Jewish wives of Swislowitz were quite ignorant of jealousy as an institution. It never occurred to them to suspect their husbands, and in their pitiful vocabulary even the word jealousy was unknown. But Nature asserted her outraged rights without regard to vocabularies. A Swislowitz housewife might speak without grammar and think in naked concepts. But in respect of her loneliness my aunt was no exception. There were many Jewish wives who, in those days, led the lives of "living widows"; there were many agents who spent three-quarters of the year on the Niz, and teachers who passed many years labouring in some stuffy *cheder* far from their families. Their wives were in effect half divorced from them. But the Jewish population did not seem to suffer from these separations. There was a compensatory factor in the universally large families brought into the world by the shopkeepers and workers and teachers whose occupations did not take them away from home.

My aunt Liube Henye had four children, two girls and two boys, and died in giving birth to her fifth child. The disaster shook our whole family. Little Toibe, my grandmother, wept longer and more bitterly than any one else. My uncle arrived from Dinaburg after the funeral, and it was seen that he too had been deeply affected. The tears which rolled down his cheeks were for the mother of his children, who had now been left orphans.

Some years after the death of my aunt, my uncle Meyer founded the first *cheder mesukan*, or modern and improved *cheder*, in Swislowitz. The very title was still unknown in our town. Both his sons were older than his daughters, and when the problem of their education became an urgent matter my uncle put all the teachers in Swislowitz through a tacit and tactful examination. He finally chose Judah Artzer, and, having consulted with my father, included me among the pupils of the first "modern" *cheder*. My uncle, the initiator of this new institution, remained for years its controller and inspector. Twice a year he came to see us, looked into our studies, examined us, and laid down the course for the ensuing term. Four pupils in all made up the *cheder:* Gershon and Levi, the two sons of Uncle Meyer, Areh, the son of Uncle Schmerel, and myself.

It was thus that, in the institution which my uncle had founded, Judah Artzer became my new spiritual guide and mentor. Until this day my memories of my new teacher are among the happiest and most grateful of my life.

CHAPTER ELEVEN: THE NEW SCHOOL

THERE were about twenty *melamdim* or teachers in Swislowitz. That is to say, there were twenty young men who, having exhausted or lost the meagre dowries of their wives in various enterprises, and having in the meantime become the fathers of families, betook themselves to teaching for a livelihood. They might with the same moral right have betaken themselves to the trades of the broker, the raftbinder, or the drayman, but they chose the line of least resistance. To become a teacher you needed neither capital nor training of any kind. In the worst case, you could begin as an elementary teacher, for every one knew at least sufficient Hebrew to teach the alphabet. With a bit of luck, you might know more than that, or learn a little more while you were teaching infants, and thus lift yourself to a higher class. Not for nothing did a famous Tanai (teacher) say that he had learned more from his school-mates than from his teacher, and most of all he had learned from his pupils. Some of the teachers of Swislowitz took the Tanai's words quite literally. They learned to teach at the expense of their pupils.

There was a story current in our town concerning one such teacher, whose stock of knowledge enabled him to guide his pupils through the alphabet as far as the simple reading of Hebrew words—and no further. But the man was ambitious, and he suffered in spirit. On a certain day he suddenly

declared that he would also take on pupils for the Pentateuch—that is, he would teach them the Five Books with
translation: and as he offered the lowest terms in town, there
were found fathers willing to entrust their sons to him. The
teacher had discovered a way out. Late at night, when
the town slept, he received the visits of a Yeshivah student,
and took lessons in the Pentateuch. The thing was kept a
secret; by night he was a pupil, by day he was a Rebbi. As a
Rebbi he could not go very far, and it was all he could do to
keep one or two portions ahead of his pupils. Fettered as he
was, he kept the arrangement up for a time. But as evil luck
would have it, his Yeshivah student took sick, and failed to
appear. Trembling for his secret, the teacher hesitated to
call in another instructor. For a few days he worked on his
tiny reserve stock of Pentateuchal learning, hoping that the
student would recover in time. But the student was seriously sick, and the Rebbi came to the end of his rope. But he
still held out. Instead of going over to a new portion of the
Pentateuch, he took to revision. He revised once, and twice
and three times, and still his midnight teacher remained sick.
For several weeks the *cheder* agonized in the throes of disso-
lution, until it came to an open scandal. The *cheder* was
dissolved in the middle of the term. A Jewish school died because the Rebbi's stock had been exhausted.

I have known of three cases of this kind, and I think them
all worthy of mention. The first case, concerning the elementary *melamed* in Swislowitz, was told me at second hand,
for the incident took place before my time. Of the other two
cases I was a living witness.

The second incident had as its centre a colleague of mine,
a prominent personage who later played a leading rôle in the
Jewish national movement. At the time, however, we were
students in Berlin, and we shared a single room. My friend

was hard up and on the lookout for any kind of work. He had more enterprise than good fortune and more courage than *savoir faire*. One day he came across a want ad in the paper calling for a teacher of elementary Spanish for a boy of six. The same day he rushed off to the beginners class in Spanish at the University and for three days crammed feverishly. On the fourth day he presented himself at the address given in the newspaper, hoping desperately that he had not come too late. The door was opened by a man around forty years of age—the father of the boy. The usual courtesies had been exchanged in German when, to my friend's indescribable horror, the father went calmly over into Spanish. My friend was literally dumbfounded. Silently and suddenly he reached for his hat, jammed it on his head, and fled from the house, forgetting even to say "Good day" in German. He told me that he had never in his life acted with such instinctive swiftness. But he found the incident as a whole quite natural. He only wondered where his unnatural celerity had come from.

The third transmigration of this situation I came across in America during a visit to a city of some millions of inhabitants, among whom are three hundred thousand Jews. I had lectured before an audience of women on the development of modern Hebrew literature, and at the close of the lecture the chairman introduced to me a young lady who, she said, was "a great patriot of Hebrew." Her intentions were touchingly delicate: she wanted to have me know that in her social circle, too, there were friends of the Hebrew renaissance. I entered into conversation with the young lady. It appeared that she came from a wealthy Jewish Reform home, and had turned Hebrew teacher *pour l'art*. Hers was a beginners' class in a well-known Reform temple. But she told me the truth with disarming simplicity. She really knew no Hebrew, but she was set on being a Hebrew teacher. So she had found a teacher for herself, took two lessons a week, and transmitted the fruits of her studies regularly to her class. She said she had never felt any uneasiness, or had ever experienced a shortage of knowledge. On the contrary, she was always able to keep up her sleeve a little reserve for emergencies and for display. I recognized in the young lady the reincarnation of the Rebbi of Swislowitz and of my fellow student in Berlin. All three were expressions and symbols of the psychology of exile, the gipsy carelessness and shiftiness of an uprooted and homeless people.

I return to my Swislowitz teachers.

Among the twenty of them there were perhaps three or four who were teachers by profession—which does not mean, of course, by training: it only means that they chose the profession deliberately and out of love for it, and took it seriously. Two of these men were well worth remembering. The first was Azer the *melamed*, and the second Judah Artzer. Azer was the older man—at that time round forty years of age and with a well-established reputation in his profession— a fixed star. Judah was a beginner, around thirty years of age—a rising star. But his name began to get around only when he took over the new *cheder* which my uncle founded. Before many terms had passed the reputation of Judah Artzer outshone that of Azer the *melamed*. They spoke of him even in Babrusk, and he received invitations from that town to leave Swislowitz. They made him golden offers—but he remained true to his little *cheder*. He was devoted to me in particular, and I believe he dedicated his best energies to my education.

There was a curious contrast between these two teachers of Swislowitz. Azer was known as one of the most miserly men in town. He could never bring himself to part with a kopeck save under dire compulsion; he ruled his house with an economic severity which kept it on the border-line of starvation: he counted the beans that went into the pot, and allowed about enough food to keep body and soul together. Judah was instinctively generous. He liked good tobacco, and distributed his store of it right and left. Azer saved his money, penny by penny, and with his first few roubles opened a loan office, lending out at weekly interest. He grasped the essential secret of money forthwith. He knew that money must never lie idle, but must be perpetually at work, must always "increase and multiply."

In my day it was already rumoured that Azer the *melamed* had a capital of four hundred roubles. With all his niggardliness he could never have saved such a sum from the fees he charged. He had made it mostly in usury. His roubles increased like yeast; and small wonder. He would lend out ten roubles and begin by deducting two roubles and forty kopecks as interest: the borrower getting only seven roubles and sixty kopecks. On this he paid twenty kopecks a week for a year's time. And the kopecks that Azer gathered in did not rest. They were immediately put out at interest. And so the kopecks begot the rouble, the rouble the hundred. Azer the *melamed* might have become one of the richest men in town if things had gone right; unfortunately for him, however, there were "bankruptcies" to be reckoned with.

The practice of appealing to the Russian courts for settlement of cases between Jews did not exist in my town in those days. The appeal was made, instead, to the Torah, to Jewish Law, as interpreted by the Rav of the town. And Azer was forever haling somebody before the Rav, appealing to the eternal principles of the Torah, and invoking, in the arguments, all his considerable knowledge of our lore. He forgot only one thing: that the taking of usury is strictly forbidden by that Torah to which he appealed. Judah Artzer was in this respect at the opposite pole. He was ready to give his last kopeck to any friend, and he was for that reason perpetually in debt even though he had the best-paying *cheder* in town.

The difference in character between the two men also expressed itself in their respective attitudes toward Judaism. Azer the *melamed* guarded with the same embittered closeness every one of the outer laws of religion, and brought his pupils up in that same spirit. For instance, during the Prayer of the Eighteen Benedictions, which has to be repeated standing in one place, and without interruption, he made it a point to remain standing longer than any one else; and woe to the pupil who was over-hasty in resuming his seat. Judah cared little for these refinements, and was much more concerned that during their prayers his pupils should distribute the accents correctly on the words. In brief, Azer was a zealot for the letter of the Law, Judah more devoted to the spirit of it. Azer was the true teacher of Talmud—but a stranger to the spirit of the Bible, lacking understanding of the Prophets and of their ethical artistic influence on the mind of man. Judah, who later became, as a Talmud teacher, the equal of Azer, remained to the end a man of the Bible, a lover of the Prophets and steeped in their spirit. In one sense they could have been called the Hillel and Shammai of Swislowitz: Judah was Hillel and Azer was Shammai. The resemblance, if it is true, must of course be taken in miniature. But then, was not the entire life of Swislowitz a miniature? One day God wanted to make Himself a vest-pocket edition of the world, and He created Swislowitz.

It goes perhaps without saying that the two men were not friends. It never came to an open quarrel, but it was well known that Azer had no use for Judah's attention to the profanities of grammar, and regarded with dislike and contempt his pedagogic methods and his general attitude toward his pupils. Judah, for his part, had little faith in Azer's piety, and as little use for his approach to the Talmud. The respective pupils of the two *cheders* felt the enmity of their teachers in their own bones, and as is always the case, the hostility of the schools was more open than the hostility of their founders. It was thus in the case of the schools of Hillel and Shammai: it was thus in the *cheders* of Azer the *melamed* and Judah Artzer. In time this hostility developed into something like genuine hatred. We were fiery in our defence of our Rebbi, and fierier still in our contempt for Azer and his brood. At first I was perturbed by the fact that my older brother Meyer attended Azer's *cheder*, but in time I equalled my schoolmates in loyalty to our *cheder* and hatred of its rival.

For the first time I felt myself drawn toward the man who was my teacher, and I remember how happy the feeling made me. Nothing contents a child more than the process of its own growth, and its constant desire to become a "grown-up" both mentally and physically. And nothing bribes a child more easily than the habit of taking it seriously, and helping it honestly to grow, to develop in understanding and in knowledge. And I felt at once that my new teacher was genuinely interested in me, not because he was paid for it, but because he looked upon me as a little man, and he wanted me to become a big one.

My uncle had made Judah promise that, without the consent of the parents, he would not increase the number of his pupils beyond the four he set out with. And the number remained stationary. In compensation Judah received, for every pupil, the then incredible fee of twenty-five roubles a term, a total income of two hundred roubles (one hundred dollars) a year. This was regarded as very high payment for any employé: for a Rebbi it was unheard of. Had not our earliest teachers decreed that *melamdim* and scribes had to be content with little, that they ought to do their holy work for the Glory of God? It is written, further, that one ought actually to accept no money for tuition. It is quite impossible to estimate the value of learning, impossible to translate the worth of the Torah into filthy lucre. A way out was found. The teacher was compensated not for the inestimable work which he did, but merely for the time he had lost and the income he had forfeited by not devoting himself to worldly business. He received, as it were, damages. And so it came to this: he received for his day's work what he might have made chopping wood or carrying water. He was not paid for his work as a teacher.

I need hardly say that in the above subterfuge there is a good deal of sophistry; but it does express the attitude of the ancients toward the sacred character of learning, and the sanctity of the profession of the teacher. In this respect, then, Swislowitz lived up to the most glorious traditions of the past, and saw to it that none of its teachers should earn a decent living. The average earnings of a Swislowitz teacher amounted to one hundred roubles a year. When it became known that Judah was to make two hundred roubles a year on four pupils, the town went up in the air, and did not come down for several weeks. And there were several respectable householders who remonstrated with my uncle for his reforms, and pointed out the dangers of corrupting the profession.

In addition to the twenty-five roubles a term, Judah also received from each pupil fifteen roubles to enable him to rent a *cheder*. This was another of the newfangled ideas of my uncle Meyer. He was opposed to the universal practice of making the living-room of the Rebbi his temple of learning. He argued that when the Rebbi was engaged in teaching, he ought not to have his family around him, forever distracting him from his difficult duties. Likewise it was bad for the children to be mixed up in the family affairs of the Rebbi.

We rented the room in the cottage of Feige Riveh, a lady I have already mentioned as one of my mother's chief assistants in her medical activities, and the foremost specialist in Swislowitz for expelling and combating the evil eye. Feige Riveh had a second husband—also married for the second time—a huge clumsy Jew known as Abraham the yellow. This man was a jack of all trades, able in nothing, and finding employment only from time to time.

Feige Riveh was a public figure among the gentiles of Swislowitz no less than among the Jews, and for the identical reason—her reputation as an exorcist of the evil eye. Abraham the yellow used to benefit by his wife's standing, and would pick up bargains among her gentile clientele—now a young calf, now an ox, now a wagon-load of hay or a bag of wheat. Sometimes he worked in the woods, with the raftsmen—a part of the trade which needed little intelligence or training. Sometimes he did a little business as a broker, and in between whiles he earned an honest rouble or two as a marriage-maker. This last profession was the only one which he loved independently of its earnings. More than anything he loved to urge a match on two young people precisely when both of them were present. He would praise the bride to the bridegroom and the bridegroom to the bride, lavishly, joyously, with genuine artistic feeling. And as he proceeded his eyes narrowed down contentedly, like those of a happy cat, and the freckles on his vast face began to glow like the faces of the young people he was extolling.

He was not very lucky in his matches, and rarely succeeded in bringing them to a consummation. On one occasion he worked on a case for as long as six months. He was trying to persuade a bridegroom of Swislowitz to take a bride from Lapitz—a village some thirty Russian miles from our town. He would not leave Swislowitz until he had wrung from the bridegroom a reluctant half consent: and this he obtained by dinning into the ears of his family the praises of the bride, distributed among detailed descriptions of her appearance, her family, her education, her wit, and her abilities. Finally Abraham left for Lapitz to begin convincing the bride's family. He came back the next day, dumb. Not a word on the subject could be obtained from him. Before long the truth leaked out. He had never been in Lapitz before. He had not known the family. He had worked on a rumour. When he got to Lapitz he discovered that the rumour had changed sex *en route*. In Lapitz too the eligible party was masculine. And for weeks the Jews of Swislowitz had something to laugh about: "Abraham the yellow is the most dangerous marriage-broker in these parts: he seeks husbands for men and wives for women."

On top of his other virtues Abraham the yellow was a henpecked husband. This huge, lumbering clown, nearly twice the height of his wife and four times her weight, used to tremble before the sharp glances of the tiny, mercurial creature—a fistful of bones and nerves—that was Feige Riveh. A great talker, he suffered from repression in the presence of his wife: no sooner did he feel her eye fastened on him than he would stop in the middle of a sentence, and turn two pitiful, cowlike eyes on her, with the question, "Feige Riveh, do you think I am talking nonsense?" And if she made no answer, he went on, timidly. But if she said, quietly, "You know what I think," he collapsed into silence, without ending the story.

Four persons made up the family: husband and wife, a daughter (a quiet, frightened girl), and Feige Riveh's son by her first marriage. Their house stood in a gentile street, and the room which we had rented as the *cheder* stood apart, protruding into the garden of a gentile neighbour. So we were sundered from the outside world: behind us we were cut off from the other half of the house by an intervening room: on three sides of us was the garden, with its high fence. And in the midst we were alone, Rebbi and pupils, with our books, an intimate happy corner of our own.

When Judah opened the class, his first point was to return to the beginning, as if we had never been to a *cheder* before. Had he been able to do it, he would gladly have erased from our memories all that we had learned till then. He went over the ground once more, teaching us the simple reading of Hebrew, eradicating the errors we had picked up from our teachers in the first three terms. He thought our reading atrocious, and said again and again that it was the hardest thing in the world for him to sit by and see the Hebrew language submitted to such torture. He did not mean to insult our previous teachers. We children felt that he was utterly sincere in his strictures. During the first weeks, when we read Hebrew to him and misplaced the accents freely, he would start at every error, catch his breath, and pull faces as though some one had stuck a pin into him. He told us, "Children, if any one of you should be saying prayers in Shuhl, or reading a chapter out of the Pentateuch or the Bible, I want every listener to know, by your reading, that this is one of Judah Artzer's pupils."

During the summer we spent ten hours a day in *cheder*, and in winter it was nearly twelve. In the summer we began

around nine in the morning and continued until the afternoon prayer; in winter we began at the same hour and went
on until nearly nine at night. But that was during the first
terms. Later on we began just as early, but did not finish
until ten and eleven at night. Not more than one hour was
taken up by meals. We had somewhat less than eight hours of
sleep. For play we had Friday afternoon, half the Sabbath,
the Holy Days, and the end of the term. During the winter
we used to say the afternoon and evening prayers in the
cheder, instead of going to Shuhl, in order to save time. With
Judah Artzer teaching occupied first place.

The hours of study were systematically laid out and, what
was unusual in a *cheder*, strictly followed. The subjects for
the first two terms were Pentateuch, Bible, grammar, and
writing. The Five Books, or Pentateuch, we learned, from
the outset, together with the famous mediaeval commentary
of Rashi. That is to say, we not only learned what he has to
say on every verse of the Pentateuch text, but we studied his
own text, too, independently. Now the text of Rashi is
printed without the guiding vowels under the letters. Partly
on this account, and partly because the language of the
commentator is a mixture of pure Hebrew and of Aramaic—
entire phrases having been lifted from Talmud and Midrash
—we spent more time on Rashi than on the text proper. But
in this way, without knowing it, we began to make acquaintance with a new language—Aramaic—so that later on,
when we came to the study of the Talmud, we were not altogether helpless.

The general impression is that Hebrew was the sole study
in the *cheder*—but it is erroneous. Side by side with Hebrew
there moved half a dozen minor dialects, beginning with the
language of the Mishnah (the authoritative compilation of
the traditional law which had grown up, in Palestine, around

the Bible proper), a continuation of classical Hebrew, but with a vocabulary and grammar of its own, and ending with the rabbinic language of Rashi. It is these dialects which have made the ancient Hebrew so supple and colourful and susceptible of development. Biblical Hebrew alone would have left us incapable of progress, and we would have remained forever bound to the affected style of the biblical phraseologists.

Grammar was an absolutely new experience for us, as it was something new in the experience of the Jews of Swislowitz. A table of verbs (an analysis of the sacred Hebrew tongue into its base mechanics—the profanity of it!) was handed to each one of us, and I conceived a tremendous affection for this part of the studies. I loved the discipline of the conjugations. We learned these by heart in between the courses, and we repeated them at odd moments at home. I was forever jingling the words, so that my mother had to beg me to stop my eternal *pokod, pokadti, pokadto* . . . I believe that the feeling for pure logic developed in me very early, and I felt grammar to be the logic of speech. I realized vaguely that language was no longer a lawless, accidental sort of affair. The long lines of the conjugations in my table of verbs became like the alleys of a neatly planted and disciplined garden, and I strolled between the lines of flowers: on one side flowers of the past, on the other side flowers of the future; in between, the line of the present. And I myself was a verb—a *poal*—a thing that works.

I look back on those days and wonder at them. Ten hours a day we sat glued to our places, studying; where did we get the strength, the endurance, to pass through so rigorous a regimen? I do not mean to say that in this respect our *cheder* was more severe than any other. In other *cheders*, too, the pupils sat shut in for ten and twelve hours a day. But there was a difference. In other *cheders* the pupils numbered between ten and fifteen; they were divided into groups, so that the *cheder* became a school with several classes but with only one teacher. So that while the teacher would be occupied with one class, the other classes, even though they revised their lessons, could relax. They let their studies run downhill then, like an automobile with the engine shut off. But our *cheder* consisted only of one class, so that we were forever under the eye of the Rebbi, and we worked intensively through the ten and twelve hours. Moreover, our Rebbi was one of the exceptions in the town: he took his work with the utmost seriousness. He watched us closely, and refused to let us get by with mere repetitions of what he told us: he wanted to hear our brains at work in our voices, as we chanted the text and the translations.

Amazing as it must sound to "moderns," it never occurred to anybody that the strain might be excessive. It did not even occur to my uncle Meyer, who was a modern man, with a modern outlook. It just did not occur to anybody that much study can be bad for your health. The world in which I lived was a stranger to the idea of excessive mental strain: the word "strain" was applied only to physical effort.

And the truth is that much study seldom leads to sickness. Our greatest teachers, the Tanaim, the Amoraim, the Gaonim, all passed their entire lives in study, and yet of not a single one of them is it recorded that he fell sick from too much study. But we did not have to go so far afield. There was the Rav of our town: did he not pass sixteen and sometimes twenty-four hours at a single stretch in study? It was quite true that the Rav of our town was sick enough from time to time: but that was because he rarely received his miserable salary on time. It was equally true that the Yeshivah students were pale, lean, and sick-looking: but that was because they were short of "days." But no one had ever traced a sickness to excess of study.

A shortage of "days" needs a little explanation. The students of the Talmud (loosely referred to as Yeshivah or Academy students, although they had no academy to attend in our town) were frequently so poor that they literally lacked bread to eat. It was the custom throughout all eastern Jewry to assign these students to various homes for the different days in the week. On Monday a student ate at one man's house: on Tuesday at another's: on Wednesday at the house of a third. This was called the process of "eating days." But it fell out more than once that the roster of Jews who could or would take in a student for a "day" fell short of the needed number. And then one student would lack a Monday, and another student would lack a Tuesday. And a pallid student, with wilted body and sunken eyes, would go around looking for his lost day, and inquiring for a fellow student who might have a superfluous one.

How closely we youngsters of six and seven guarded our time may be seen from the fact that even during the long summer days we were not allowed to go bathing until the hour between afternoon and evening prayers. It is easy to understand, then, that our *cheder* rapidly outstripped every other *cheder* of the same standard. Our Rebbi literally crammed us. In the first term we had the first three books of the Pentateuch, together with Rashi's commentary for the first sections of the first book; the last two books of the early Prophets, the first two books of the Bible (meaning, in this case, Joshua and Judges); and the entire table of verbs. By the end of the second term we had taken in the entire Pentateuch, all the earlier Prophets, the two books of

Samuel, the two books of Kings: and we had already formed some idea of the laws which govern the vowels: an important part of Hebrew, since in advanced writing the vowels are omitted, and the reader must know what they are by the laws of grammar alone.

I cannot remember within one term how old I was when I finished my first year with my new Rebbi; but the doubt does not cover more than a term or half year. I cannot, however, have been more than seven or eight years old. Two of my schoolmates were a year older, and the third was of the same age. I was, however, the leader, and this was shown by the attitude both of the Rebbi and of the class. It was true that we all followed the same course of studies, and learned the same things. But this was so only in regard to the area we covered; it did not hold with regard to the depth to which we penetrated toward the meaning and spirit of our studies. For in this regard I was always far ahead of my schoolmates. The Rebbi said openly that if he could only find another pupil to match up with me, he would make a separate little class of two. He could not make a class of one, because a boy, he said, had to have at least one comrade in study. Curiously enough, he would say these things openly in my presence and in that of my schoolmates: and I do not remember a single sign of envy on their part. This may have been due to the fact that my superiority was so marked that envy lost all meaning; calculation in common terms—which is the source of envy— had become impossible, and envy therefore yielded to admiration. But the friendliness which my schoolmates manifested was mutual. I was neither haughty nor impudent toward them, and neither the praises of my Rebbi, openly uttered, nor the compliments which I began to hear in increasing numbers, both at home and in the Shuhl from the grown-ups, affected me in my attitude toward them. I was as fond of their company, as fond of play, as ever. It seemed to me that even my studies were a part of my play.

I cannot remember that I ever overstrained myself; my brain never became weary. It seemed to me that my brain was always at play, and the things I learned just leaped into my mind. One of my playmates, as I recall, had to work so long, so arduously, to acquire the conjugations, that it was painful to watch him. He gave us the impression of a man chopping wood, the perspiration streaming from his face: it was as though, by hacking away with the repetitions, he could hack a way into his own brain. And he had to repeat the same process with every verb separately. But the trick of the rule, the secret of the principle, came to me so simply and so easily that the separate verbs lost all terror for me. They were like tamed horses, all ready to be put under the same yoke.

In grammar it was the logical faculty which played the main rôle; but in Bible study it was the psychological factor. Here too I went much deeper in my studies than my schoolmates. I looked, as it were, for the "rule" and the "principle" of the story—the inner connection and not the individual parts. The words were bricks, the verses were lines of bricks, but there was an invisible mortar which held everything together and permitted no changes or substitutions. I never studied the Pentateuch and the Bible with the express intention of knowing them by heart; yet none of my playmates knew them as nearly by heart as I did. It was not memory which played the chief rôle, but the logical indices to the text, worked out in my own mind.

Back of the faculty which helped me to learn and to remember much without putting myself under an undue strain, was my living relationship to all that surrounded me, and particularly to the world of nature in all its forms. I sought life in all things, and found it. I remember some one telling me that stones too could grow, and that all big stones had once been little; and I was happy that one more way of life had been added in this world to others. It was always patent to me that the woods and fields lived not only in the sense of growth, but in the sense of the possession of an individual spirit, which could weep and laugh, as it could suffer and be happy. And later, when I learned the book Shirah, I found nothing forced or unnatural in the thought that the trees have their verse of praise, and the fields theirs, and so on.

Often enough I went alone into the woods to listen to the trees saying their verse of praise, as the book Shirah tells. Not that, even then, I expected the tree to lift up its voice and, with a human tongue, repeat the exact words of the Bible. But of course there was a distinct, fixed language of the trees, inaccessible to us. Why, King Solomon understood it.

My joy in life itself, and the growing of life, shone back on my own body. I wanted to measure my own body's growth, too. For many mornings I measured myself against a mark I had made on the door—it was my first duty after I had got out of bed. Once I heard my mother say that the cucumbers in the garden had grown up overnight. More than one night I stole out, and lying between the planted rows, watched in the quiet moonlight the long, green young cucumbers. I wanted to catch them red-handed, in a spasm of growth. And every now and again I would imagine that I had seen them throb in sudden expansion, and a thrill of joy ran through me.

The current of my feelings toward my studies ran from the same source. I remember that even in the *cheder* of Mottye the bean, when I first learned about Adam and Eve, I did not feel that they were far-away people, who had lived thousands and thousands of years ago. Together with them I walked in the scented alleys of the Garden of Eden, and together with them suffered disaster. I heard the voice of God, a lamentation, calling, "Where art thou?" and I trembled from head to foot. The shame of Adam ran over my whole body; it seemed to me that I had committed the great evil, I had tasted of the Tree of Knowledge; and I felt myself, to know if I was naked. I floated in the ark with Noah, and saw the gates of Heaven open above me. I saw the dove come flying back over the waters, bearing the leaf of olive in its mouth.

Until I came to Judah Artzer my imagination worked for itself, in a vacuum, for neither one of my first two Rebbis knew how to feed it, or cared to. They had no living relationship to the stories of the past, and where I had managed to establish a contact, it was by the brute will of the imagination. How different Judah was! He himself was given to seeing all things in a living form. He did not simply translate the stories of the Bible, but added to them a conviction and an intimacy of experience which gave them colour and passion. I heard in the Rebbi's voice a far-off ringing echo of my own being, and new strength drew me to my studies. The opening sentences of the chapters were like gates that gave upon new stretches of life.

CHAPTER TWELVE: I ENTER A NEW WORLD

Until I found my new teacher my development had been determined chiefly by the small, poverty-stricken, and colourless life of Swislowitz. It is true that on occasions the things I learned in *cheder*, the stories I heard from my mother, and the pictures of the big world which sprang out for me from the talk of the older people, did lift me out of my environment. But the illusions lasted only for a moment: there was no thread on which to string them, and they never poured themselves into a single powerful stream to carry me away. I lived the realities of Swislowitz, and I dreamed the dreams of Swislowitz, as pitiful, as meagre, as its realities.

A complete break came in my inner life with my entry into Judah's *cheder*. It came not at once, but by a process of steady preparation. I am quite certain that my Rebbi did not quite understand what he was doing to me. Least of all, I think, would he have desired to uproot us from our environment and transplant us into another soil. But this is exactly what happened—and of its own accord. It happened, in a certain measure, with all my schoolmates; but it happened in the strongest measure with me.

With every new chapter of the Bible that I learned, with every new hero I came to know, with every incident that I lived through, I was drawn one step farther from the soil into which I was born, and closer to the sacred soil of ancient heroes and ancient heroisms. Fragment by fragment a new life grew up within me, a life which began in Ur of the Chaldees, stretched through Mesopotamia, wound its way across a gigantic desert, held war with the most powerful kings, and at last found a resting-place in Palestine—the first half of a vast world-drama. I learn steadily, and become a more intimate part of this life. I forget completely that these are the stories and descriptions of a world which has passed away these thousands of years. Strange paradox! The more clearly I understood the meaning of the words *past, gone,* the more potently did I feel the presence of that world. It captured me, I became part of it—I could not free myself!

And when the books are closed, when the *cheder* is shut and, with my Rebbi or my companions, I walk homeward, I must exert myself to return to the world of reality. I do not notice what is happening around me. My mind is with the heroes of old, and I make a deliberate effort to bridge the gulf between Abraham our Father and Abraham Kazar, between Moses our Teacher and Moses the shoemaker.

So day by day I am drawn more deeply into this double existence—the material world of Swislowitz and the dream-world which issues from the books of the Bible. In my sleep my dreams become confused, and I no longer know from which of the two worlds they are drawn. I can well remember seeing in a dream of my childhood the splitting of the Red Sea. The water rises like two walls on either hand, and in the midst is a broad path of sand with millions of smooth pebbles, like the banks of the Swisla. In the midst the Jews march along, dressed in holiday attire, the men with prayer-shawls over their shoulders. Among them I recognize my grandfather, the Rav of the town, and many other familiar figures, and it does not occur to me that my grandfather had nothing to do with the passage of the Red Sea. Two worlds have mingled within me, and I no longer distinguish where the one ends, where the other begins.

There is only one passage in the Bible which can describe the strange state in which I lived in those years when I was passing from childhood into adolescence (for we were adolescents at the age of twelve)—the passage which tells of Jacob and Esau in the womb of Rebecca. *And the children struggled together within her. . . . And the Lord said unto her, Two nations are in thy womb and two manner of people. . . .* Two brothers, two worlds, in the mother-womb. And when Rebecca went past a Jewish House of Prayer and Study, Jacob trembled and struggled within her; and when she passed by a church, it was Esau who trembled and struggled to get out. That was what the commentator, Rashi, said; and that was what the Rebbi taught us. Where churches and Synagogues existed in those days was a mystery, and it still remains one. But I see now that our sages had the trick of my own childhood—they pulled the world which was ancient even in their days closer into their own lives. They too lived in a double world. At that time, within me, the struggle was not between Jacob and Esau (that struggle was to come in later years when I became acquainted with the world of Esau), but between two Jacobs. One little Jacob was the child of Swislowitz, the *cheder* boy, oppressed by the narrow life which encircled him; the other little Jacob came from a mighty and tumultuous world. For I was acquainted with many others besides the Jewish heroes of old. I knew the giant Og, king of Bashan, and Sihon, king of the Amorites; I knew the most wonderful magician of all times, Balaam, and the mightiest warrior, Nebuchadnezzar of Babylon. And on the threshold of the *cheder*, as I entered and left, the two brothers held war. Within the *cheder* the Jacob of the great world was triumphant; outside, the Jacob of Swislowitz

211

asked for his place in the sun, and struggled to assert himself.

After all, the significance of a classical education lies in this: that the child is introduced to a world that existed a long time ago, so that he may learn how, in ancient times, there already existed a rich life, an organized society, with its own art and knowledge and its own ideals of justice and beauty. For most of those who believed in a classical education, the instruments employed to this end were Greek and Latin, and a knowledge of the best books in those languages. Thus civilized man might learn how the process of life stretched link by link from generation to generation, from epoch to epoch, from the beginning down to his own day. I am quite certain that the ordinary classical education, too, gives rise to a conflict within the mind of the child, like the one which I experienced.

But I cannot for a moment admit that the conflict would be at all comparable to mine. Latin and Greek have remained dead languages even to the most gifted of students. They cannot compete in this respect with the mother-tongue of the Talmud. And then the life which is portrayed in these languages is an alien life, and only the rare genius can identify himself with it, find his way about. Language and content are like the faint echo of a life that has uttered itself long ago and has died—the passing shadow of an eagle on desert sands. Thus the conflict which must have been awakened by classical studies among gentiles was a weak one, a contact rather than a conflict. Yet even that contact was enough to rouse a world-wide movement against the classical education as such.

I cannot enter here into a discussion of the rights and wrongs of the arguments on both sides. I only wish to stress the fact that the Jewish *cheder* was a classical school.

Whether it was good or bad is another question; but it was classical in aim and scope. The programme of studies carried the Jewish child back to the classic age of its people. The Hebrew language which we learned, the books that we studied, belonged to the classic epoch of our history, and the effect on the Jewish child was infinitely more powerful than the effect of the non-Jewish classical education even in countries which regarded the classics as the chief and perhaps the sole substance of education.

Two considerations, the one quantitative, the other qualitative, explain this difference. The actual time spent in the *cheder* on Hebrew and Hebrew subjects was between three and four times as long as the time spent on both Latin and Greek in the best high schools of Europe. The *cheder* boy was simply steeped in Hebrew from morning till night. And in passing, he also learned, as I have already noted, several important Hebrew dialects.

But the qualitative element was perhaps even more important. In Hebrew, the Jewish child was learning the history of his own race. These were not the stories of an alien world, but events and individuals who had some sort of inner relation with father and mother. A third factor, of less importance, should be remembered. At the time of which I write the Hebrew language played a much more important rôle in the daily life of the Jews than it does today. Contemporary Hebrew literature was, it is true, very poor; the language had not yet been adapted to modern life, and the efforts of writers at modern self-expression were clumsy in the extreme. But I allude now solely to the daily life of the Jewish householder. At that time, fifty or sixty years ago, nearly all Jewish shopkeepers kept their accounts in Hebrew, Jewish merchants corresponded in Hebrew, and among the better classes bride and bridegroom exchanged notes in the same language. And if they could not write Hebrew, they would have their love-letters written for them by their teachers or by special scribes. And the Song of Songs was ransacked in every corner for quotations—from "Let him kiss me with the kisses of his mouth" to "Flee, my beloved."

It is not my business to pass judgment, to estimate the value of that system; but the system ought to be understood by all those who wish to know something concerning our immediate past.

As far as I am concerned, personally, Hebrew became an absolutely living tongue. The transformation had already begun, I believe, with the second or the third term with Judah. I have an unmistakable "marker" of the time when Hebrew had become a living tongue for me, or, rather, when I had awakened to it. When a language has become real, it is no longer necessary to translate it, and I remember that in my third or fourth term I was already reading the Bible without translating it—and my Rebbi let it pass. It was only in the most difficult passages that he would stop me and make certain that I knew the meaning. The translation had by now become superfluous ballast, which only impeded my progress. I was impatient, eager to run ahead, and the translation had been clinging to me for some time like heavy winter clothes when the spring is already here.

My three schoolmates were by nature slower than I, and the difference in the rates of progress made the Rebbi's task difficult. He was like a skilful driver who must find a compromise between his horses, holding in the swiftest—but not checking it too brutally—and encouraging the others to greater speed. In a general way, too, my schoolmates were quieter than I—two of them were almost phlegmatic in character. Thus, because they were driven fairly hard to keep pace with me, they had not the time either to reflect or to stand up and ask questions, and so they swallowed whole whatever the Rebbi handed them out of the Bible. I, on the other hand, found the tempo of studies slow; so I had perhaps too much time, during the actual work, to look around and to think things over. So from the beginning—and this went back to my earliest years—I used to ask puzzled question after question. I manifested in childhood the logical faculty which I had inherited from my father—manifested it long before I had the slightest idea that logic was something in and for itself, with formulated laws of its own. (Our Rebbi taught us the elements of logic, in my eighth year, out of the textbook of Ben Ze-ev.) But even then, when I became confused, it was my habit to reconstruct the first syllogisms of a case, just as I learned to do years later, and to thread my way cautiously through the labyrinth of arguments. My mind moved swiftly and smoothly, and always felt the quick jolt when it ran over a break on the logical path. Nor did I have long to wait for such jolts; there are logical breaks enough in the Bible stories, whether in the Five Books or in the subsequent parts.

But in addition to the questions which sprang up in my mind because of logical contradictions in the text, there rose in me questions directed to the psychological aspects of the stories. I was interested in the principles of justice which the stories illustrated, and whenever a struggle arose I could not remain neutral, but had to ally myself passionately with one of the two sides: this was my inheritance from my mother. My older playmate, Gershon, used to ask me, bewildered, what business of mine it was who was in the right and who in the wrong: it was only a story, after all, and the outcome settled no point of law. But his question was in turn unintelligible to me. For the stories were living things to me, and where there is life there is a principle of justice.

215

And thus I was drawn into heated arguments with my Rebbi, defending one of the parties in a biblical drama, attacking the other, without regard to the orthodox view.

My Rebbi was never angry with me—neither for my questions nor yet for my arguments—not even when the latter made the sweat stream down his brow. On the contrary, I could sense that he found a special joy in my restlessness and excitement. Often, when he felt that he had answered a difficult question weakly, he would laugh at me with his eyes, and on his face I read that marvellous answer which God once gave to an obstinate questioner, "My sons have conquered Me!" For Judah was an honest man. He never abused his authority, and never did he say to me, "If you were to know everything, you would grow old too quickly. . . ." He treated me like a young comrade, gave my thoughts free rein and my tongue free play. His *cheder* was for me the best debating-school I have ever known.

Among the countless stories in the Bible which provoke a partisan feeling for the one side or the other, I choose only three to illustrate the workings of my mind at that time. Two of them I had already heard in my first *cheder*, but I do not remember that they awoke a conflict in me at that time. The third story I learned during my second term with Judah. I have chosen these three stories because they are in my opinion the most important and most characteristic, and also because I never obtained a satisfactory answer to the questions they provoked—neither in my *cheder* years nor in the years that followed. Long after my confirmation, when I left the *cheder*, the questions still haunted me and gave me no rest.

They are the stories of Sarah and Hagar: of Esau and Jacob: and of Saul and David. In all three stories I espoused the "wrong" side. I was for Hagar and against

216

Sarah, for Esau and against Jacob, for Saul and against David. I left the strait and narrow path, and began to tread a dangerous road.

I could not bring myself to forgive Sarah for her treatment of Hagar. It is clearly written: *And Sarah said unto Abraham, Behold now, the Lord hath restrained me from bearing: I pray thee, go in unto my maid; it may be that I may obtain children from her. And Abraham hearkened to the voice of Sarah.* So who, I argued at the age of seven, was to blame but Sarah herself? It was she who had persuaded Abraham to his new marriage. What right had she, then, to vent her anger against the poor servant-girl? The answer that *When Hagar saw that she had conceived, her mistress was despised in her eyes,* did not content me. I could not understand the text. It was inconceivable to me that Hagar should have borne herself haughtily against Sarah. Suppose one of *our* servant-girls was to try and bear herself haughtily against my mother . . . the mere idea was absurd! And all my sympathies went out to Hagar, and I conceived a love for Ishmael, the little "wild man" with black curling locks— the rascal who never went to *cheder,* but ran around in a short smock, bow and arrow in hand, as we did on the New Year of the Trees: not a Jewish boy, and yet not a gentile boy: but gracious and charming and lovable.

What I resented, too, was that God had given us such an old grandmother as Sarah, so wrinkled and so bad-tempered. My grandmother Toibe was much nicer. She would surely never have driven a servant-girl out of the house into a wilderness without a spring. There was, for instance, Pessye the deaf, who served my grandmother for so many years: not a good servant, because she hardly ever did what she was told, first because she was as deaf as a clod, and second because she was incredibly obstinate. Yet she remained thirty years with the family, and when my grand-mother died she conducted the house for my grandfather, and it never occurred to me that any one could be angry with Pessye. After my grandfather's death she was "in-herited" by my mother, and she served us for several years. My grandfathers and my grandmother always confused themselves in my mind with the patriarchs and the matri-archs. I transferred the respect which I felt for the ancient fathers of our people to the oldest members of our family: and from the "Old Men" of our family I learned to under-stand and to feel more intimately the patriarchs.

The story of Jacob and Esau gave rise to a much more furious argument, for after all, the grandmothers are not as important as the grandfathers. Granted that Sarah was not one hundred per cent. perfect: but then Abraham was such a saint, so hospitable to wayfarers, such a lovable, gentle fellow, that he atoned for the sins of Sarah. But what was to be done about Jacob? Was he not the last in the chain of the patriarchs, the last, the most active, and the most productive of our grandfathers? Jacob should be immacu-late, pure as a ritual citron—and here he was, cheating his older brother out of his birthright, and his father out of the blessing. And how did Rebecca, the sweet, lovely girl who stood with her vase upon her head by the well-side, Rebecca the gentle, who pitied the thirsty camels and drew water for them, that same Rebecca of whom Rashi tells that when she went in to Sarah soon after her marriage with Isaac, the tent was flooded with light—how did she come to help her son to steal the birthright? And from whom? A blind old father!

The tortuous excuses and explanations of my Rebbi were without avail: he told me from learned and sacred sources that Rachel knew, by the help of the Holy Spirit, that red-haired Esau would come to no good: in the morning he never poured water over his finger tips, as all good Jews should the moment they step out of bed and before they say their first prayer: he went around roistering for days at a stretch: he sat down to a meal without washing his hands, and never said grace after it. A bad lot. And that was why she arranged that Jacob should get the benediction; for Jacob sat from morn to night in the House of Prayer and Study of Shem and Eber, learning what good Jews should learn. I replied that all this might be very true, and the Holy Spirit was an important matter, no doubt; and I too loved Jacob greatly, but a swindle was a swindle, and excuses could not wash away the blot. I refused to yield. And long after I had left *cheder*, that is, after my confirmation, I turned the story restlessly over in my mind. Jacob was for me one of the most fascinating figures of that ancient world. I marvelled at his strange endurance, both in his love and in his life-struggles. I marvelled too at his dream, the greatest of dreams, bringing Heaven and earth together. But most of all I marvelled over the story of his battle with the angel and of his victory. But the blot remained a blot, a disturbing factor in the life of the hero. I was not less disturbed when in later years I heard Christian teachers refer to Jacob— precisely because of this blot—as a negative character. I was still more disturbed when it came my turn to teach the Bible to half-grown children and I was false to myself and choked over the first chapters of the story of Jacob.

Something of a like nature took place with me when I first read and afterward saw on the stage *The Merchant of Venice*. I was drawn instinctively toward Shylock, the victim of merciless robbery. They stole his daughter, they stole his money. But that pound of flesh which he demanded almost literally stuck in my throat, and I could not gulp it down.

I am grateful to four men who, through their works, resolved in me the Jacob and Shylock conflicts. Vladimir Soloviev, the Russian philosopher, by his classic analysis of Jacob, in *The National Question from the Moral Viewpoint*, returned my hero to me, whole; the poet Richard Beer Hoffman, in his play *Jacob's Dream*, helped to draw me closer to him. The Shylock conflict was resolved in me in part by Heine's essays on the plays of Shakespeare, but still more by a performance of the rôle by Schildkraut in the Deutsches Theater in Berlin. The interpretation which the actor gave to Shylock that evening was such that a number of visitors —probably bitter anti-Semites—rose in the middle of the performance and left in a rage. I mention this incident only because it was a psychological throw-back to the struggles of my *cheder* days.

In the long, epic narrative of David and Saul I refused again to follow the trodden paths. I could not under any circumstances understand wherein Saul had sinned. Samuel the prophet had bidden Saul wait for him with the sacrifice. And Saul waited. But Samuel did not appear at the appointed time; so Saul sacrificed without him. Was this a punishable offence? Or if Saul could not bring himself to destroy Amalek root and branch, leaving no trace of that people, was he therefore to lose his throne? I was on the side of Saul, too, in his struggles with David. It was clear to Saul that the kingdom would pass into the hands of David: that was enough to explain why the evil spirit terrified him, so that his mind became confused. But in single and lucid intervals the old Saul awoke in him, and how great, how pure, was the soul that then spoke from him: *And Saul knew David's voice, and said, Is this thy voice, my son David . . . I have sinned, return, my son David: for I will no more do thee harm, because my soul was precious in thine eyes this day: behold, I have played the fool, and have erred exceedingly.* Children are sensitive. They have a feeling for the natural and for the artificial. They give themselves instinctively to that which is honest, and to me no one was as honest —as naïvely honest, perhaps—as Saul, and no one's fate was as tragic as his.

The Rebbi was compelled *ex officio* to be on David's side. He uttered his formal verdict on the case, but in my heart there was a suspicion that in secret he too sympathized with Saul. I suspected my Rebbi not because I had no faith in him, but because I had too much faith in him and believed too implicitly in his sense of justice.

CHAPTER THIRTEEN: I BEGIN THE TALMUD

As FAR as I can remember I must have been seven years old —certainly not more than seven and a half—when I began to learn the Talmud. And I did not begin with the usual light anthology pieced together from the various tractates—as was the practice in all *cheders*—but with the body of the Talmud itself. I started at once on the tractate Berochoth— Benedictions. My Rebbi asserted that he had no fears for me; only weak and timid children must be led carefully into the waters of a cold lake. Sturdy children could be plunged in at once—they could endure it.

But the beginning was not so easy as my Rebbi had imagined, and I was not very happy while I floundered around in my first attempts to swim. The material itself was not difficult for my young—my too young—brain; but there was a psychological resistance. I was too closely bound to the world of the Bible—a world governed by the emotions, a world of marvellous stories and incidents which spoke an inner language of their own to the tender soul of the child. The Talmudic world, and especially the legalistic-theological province of it called Halachah, is at the other pole from the world of the Bible. It is a world dry and logical as a square root; it is governed not by the emotions, but by a stern and sombre logic. The jest, the parable, the maxim, the fiery phrase, disappeared; their place was taken by the intellectual syllogism, cold and inflexible as a bar of iron. And the transition from emotion to intellect was painful.

When my brain grew weary with the strain of logic, I used to plead with my Rebbi to close the Talmud and return with me to the Bible. My Rebbi understood me well, but he seldom yielded to me. On the contrary, with the passage of each month he decreased the allotment of the Bible, increased that of the Talmud. He comforted me: "Wait a while; you will soon find out how lovable and delightful the Talmud too can be." And before long the taste for it came to me—but not as my Rebbi had meant it. For several terms had to pass before I got the swing and joy of the dialectic Halachah. But as against this the Hagaddah, the folk-lore section of the Talmud, contented me enormously. I might almost say that the Hagaddah made complete restitution for the losses I had suffered in the Halachah. A new world opened again for me in the Hagaddah, and this time not a distant world, but one that was intimate and my own. I felt the breath of the prophetic world borne over me again— the fainter continuity of the first ecstasies which I had learned to know so well. Heine has defined the distinction in an excellent simile. The Halachah, he says, is like a fencing-school where the swordsmen of Pumbedhita and Nehardea, armed with the sharp, flashing swords of logic, compete for the supremacy. And the Hagaddah he compares to the hanging gardens of Queen Semiramis, strange and marvellous trees growing in tangled richness, hiding among their branches the secrets of creation. And when the athletes in the arena grow weary of the struggle, they leave the Halachah for the Hagaddah, to find refreshment and rest. I would compare the Halachah to the ocean, and the Hagaddah to the Gulf Stream which cuts across it.

It did not take long before I was as intimately at home

in the Hagaddah as I was in the Bible, and swam around in it as if it had been my natural element. But the Hagaddah did not represent a new phase in my development, for it fused completely with my experience of the Bible. Or, to change the figure, I had entered into a new temple, but the foundations underfoot were old and familiar. The basic feeling was that of the Bible. Or again, the Bible was the root, and the Hagaddah was branch and leaf, drawing sustenance from the Bible.

The individual conflicts which arose in me—those that I have already spoken of—did not disturb the general harmony of the Bible (in which I now include the Hagaddah), and I may truly say that the Bible as a whole became the cornerstone of my later life. I devoured, like a famished soul, the individual books: digested carefully the chapters, verses, and individual words: and I did not observe that it was not I who swallowed them, but they that swallowed me up. I did not conquer them, but they me. They determined the path of my life, dictated the currents of my thoughts. I had drawn them into myself, but they had drawn me up into them.

So intimate was my relation to the world which these ancient books reconstructed for me that I often had the feeling that I could step into the arena of events and influence the outcome again. This was neither the impudence of youth nor yet a delusion of grandeur such as might take hold of a *cheder* boy who heard nothing but compliments in the school, at home, and in the street. For, mingled with this sense of intimacy and personal immediacy, there was a respect and worship amounting to terror in the presence of these gigantic figures. I was part of that enormous world, but a tiny, insignificant part; and when I raised my eyes to the figures that bestrode it, I trembled.

Like all those whose thoughts have transported them into
a world of the past, I learned very early to turn my gaze
inward upon myself. The world of reality around me became
poor, anaemic, a miniature world in comparison with the
world which I carried around within me. The pitiful present
could not compete with the rich past, stretching through
long generations from Abraham our father up to King
Zedekiah, through heroic events, dramas and tragedies. I
have mentioned two bounding-lines in this world—Abraham
and Zedekiah; for I no longer looked upon that which occurred before Abraham as part of Jewish history. I had
become more intelligent, and knew that a part of the Five
Books belonged to the other peoples of the world. But on
the other hand the destruction of the first Temple by
Nebuchadnezzar and Nebuzarodon was the last point of
history; for as to those events which occurred in Babylon,
and, after Babylon, in Judaea, when we had reconstructed
our state, I had the most nebulous ideas. Something I knew
from the accounts of Ezra and Nehemiah, and there were
fragments of the Roman rule imbedded in the episodes of the
Hagaddah; but the continuity was broken, and the period
from the destruction of the first to the destruction of the
second Temple was a mist in my mind. The two books of
Ezra and Nehemiah, which are really one book, made me
think of the last spoonful of dough which my mother scraped
out of the kneading-trough. The voice of the "young lion"
is heard no more. The bitter rage of the prophets has died
out, and no longer falls on the ears of mankind "like a
hammer which shatters the rocks." In Ezra and Nehemiah
the voice of the protagonists is gentle, entreating; they write
diplomatic begging letters to foreign kings. It seemed to me
that with Ezra and Nehemiah a curtain was drawn across my
world, and instinctively I felt that behind that curtain, in

225

the years beyond, there must be a world as rich in storm and wonder and catastrophe as that of the Bible; and I begged my Rebbi to tell me more, more—what happened when the Bible was closed?

My Rebbi had an answer for me: "The Bible was written with the Holy Spirit, when the prophets still lived and the word of God flowed from their lips. But with the death of Haggai, Zachariah, and Malachi, the last three links in the golden chain of prophecy, the well was closed and sealed. No new prophets arose after them. That is why we have received no new sacred books. The Talmud is sacred, of course, but not with that first unforgettable sanctity. The voice has died away, and all that we hear is the echo."

CHAPTER FOURTEEN: I BEGIN TO WRITE

I BEGAN to learn writing when I was six years old: at first half an hour and then a whole hour a day. In this branch of his duties, too, Judah was thorough and exact. He wanted his pupils to develop a clear and beautiful script, and in the detailed attention which he gave to the shape of every letter, to the spaces between letters and words, and to the proportions of the letters, he developed a complete philosophy of his own. The script, he said, was the vessel, the thoughts were the contents; it was necessary from early childhood to develop a beautiful script, for beautiful vessels attract beautiful contents, and learning to write finely, we would also be led to think finely. But my Rebbi was dead set against the practice which still survived among certain schools—a memorial of the old Oriental days—of adding flourishes and arabesques and curlicues to the letters. He thought the practice harmful. "You learn to twist and embellish the letters: afterwards you will also twist the thought."

We used to do our writing with goose quills. My Rebbi whittled them, and from him I learned the mediaeval art of transforming a feather into a pen. When we had been writing for a couple of years we graduated to steel pens. The change was uncomfortable. A goose-quill pen is softer, travels more lightly over the paper, and follows more readily the commands of the fingers. Steel is hard, sharp, and obstinate. The writer can fashion his goose quill to his taste and character, but a steel pen has a will and character of its own; its mother is not the living bird, but the dead machine, and such as it was when it left the machine, it remains. With the goose-quill pen it is still possible to put a certain art and life into the letters; with the steel pen you may attain a higher or a lower level of technical proficiency—nothing more. Thus, with the appearance of the steel pen there have vanished those marvellous old scripts which sometimes made letters so beautiful that they seemed to beg to be framed and exhibited. But the steel pen is the symbol of an entire epoch; it represents the transition from the soft to the hard, from art to technique; and even Swislowitz had to yield to the triumphant machine. I need hardly say that I did not understand, in those days, anything about art or the machine, and had not the faintest foreshadowing of the struggle that was taking place in the world about me: I did not know that a hard civilization of steel was overtaking us, and that the successor to the goose-quill pen was the embryo of the new *golem* which was to conquer mankind. But I do remember that for a long time I longed to go back to my goose-quill pen; I longed for its softness, its kindly, gentle character. For a long time I hated the steel pen which had replaced it, without my invitation, even without my permission.

In any case I am glad, even now, that I learned to do my first writing with a goose-quill pen. Something has remained in my handwriting which is not wholly the machine.

The half-hour or the hour which we devoted to writing in *cheder* was insufficient for me. I did a lot of writing at home. In *cheder* we had to follow the copybook text prescribed by the Rebbi: at home I wrote "out of my head" . . . and often entire verses from memory. But writing out of my head was nicer: and very early I developed a desire to express my own thoughts. Whenever the biblical verse coincided with my thought, I set it down whole. But where they diverged, I laboured to find fragments of verses, or detached words from the biblical text, and pasted them together to render my meaning. I cannot tell whether my eagerness to write sprang from my love of my own handwriting—which is often the case with children—so that I was thus driven to find content, or whether it sprang from the more primordial desire for the expression of my own thoughts. In any case, I covered with my close script every clean piece of paper I could lay hands on. I do remember, however, that at home, where I was free to choose my own text, and write whatever I liked, I enjoyed myself much more than in *cheder*. But· even what I wrote at home I carried to *cheder* the next day, for correction in spelling and grammar. And how happy I was when my Rebbi could not find a single mistake to correct. In such cases he could not restrain himself; he would compliment me to my face, foretell that I would be a writer some day; and his compliments intoxicated me. My liking for writing became a passion. On winter nights, when I returned from *cheder* after ten and twelve hours of study, I would eat quickly and sit down again with my pen. My father and mother protested, and tried to make me go to sleep, but I begged them, with tears in my eyes, to let me write another few lines.

One thing is quite certain to me; the first language which I used in writing was Hebrew. The fact is, it never occurred to me to write Yiddish. Everybody knew Yiddish; what was the marvel, then, of writing in that language? Besides, I knew no ready-made verses in Yiddish, and Yiddish books—apart from my mother's devotionals—were unknown in our house. Without biblical verses, too, the things that you wrote would sound just like the ordinary things that people say.

Everybody would understand them, and no one would carry the letters around and ask their meaning and shake his head over the wonder of it. In one word, all my ambitions lay in the Hebrew language, for that alone would give me the opportunity to satisfy my pride by giving me the foremost place among my schoolmates. But I doubt whether this was the sole motive which drove me to live myself out in Hebrew. I believe there was a deeper force at work. Although everybody around me spoke Yiddish, it was Hebrew, *as a language,* that I knew better in my childhood. For a language does not consist merely of words. It is built up by pictures, by ideas which the words awaken in us. A language must possess, beside its ordinary, everyday side, a holiday side, a spiritual aspect. A language is rooted firmly in the mind of a child only by the book; there is no other way of giving a literary force to language, and no other way of making it writable. The language which is not reflected in classic books is doomed to remain a language of the street. It was therefore inevitable that Hebrew should become, for me, the language of the written word. For I learned it from books, from sacred books, the contents of which had become flesh of my flesh, bone of my bone.

I remember very clearly my first essay in Hebrew: that is, the first one which my Rebbi carried round the town to glorify his pupil.

Among the Jews of Swislowitz there were no thieves. Among the gentiles there were a few real professionals— chiefly horse-thieves. All of them were known and feared, for between their thefts of horses they would not refuse to execute minor jobs, too. The big robberies, however, were committed not by our local craftsmen but by the masters of Babrusk, who used to pay us a secret visit now and then and leave ruin behind. A merchant of Swislowitz would wake one morning, go down into his store—and discover that every scrap of merchandise had been removed; nothing left but the bare shelves. More than one merchant of Swislowitz was ruined for life in this manner. As it happened, the thieves of Babrusk were only Jews, and they concentrated only on Jews: they were probably actuated by an obscure family feeling. (The subject would, by the way, make an interesting study. I believe that statistics would prove that Jews prefer to rob Jews. They feel safer.)

Among the Jewish thieves of Babrusk there was a famous ring-leader by the name of Chaim Gimele. He was not only a burglar, but a highway robber. More than once he would descend with his band on some drayman travelling the road toward Babrusk, and remove the entire contents of the cart. It never got as far as the shedding of blood, but "dry" blows were exchanged more than once. Benjamin the storekeeper, a son of my second Rebbi, Abraham Kazar, returned one day from the Babrusk road beaten up and with an empty cart. He had been waylaid by Chaim Gimele and his gang, who had taken both the merchandise which he was taking to sell in Babrusk, and the cash money which he and his passengers carried with them. Benjamin got badly beaten up because he had protested, had appealed to the sense of justice in the robbers: and this was Chaim Gimele's greeting to the other Jewish shopkeepers of Swislowitz. The extraordinary thing was that everybody knew who the thief was, and yet nobody ever thought of prosecuting him. Had it been possible to get him to a Din Torah—to a Jewish tribunal—it would have been done. But not the gentile courts. After all, the merchant would not get the goods back. The Jews of Swislowitz put robberies, thefts, and fires in the same class.

This was the story which was the theme of my first Hebrew essay. And it ran somewhat as follows: "And Benjamin the son of Abraham drove forth in his chariot on the way which goeth to Babrusk. And he came to Barishanke and rested there. And it happened that when the sun went down robbers fell upon them, and the chiefest among them was the great robber Chaim Gimele. And they said to Benjamin, Give us all that thou hast, but thy soul thou mayest keep. And Benjamin said, This would be a great sin, but they would not hearken to his voice. And they took from him all that he had, leaving neither a thread nor the latchet of a shoe. And they smote him grievously. And Benjamin returned home, weeping, and the city of Swislowitz was in great confusion."

The beauty of my language made a terrific impression. In particular the scholars of Swislowitz were delighted with the inverted phrase: *Give us all that thou hast, but thy soul thou mayest keep*—the very opposite of what the King of Sodom said to Abraham. It showed that I was not only capable of inserting a biblical verse, but I could also turn it upside down as need dictated. This was regarded as evidence of intelligence and talent. I ought to say that the only newspaper then received in our town was the Hebrew *Ha-Zephira* of Slonimsky, and the majority of its correspondents stood on about the same literary level as I reached in my "essay." It was therefore proposed that I ought to send my essay to the *Ha-Zephira* for the greater glory of Swislowitz. The proposition took my breath away; the possibility of being printed had not occurred to me, but when it was spoken of I was thrown into such confusions of joy that I hardly knew what world I was living in. Like everybody else I pitied poor Benjamin the shopkeeper, but in my subconscious I was thoroughly happy that the incident had taken place and that I had been able to describe it so well.

When I was nine years old the complete foundations of my Hebrew education had already been laid. I knew the Bible by heart from cover to cover—and stood up under all the weird tests which were devised for us. Here, for instance, is one. We used, in school, the Letteris edition of the Bible, as issued by the London Bible Society. The book would be opened at a given page, a word would be chosen, and then a needle would be driven through the pages as far is it would go. I was then asked which words the needle had pierced on the various pages. And with the rarest exceptions I guessed every one of them. I understood well all the commentaries, both those of Rashi and of Mendelssohn and his followers. As a grammarian I was accounted the best in the town, and even my Rebbi would often ask my opinion on difficult passages. He treated me now not as a pupil, but as a comrade and equal. As far as Talmud was concerned, I knew thoroughly the three Tractates, Benedictions, the First Gate, and the Middle Gate, and could quote long passages from them by heart. From the translations of Kalman Shulman I had already formed some idea of history and geography. But my best gifts, which were for mathematics, were still dormant. There was no one to waken them; and so the foundations of my education were still one-sided and purely literary. It might be thought that I ought to say "theological-literary" rather than purely literary, for my education was drawn not from profane but from sacred books. But I deliberately omit the word "theological," for the emphasis of my education was on the literary and not on the theological side. This was due to the character of my teacher and to his consistent attitude toward study—an attitude which was completely worldly. The theologic element was introduced only to the extent that the Bible dealt with a theocratic order of society.

CHAPTER FIFTEEN: PLAY AND DREAMS

THE love which I had for my studies enabled me to sink in them my energetic and playful nature. I am quite certain that if I had not been absorbed almost completely by my *cheder* work, I would have been the greatest young nuisance in town. For I was brimful of energies which could not be suppressed. Nine-tenths of them went into my reading and writing, and one-tenth was left free. Human energy is like capital; it must be kept in constant circulation—for that is the law of its being. But even that tenth—perhaps there was a little more of it—was enough to make a young Czar of me. The form of government in a country always has a deep influence on the minds of the young—and the highest worldly power we could think of was the Czar. But my rule was not absolute; I had a rival who also pretended to the throne—Benye, the son of Chanah Necheh, a playmate one year older than myself, and a pupil in the rival *cheder* of Azer the *melamed*. This boy, it will be seen later, played a real rôle in my life.

There lived in our town a family by the name of Getzoff which was not organically bound up with the Jewish community of Swislowitz. The family came all the way from the metropolitan city of Minsk, and brought with it a metropolitan atmosphere which did not harmonize with the way of life of Swislowitz. The Getzoffs were of rich stock, but it appears that they had come down in the world; so they had been exiled to Swislowitz. There they were entrusted with the post, which used to go twice and then four times a week to and from Osipowitz—a station on the Liubi-Ramne railroad, some thirty miles from Swislowitz. The head of the family, Leib Getzoff, or, as we called him, Leib the postman, was a small Jew, a bewildered sort of man, and a natural simpleton. The tone was set at home by his wife, Hannah Necheh, the Pinsker, who looked aristocratic and tried to convey as much aristocracy to the conduct of her house as the atmosphere of Swislowitz permitted. The Getzoffs had quite a handsome house, with two wings. In one wing they lived, and in the other they conducted the post office: for the mails were a governmental matter and had to be treated with respect. Plebeians, before entering the post office, would remove their hats outside the threshold, above which hung the image of the double eagle, with wings outspread over half the verandah. The postal teamster who carried the mails to and from Osipowitz wore a sword and a revolver, symbols of his governmental functions. This circumstance alone sufficed to create the impression that the Getzoffs, who lived in such intimate contact with representatives of the state, were themselves part of the government, by virtue of which they were raised to a privileged position. Apart from this, Hannah Necheh really was the best-educated woman in Swislowitz. This may not have meant very much, but she was treated, nevertheless, with great respect.

My playmate Benye was Leib Getzoff's youngest son—but he went by his mother's name: Benye, son of Hannah Necheh. He was the best-dressed youngster in town—for Hannah Necheh always followed the Pinsk fashion-books. Moreover, he had a Russian tutor, at a time when we others did not even know the Russian alphabet. It was Hannah Necheh's dream that her youngest son would some day enter the Minsk High School, for she saw that her older children had come to nothing in Swislowitz. The boys had become carters, draymen: true, rather refined draymen, but draymen for all that. And so the aristocratic mother wanted to save her youngest son, make a real person of him according to her taste and lights.

This same Benye was my rival. When I organized an army of between thirty and forty boys, and they unanimously raised me on their shields and elected me imperator, Benye protested violently and asserted that under no circumstances would he acknowledge my rule. "I already know Russian," he argued vehemently, "and I'm better fitted to be Czar." I offered Benye the portfolio of first minister, but he refused to compromise. In the end we had to quarrel, and the army was split into two enemy camps—and mine was the larger. But Benye had his way: he was Czar of an army of his own.

The war lasted without let-up for a period of three years. Every Sabbath evening, when the sacred day had closed, we used to muster our forces under Castle Hill, array them opposite each other, and send out one warrior from each side. The heralds halted at several paces from each other and repeated the following:

> What's yours is yours,
> What's mine is mine,
> Your King is rotten,
> My King is fine:
>
> My King can swim
> And yours will sink:
> My King is a hero
> And yours is a ———.

After these provocations to mortal combat the two armies closed and belaboured each other mercilessly, until one of them acknowledged defeat. That ended the battle. Truce was declared and we played like good friends until the next engagement. It was understood among us that whatever might happen it was impossible to complain to the older folk. This treaty was severely observed: would that the modern states were as honourably exact. . . .

Sliding on the ice was another great pastime. No one among us had a pair of skates, so we slid in our shoes: and I have already described the virtuosities which we achieved in this branch of sport. Better than the pool in my grandfather's yard was the Swisla, when it froze over: but sliding on the Swisla had to be done in secret, for it was a dangerous game.

It was dangerous even in Grandfather's yard. One Sabbath evening, between Tabernacles and Purim, we gathered there for a sliding-fest. Determined, as always, to take the lead, I displayed all the tricks, the variations and ornamentations, of the virtuoso. In the midst of a complicated manoeuvre I fell face forward, smashing my head against a stone. I felt no pain, but the warm blood streamed over my face. My playmates led me into my grandfather's house and stuffed up the hole in my forehead with soft bread: this was on the advice of Pessye the deaf, my grandmother's servant. When the blood had been washed away, I shoved my hat close down over my forehead and went home. I still felt no pain, but there was a throbbing in my temples. After the closing ceremony of the Sabbath eve, I still had strength enough to sit down to a glass of tea, but my mother, watching me closely, began to suspect that something had happened. I refused to say anything, and my hat covered the traces of the disaster. An hour later my Rebbi turned up:

my playmates had told him the story. My mother took the soft bread out of the wound, washed it again, and sprayed it with *eau de cologne*. She declared that the wound would soon heal—and in medical matters her word was accepted without question. My Rebbi scolded me for my carelessness, and, dazed and confused, I went to bed early that evening.

I remember as in a dream that I went through a hard night. A whole building had collapsed on me and was choking me. I was pulling my limbs out one by one from under the ruins. A fallen beam lies on one of my legs: I pull and pull, without success. I begin to scream for help. And suddenly I hear my mother's voice—she is crying. . . . That is all I remember. I had, as a matter of fact, wakened my mother in the middle of the night, and my mother was crying. I lay for two weeks unconscious, in high fever. The soft bread which had been kneaded with dirty fingers and stuffed into the wound did its work. I was ultimately cured by "Doctor" Schwartz, a *feldsher* or half-trained village doctor, but a skilful and careful healer. I remained in bed for two months. My mother said that I was saved by a miracle, that I already had one leg in the other world—and that only God and Doctor Schwartz had pulled me back. The wound left a scar on my forehead, like a deep measle pit; this was always mentioned in my Russian passport—the Russian police was very careful in its day not to confuse me with anybody else. In Swislowitz they began to call me "the marked man"—because of the scar. So I was marked in two places—on my forehead and in my passport. Since acquiring a more civilized passport, the second mark has disappeared. But the first remains—a reminder of an evening of sport long, long ago, in my grandfather's yard.

Apart from this accident, which cost me three months in bed, and from which I escaped with my life only by a miracle, I was laid up only twice in my childhood—once with typhoid fever and once with malaria. The typhoid ran its normal course: it took away a month of my time and the hair of my head: the latter I recovered immediately on becoming well. But the malaria was an obstinate visitor. It was the ordinary malaria indigenous to those parts. How widely Russia suffered from malaria is evident from the popular folk-saying, "Malaria is no sickness." Respecting no one, it was in turn respected by no one. My attack lasted on and off for a couple of years, with intervals of a month or two. The frequent attacks interfered with my studies, but during the intervals I exerted myself doubly to make up for the loss. An attack would generally last for one day: rarely for two. And as malaria was very common in our parts, the innocent question, "Have you had a good day or a bad day?" came to have a very specific meaning, namely, "Did you shake very much, or only a little?" And in the autumn months Swislowitz as a whole lived between one shake-up and another. There was even a town joke on the subject: one man would suddenly ask another, "Would you like to have a good day tomorrow?" The unguarded answer was, "Certainly! Who wouldn't?" Whereupon he received an excellent piece of advice: "Get your fit of malaria today, and shake well. Tomorrow you'll have a good day."

As it happens my malaria came in very useful in later years, and I derived from it certain advantages which did not occur to us in Swislowitz. In the eighties of the last century there arose the Chibath Zion (love of Zion) movement, and the ideal, the return of the Jewish people to Palestine, and the abandonment of the exile, sank into the uttermost depths of my soul. The entire course of my studies until that time, everything that I had heard and learned, all my dreams and fantasies, had prepared the ground for this thought. The Messianic dream of long generations found expression in it: I was carried along as by a tremendous whirlwind, and without questions, without reservation, I placed myself at its service. I did not have to look for new sources of inspiration. Did not the old prophets suffice? Was there no balm in Gilead? Are the prophecies of Isaiah not sufficient, and are there not in Jeremiah and Ezekiel and in the minor prophets verses enough that send out streams of fire and light up the souls of men?

As a boy, I threw myself into the struggle with all the weapons drawn from my mother's piety and my *cheder* education. Too young to be a knight of the movement, I was a page who carried the long trailing robes of the queen. But burning with youthful impatience, I waited for the day when I could play my part in the thick of the fray.

But in the moment of its birth the Chibath Zion movement ran up against a furious opposition, and the numbers of its enemies grew from day to day. The story of that movement comes in the later part of my life: I mention it here only in connection with the attacks of malaria which disturbed my childhood.

The movement was still in its swaddling-clothes, and the arguments both of its leaders and antagonists were extremely primitive. Among the arguments of the antagonists the malaria question in Palestine occupied an important position. "Palestine is a malaria country: the colonists will unquestionably die of the disease." And I was able to answer bitterly that our Palestine was at least better than Swislowitz and Pinsk, and that the colonists in Palestine would not shake and shiver half as much as we did. And when I became altogether excited, I denied that malaria was indigenous to Palestine: it had been **carried thither from**

Swislowitz and Pinsk and Babrusk and Homel—places famous for their malaria.

Some forty years later, as a member of the World Zionist Executive, I went through the Palestine malaria in Jerusalem. During my sickness, I received the visit of an old friend of mine from Ekaterinoslav. I asked him whether he had gone through his malaria yet. "Certainly," he answered; "to have the privilege of living in Jerusalem, and not to pay for it with malaria, is only for the saints." More than once, going through the colonies of Palestine, I would see a worker in the fields lay down his tools and retire to his tent. He was going to "shake": the shaking finished, he returned to his work. And the fact is that in Palestine we were more successful in our experience with malaria than in many, many towns and villages of my native country.

The subject of malaria brings to my mind an episode of my childhood which made a profound impression on me as evidence of the respect in which my mother was held by the gentiles of Swislowitz. I am aware that a writer's descriptions of his mother are suspect, but I cannot help myself if, in all objectiveness, I must remember that my mother was exceptional, and that strangers, both Jewish and non-Jewish, looked upon her as a remarkable woman, who in her relationship to others recalled the type of woman, pious, godly, gentle, who is glorified in the Old Testament.

It was not long after my recovery from typhoid that my mother fell sick of the same disease. My father was away, either in Minsk or in Babrusk, on business, and returning after a week's absence, he found my mother in a dangerous condition. I cannot forget what happened when my father received the sudden tidings. He wept like a child. He threw off his travelling-clothes and went at once to my mother.

She barely recognized him, and only with effort could she pronounce his name. My father, unable to restrain himself, broke into a loud sobbing. There was standing on the table, I remember, a glass of tea to refresh him after his journey. He did not drink it. Instead, he put on phylacteries and praying-shawl, and began to pray with a passion and abandon which I had never seen in him before. When he had ended his prayers, he approached my mother's bed, and said to all of us, "Lord of the universe! Perhaps I have sinned, and this is the punishment You have prepared for me. But I pray to You: punish me as You will, but leave my wife Elke: do not punish the innocent for the sins of the wicked. . . ."

During one of those days—it was in the middle of the week—the bells of both Orthodox churches began to toll over the town. It was not a festival, nor had fire broken out. The Jews were startled. We were living at that time in our new house opposite the church of Yuremitch, and looking out of the window, we saw the gentiles streaming toward the church. One of us went out and asked a passerby what had happened. And the answer was, "We are going to pray to God for Elke." They did not say it boastfully, for they found it altogether natural. Later we discovered that the man who had initiated these prayers for my mother was that same Stepan Harnai, the God-seeker, who loved so much to discuss religious questions with my mother.

My mother did not forget. Years later, when my older brother Meyer was married—the wedding took place in our home—my mother suddenly disappeared after the wedding supper, and was absent for above an hour. We became restless and sent out to look for her. The wife of the gentile water-carrier (we had two water-carriers: the other, it will be remembered, was Asher Pakess, the simpleton) had been brought to bed of a child. My mother had taken a hen with her and prepared a pot of soup for the woman. She stayed till the soup was ready, fed the woman, went over to the cradle of the new-born child and fixed something there, gave instructions to the mother, then turned back home, and sat down at the wedding table as if nothing had happened.

My mother's sickness lingered obstinately, and at last my father lost faith in the local healer and sent for two doctors of Babrusk. Both of them wore military uniform; one was a gentile, the other a Jew by the name of Kahan. This was just after the Russo-Turkish war, and the government had not yet had time to drive all the Jewish doctors from their positions. I looked upon a Jewish doctor for the first time in my life—and one that wore epaulettes, too. I was so amazed that I could not take my eyes off him. How could a Jew reach such a lofty position? And I was still more amazed when I heard the doctor speak with my mother in Yiddish. Uniform, epaulettes, spurs—and Yiddish! This was an incredible and incomprehensible combination. But the measure of my astonishment flowed over when the doctor, on leaving, wished my father a *refuah shlemoh*, a complete recovery, in right good Hebrew. Epaulettes and Hebrew were an even stranger combination than epaulettes and Yiddish. My father told us afterward that this Doctor Kahan was a former Talmud student, and that he was not only a good doctor but had a sound Jewish education. For the first time the idea stole into my mind that one could first be a Jewish student and afterward a doctor. Who knows? Perhaps the single visit of that doctor, Doctor Kahan, opened a new channel for my thoughts, and widened my whole outlook on life.

CHAPTER SIXTEEN: THE THRESHOLD OF A NEW WORLD

I was nine years old when I began to learn Russian. It was again my uncle Meyer Wendrow who insisted on it. He lived in the big world, in Dinaburg, and his position brought him into close contact with the higher military world, where it would have been impossible to get along without Russian. His dream was that his two sons, my schoolmates, should in time take up their studies in a technical school and become architectural engineers. Before they could take up such studies, they would have to pass through a secondary school, and he was anxious that before they entered the Russian schools, they should be possessed of a thorough Jewish education. In those days every Maskil, or modernist, "enlightened" Jew, had the same ambition for his children, a combination Jewish and general education. Thoughts like these were far from my father, and he did not think of sending any of his sons into the liberal professions. He wanted them to be able merchants, timber dealers. It was my mother's dream that I should become a Rabbi, a Gaon, one of the great scholars of the time, and my Rebbi seconded her steadily. But my father agreed that I should learn Russian, for he thought it would be useful even from a purely business point of view. "It's a good thing," he said, "to be able to talk to the landowner in his own language, to draw up a contract, or address a petition to the government." The Rav of Swislowitz, whom I have mentioned so often, was one Abraham Shevelev of Slutzk. He was the only son of the most popular midwife in Slutzk, a woman by the name of Bobke, who was looked upon as being almost a holy woman. Abraham Shevelev was a Talmudist of note, and also knew well the Hebrew language and the literature of our new Renaissance. In a certain sense he was a "free-thinker"—which really meant that he was a man with a worldly outlook on life. My father was greatly influenced by this man, while my mother was a close friend of his wife. Both the Rabbi and his wife gave their approval to the idea of teaching me the Russian language.

We imported a Russian teacher from Mohilev on the Dnieper. Some two years before, my second sister, Frieda, had married one Asher Shafrai of Mohilev, and it was he who recommended an acquaintance of his by the name of Krugliansky. My brother-in-law was a great Jewish scholar, but knew not a word of Russian. He assured us that Krugliansky was a first-rate teacher, spoke Russian like a Moscow aristocrat, and in addition was an observant Jew: he would not set a bad example to the young folk in the town. And the last point was the most important. It was the teacher himself who was feared more than the direct influence of the Russian language. And a Jewish teacher of Russian was more feared than a gentile teacher, for the Jewish teacher becomes more intimate with his pupil and can influence him more deeply.

Krugliansky remained in Swislowitz two years. During the first few months he used to go to Shuhl daily and put on phylacteries, just like every one else. But at the end of the first year it became known that in his own lodgings he was given to all sorts of un-Jewish practices. The place finally got too hot for him, and he had to leave Swislowitz.

The fears of the parents for their young children were not unfounded. On some of his friends and older pupils he had a decidedly negative influence, as far as the Jewish way of life was concerned. But on us, the youngest of his pupils, he had no influence at all. We looked upon him as upon a visitor from an alien world. Our contact with him lasted one hour every day, five days in the week, for Friday and Saturday we took no Russian lessons. His pedagogic methods were in the old style: that is, he used to teach the language by translating passages from Russian into Yiddish, and he put the main emphasis on the rules of grammar, so that the course of studies was hopelessly dry and unattractive. I regarded my Russian studies as an uninteresting duty which I wanted to discharge as soon as possible; my progress was therefore very slow. But I cannot put the entire blame on the teacher: one half of it at least belongs to me. Benye, son of Hannah Necheh, was abundant proof thereof. He was not particularly gifted by nature, yet his progress in Russian was incomparably swifter than mine. I believe the explanation lies in the deep roots which Hebrew had already driven into me. I had not the strength to tear my mind loose and to absorb a strange language easily.

It was not my first Russian teacher, but the Russo-Turkish war of 1877-1878 which drew me closer to the Russian world and to the living interests of the Russian state. It was this war which first made me conscious of the fact that the Hebrew world which I carried within me was an old, old world, lying far behind me. Immediately surrounding me there was a great world of reality, the Russian world—and it was in this world that I breathed and had my being. Some two years before the war broke out the Russian government—or rather, the Czar, Alexander the Second— had decreed universal military service. The Jews naturally regarded the decree as a heavy blow. Until that time only the children of the poor, whom there was no one to defend, had been pressed into service: and now the children of the middle classes, of the finer homes, would also have to serve in the army, and the thought was horrible. I remember that a relative of ours, Leivik, the son of Pessye the candlemaker, hid himself in our house from the military "catchers." It did not help him much. One winter night the "catchers" broke into our house, dragged Leivik out of bed, bound him with ropes, and led him out to the sled which was waiting outside to carry him off to Babrusk. The scene was ghastly in its cruelty. The catchers had the look of wild animals, and Leivik himself struggled like an ox being led to the slaughter. So that there were numbers of Jews— part of them the more enlightened, part of them the poorer classes—who looked on the reforms of Alexander the Second as acts of justice. If there was to be military service, let it be borne by all; let there be no privileged classes. Poor optimists! They still did not understand that though there might be no "privileged" families, the influence of money had not been destroyed; the rich would still be able to buy their sons out of the service. That, in fact, is exactly what happened. When the war broke out there were Jews of Swislowitz, too, who went forth: but they were all poor Jews. And one of them was, in fact, Leivik's brother, Pessye's second son—the bread-winner of the family.

The Jews regarded Alexander the Second as a king who reigned in justice—particularly so after Nicholas the First, whose name made men tremble, and concerning whose cruelties there were living legends in every part of the country. But Alexander the Second was the Czar who had freed millions from slavery. And he was the Czar who tried to introduce reforms in the government, the courts, and elsewhere. He was the Czar in whose reign even the persecuted and oppressed Jews could breathe more easily. It was he who had decreed that the schools and universities should be opened wide for the Jews, and he had made it possible even for a Jew to wear real epaulettes. It is not to the point to remark that with the exception of a few modernist Jews, the masses of our people were afraid of the Jewish generosities of Alexander the Second. They were afraid, instinctively, that a break would come in their lives, that the freedom they were winning under Alexander the Second would be apter to destroy the world they lived in than were the oppressive decrees of his father Nicholas. But their attitude toward Alexander, their Czar, was a positive one. In almost every Jewish home his picture could be found hanging on the wall. And when the regular prayer was said for the Royal Family, and the name of Alexander was inserted, the words did not carry a bitter irony, as they did in the case of his son, Alexander the Third, and of his grandson, Nicholas the Second.

As far as I can remember, the Jews of Swislowitz were submerged by a wave of patriotism when the war with Turkey broke out. We had two Hebrew newspapers, weeklies, which came to Swislowitz: or perhaps *Ha-Zephira* was a bi-weekly in those days—I cannot remember clearly. Another source of news was Krugliansky, who read the Russian papers. There were great scenes in the Shuhl, particularly in the evening, between the afternoon and evening prayers. The majority were on the Russian side, but there were also a number of "Turks" who, feeling secure in this place, openly avowed their sympathies. One of the main factors in their calculations was that the Turks were regarded as Arabs, for they were Mohammedans: they were therefore, by this logic, Semites, descendants of Ishmael, the son of Abraham and Hagar: which is to say that they were actually cousins of ours. It was true that it would be better for us if Russia emerged victorious from the war, but how was it possible to pray actively for the murderous defeat of so close a relative? The call of the blood rang louder than the call of self-interest.

For quite a time the national hero of Russia was the young general Skobeliov, conqueror of Plevna, the most important Turkish fortress, which was defended by the ablest Turkish soldier—Osman Pasha. The papers were full of Skobeliov and of his heroism: the Angel of Death trembled before him and retreated from his presence. They told how Skobeliov, riding on horseback, led the army to the attack in person. The enemy marksmen singled him out and shot at him from every side. A bullet went through his hat; another killed the horse under him. He leapt on to a second horse and led the army with uncovered head. The bullets sang round him like rain, but not one of them could touch Skobeliov. The Russian masses saw in him the hero of their folk-legends, and in true Russian fashion bowed the knee to him in religious ecstasy.

Morning and evening big crowds gathered round the district commissioner's building and in the open market place. Jews and gentiles hotly debated the news from the front. On several occasions the priests held special services and a Te Deum was sung for the Russian victories. At such times the Jews would gather in the Synagogue to say prayers of thanks. The Rav of our city did not mix in war matters, but the Jews did it of their own accord. When the priests called the gentiles to the churches, the Jews gathered in the Synagogue. The element of fear did not enter into their calculations; fear of the gentiles was still unknown in those days, and it was not a question of winning favour in the eyes of our neighbours. The relations between Jews and gentiles were normal, thoroughly friendly. It was accepted as natural that if the gentiles went to church to pray for their Emperor, the Jews had to go to the Synagogue for the same purpose. Was not Alexander the common emperor of Jews and gentiles? And such an emperor! One who did not shrink from the perils of war, but went to the front and exposed his person. . . .

In the Synagogue the "Turks" gradually lost ground and became less insistent. The series of Russian victories had raised the general enthusiasm, and in the face of a rising fervour they found it hard to defend their position. But there were a few hard-bitten and obstinate "Turks," too. They admitted that according to the Jewish law they were compelled to pray for Russian victory, but they could not bring themselves to pray for the defeat of the Turks. A tragic conflict took place in their hearts. They would be happy if the war ended with a stalemate. And God heard their prayers. The peace treaty of Berlin actually did reduce the Russian victory to a stalemate.

I was swept along with the tide of emotion, and my Russian teacher did all he could to push me along. I expressed my longings for the triumph of Russia not in prayer, but in song—in Hebrew song, for I began to write Hebrew poetry at that time, under the influence of Russian victory. I put all my soul into those childish, clumsy Hebrew poems. I became of a sudden a fierce Russian patriot, and even began to take a new interest in my studies of the language. I must have written at least ten poems on Skobeliov: and one of the verses I remember to this day: *Arise, Skobeliov, and lead thy captivity captive, thou son of Dmitri.* . . . I had lifted it bodily from the oldest Hebrew poem, the song of Deborah: *Arise, Barak, and lead thy captivity captive, thou son of Abinoam.* . . .

Thus, with a verse from the oldest, finest, and most powerful song of the Hebrews, a *cheder* boy of Swislowitz made the first payment on his debt toward the great Slav nation.

The fortress of Babrusk was at one time ranked in the first class of those that blocked the road to Moscow from the west. With the building of the Warsaw-Moscow railroad Babrusk lost its strategic value and Brest-Litovsk took its place. Babrusk was thenceforth used only as an ordnance centre and as a base for manoeuvres. For this reason Babrusk was chosen as a concentration camp for captured Turks. But as the number of prisoners kept rising almost daily the fortress itself soon became too small. The military authorities began to distribute numbers of them among the population, and later, when Babrusk was saturated, the surrounding towns and villages were also pressed into service. In this way Swislowitz was privileged to quarter some two hundred real Turks, who were distributed equally among the Jews and gentiles of the town. The Turks themselves asked to be quartered with Jews only. They felt more at home there. It would be quite unjust to say that the gentiles treated them harshly, as enemies, but the attitude of the Jews was one of pity, and almost of affection.

I have already said that traditionally we looked upon the Turks as great-grandchildren of Ishmael—close relatives of ours. But there were three important considerations which added to the feeling of intimacy. First, it was no secret that the Turks, as Mohammedans, were all circumcised; second, and for the same reason, they ate no swine meat; third, the Turk never took his hat off, even in the house.

The attitude of the older folk toward the Turkish prisoners quickly communicated itself to the children, and as children we felt even more tenderly for these unhappy men whom the destiny of war had cast among strangers in a strange land. Old pictures rose in my memory. It seemed to me that our great-great-grandfathers must have looked thus when they were driven forth into Assyria, into Babylon, and among the Medes and Persians. But our great-great-grandfathers had it worse, for where they went there were no Jews to take pity on them. . . . On summer days the Turks would go down to the Swisla to bathe, and then they would sit, hour after hour, with their feet folded under them, Turkish fashion. Then I would think of the psalm *By the waters of Babylon*, and of how *we* had sat by alien waters longing for Jerusalem. Nothing was missing but the harps and the willows to hang them on. But the waters were there, and the prisoners too, and the rest my fantasy supplied.

I remember we were told that the Turks were delicate people and were not accustomed to black bread. They eat only white bread or else rice. We children would often stuff our pockets with pieces of white bread and with handfuls of rice and give them to the Turks. Conversation was of course impossible: all we could do was stuff their mouths with bread and rice. And it seems that they were delicate indeed: not one of them ever refused the little gifts which we brought to them out of our sympathy with close relatives.

The war went on, and victory was added to victory on the Russian side. It began to look as though the Slav-Byzantine dream of Constantinople were drawing nearer and nearer toward realization. And who knows what turn might have been given to world-history if Russia had not been thwarted in her ambitions, if the European Powers had not prevented Russia's ultimate triumph? The chief anti-Russian rôle was played by England. England guarded the gates of the Mediterranean, the entrance to the Near East, and it was England that put the curb on the Russian appetite. The British lion shouldered the Russian bear away from its victim. There came the peace of Berlin. The English plenipotentiary, the Jew Disraeli-Beaconsfield, was the leading spirit there, and under his skilful hands the Russian victory melted almost completely away. Not for nothing did the entire Russian press rage more against England than against Turkey, and most of all against the insolent queen and her Jewish envoy. Not for nothing did certain of the Russian papers say that the legend of the ten tribes was no legend at all; that the English were the lost ten tribes and that Disraeli was descended from King David. . . .

Who can fathom the ways of history? There are events that break suddenly upon us, like a bolt from the blue—unheralded, unexpected, only because we are absorbed in our immediate affairs and cannot sense the vast preparations which usher them in. After all her victories Russia emerged from the war almost empty-handed. Her Byzantine dream remained as far from realization as in the pre-war years. The chief responsibility for this rested with one man—the Jew Disraeli; and within three or four years the wave of pogroms passed over Russia!

As a Jew his name was Disraeli; as a Lord he took the name of Beaconsfield. It was as Beaconsfield that he acted in Berlin, but the Jews of Russia paid for Disraeli. And in very recent history, too, something similar took place. As a Jew his name is Bronstein; as lord of the Russian revolution he is known as Trotzky. In the days when Trotzky was taking Russia by storm one of the biggest and most important Jews of Russia, Jacob Maazeh, Rabbi of Moscow, said, "It is Trotzky who storms over the country, but we will pay the reckoning for Bronstein." When the organizer of the mighty Russian army was left with only two soldiers, who guarded him on his way into exile, he was engaged—so all the papers reported—on a close study of the biography of Beaconsfield. Was it Trotzky who was interested in Beaconsfield, or Bronstein in Disraeli?

The war was a great influence in my life. It drew me, as I have said, closer to the reality of Russian life, and opened a new world to me. It was no longer possible for me to live exclusively in that ancient world which I carried within, and I began to look for ways of entry into this vast life, with its stream of living events which filled all the newspapers. I was deeply chagrined that I was still unable to read Russian, and I turned with renewed vigour to the study of the language. Without any persuasion from others I asked my father to increase my Russian lessons to two hours a day, and he granted my request. But with all my eagerness, with all my labour, I found the road extraordinarily difficult. I could not enter into the language; and sometimes I had the feeling that it was a living thing, which actively repulsed me: it was as though it spoke to me, saying, "Not so fast, stranger. I was not created for you. My doors are closed." The more difficult I found it, the more obstinate I became. I wanted to take the language by storm, and a real war ensued between the Russian tongue and myself— a war which lasted longer than the Russo-Turkish war, and longer than the World War. It was years later, when I had completed my studies at the Realschule of Minsk, that my studies of Russian were crowned with success: that is to say, I was able to enter into the life of the language, and to taste at first hand the fulness of her classic writers. The reader will ask: How was it possible to pass through a Realschule without a proper knowledge of the Russian language? The answer is that my mathematical gifts made up for my lack of Russian. In those days everything was possible in Russia.

But the centre of gravity of my education still remained with my Jewish studies. It only shifted from the Bible to the Talmud. In the Bible I had nothing more to learn. I knew by heart both the full text and the chief commentaries. But there is no end to the studies of the Talmud: there is enough in that for an entire life. The Bible can be compared to a temple, a palace of the Jewish spirit, erected in the days of its youthful creativity. The Talmud may be compared to a skyscraper, built by the same spirit, but no longer in its splendid youth. For the building of a palace there is needed vision and fantasy, but for a skyscraper nothing is needed beyond logic and dry intelligence.

From my tenth to my fourteenth year the Talmud was my chief study, taking up five hours daily. In time, of course, I passed from the exclusive influence of the Bible. The final state of balance was a repetition, in riper form, of the experience of my early childhood. As my mother had spoken to my heart, and my father to my mind, so now the Bible appealed to my emotions, the Talmud to my intelligence. The Bible was my mother, the Talmud my father.

My teacher, Judah Artzer, introduced what was then a new course of studies—systematic readings in the new Hebrew literature. Through him we became acquainted with modern prose and poetry, with the works of Naphthali Herz Weisl, the Luzzatis, Adam Ha-Cohen, Shulman, and the others. On me, as on thousands of others at that time, the deepest impression was made by the *Ahavath Zion* (Zion's Love) of Abraham Mapu. This was the first novel I ever read. And I chanced to read it just at the time when the youth in me had ripened to the right point for a work in which love was the main theme. I do not remember exactly how old I was at the time, but I still feel the taste of the impatience with which I waited every day for the hour dedicated to this book. True, I was enraptured by the language and the pictures—both of them drawn exclusively from the world which was so peculiarly my own. But more than by these, I was taken captive by the heroine of the romance, Tamar. I envied her lover Amnon, for whom God had created such a creature. The realities of love were still a sealed book to me, but I felt their force and attraction obscurely, powerfully. In *Ahavath Zion* I found a vague satisfaction. I did not dream of taking Tamar away from Amnon, but I wanted to love her, too, and in just the same way as Amnon did.

That book was the symbol of the springtime in me. I felt on my forehead the dew of Hermon and the wind that blew over the snows of Lebanon. My delight was in the roses of Sharon and the lilies of the valley. *Ahavath Zion* was my morning star, and the Song of Songs was in my heart.

CHAPTER SEVENTEEN: STUDENTS IN SWISLOWITZ

THE town of Swislowitz was too poor to support a Yeshivah or Academy. But at no time did it lack Yeshivah students. They were called Yeshivah Bochurim (Yeshivah boys) even though they studied alone, without a Yeshivah director— for in the manner of their life and the choice of their studies they were not to be distinguished from the boys and young men who attend real Yeshivoth. They met the principal condition of that status: they gave all their time to the study of the Talmud, of the ritualistic and legalistic codes, and of the other branches of literature which revolved around the Talmud. In Hebrew the phrase is: the Talmud and its armour-bearers. To that class belonged only the works which were devoted to the Halachah, or legalistic side of the Talmud. The Hagaddah, or folk-lore and humanistic part of the Talmud, as well as the moralistic books of later epochs, were regarded as belonging to a lower order, fit only for occasional and passing study. The Bible occupied the last place—something to take snatches from at odd moments.

The attempts which have been made to draw a parallel between the old Yeshivoth and the modern Hebrew institutes of learning—the theological seminaries—are a direct contradiction of the spirit of history. The truth is that the Yeshivoth stood much nearer to the higher schools of jurisprudence. The old-fashioned Rabbi, and the Yeshivah students who were preparing to enter the Rabbinate, were in reality much more Jewish jurists than theologians. It is true that this Jewish jurisprudence had a strong theologic bias, the reason being that it reflected a theocratic order of society; but its chief content was of a worldly nature, and its concepts were exclusively logical. The mastery of this system needed many years of assiduous study. A Rabbi with a purely theological training, a "spiritual leader," is a new product in Jewish life: he was only brought into being with the age of assimilation. The adaptability which Jewish life showed in so many other fields extended also to the Rabbinate, which began to resemble the Christian priesthood regardless of the fact that the concept of a church is much too limited to correspond with the fulness of meaning conveyed by the words Jewry and Judaism.

The Yeshivah students of Swislowitz, as well as those whom I met in later years in other parts of the country, were therefore, from the viewpoint of Jewish knowledge, on an incomparably higher level than our modern Jewish theologians with their double title of Rabbi and Doctor. Little wonder, then, that from these sources should have been drawn our best writers, our greatest poets, and our most important scholars.

The number of Yeshivah students in Swislowitz never exceeded twelve. They were all quartered in the Study House of the Synagogue. Here they passed the best years of their youth, living under a régime which to the modern student must seem incredibly harsh. Five to six hours of sleep was all that was permitted them. Two hours a day were given to meals and prayers. The remaining sixteen were dedicated to studies. Not all of them were able to endure this terrific discipline, and move all their waking hours in an atmos-

phere of intellectual tenseness. But whether they could endure it or not, they did not dare to leave their books. They
were ashamed before each other and before the few older
scholars and ascetics who also spent their entire days in the
Study House of the Synagogue. And the weaker ones would
become tired, and drone through their studies in a state between sleeping and waking. There were, on the other hand, to
be found real giants of the spirit, remarkable for their endurance. They glued themselves to the Talmud as the Russian Cossack glues himself to his horse in time of war: only
death can dislodge him. For some of them sixteen hours of
study a day was insufficient, so that now and again they
stole an hour or two from their meagre sleep. There is a
folk saying of ours, that certain Yeshivah students have
been known to study twenty-five hours on one day by bor-
rowing an hour from the next and forgetting to pay it back.
On summer nights the townlet would be lying fast asleep,
wrapped in silence: above, a multitude of stars shine down
and from the earth only a single feeble glimmer responds—
the glimmer of the candles in the Study House. And from
the half-open window voices float, in a chant that is filled
with passion, with love and with vain longing. A strange
serenade, sung by the ascetic knights to their beloved, the
Talmud: or perhaps, who knows?—to the Divine Glory,
which wakes in the dead of night to weep for the Temple
which has been destroyed and for her children who live the
life of exiles. All the repressed longings of their lonely lives
are poured out in those nightly songs.

The Yeshivah students slept in the Synagogue and Study
House—sometimes even in the women's division of the
Synagogue. A regular cushion stuffed with feathers was
rarely to be seen among them. They slept mostly on sacks
stuffed with hay and straw. Blankets were unknown. They

covered themselves with their topcoats. In the winter they used to lie down around the two big stoves at the entrance to the Synagogue. They had to get up very early—before the first services began. And it was unbecoming to stop studying before midnight. In this wise it was made impossible for them to get more than five or six hours' sleep a day.

For food they "ate days"—a peculiar diet already explained. They ate them when they had them. And when they were short, they complained, "I am short of a day—of two days." The expression is a strange one. What they were short of was not days, but householders to feed them. . . . The significance of this indirect phrase is clear enough. It was unbecoming to blame the householders. So they blamed the days. But the mere circumstance that certain of the Talmud students did lack days gives some idea of the general poverty of the Jews of Swislowitz.

When my knowledge of the Talmud was such that I was able—in the popular phrase—"to read a page," together with the commentaries and subcommentaries, I began to come in contact with our Yeshivah students. Practically all had a "day" in our house—and sometimes two, Friday and Saturday. I became intimate with a few of them, and very often I would visit the Study House late at night, and sit down and study together with them for several hours. I was much younger than they, but they took me into their company and treated me as an equal. More than anything else I wanted to sit with them through the night of Thursday to Friday. Thursday was always reserved for the recapitulation of the week's lessons, and most of the students remained up the whole night. The test was a severe one. Sometimes I would sit into the small hours and be compelled to go home. Now and again I was able to see the night through.

The "ascetics" who have been mentioned more than once in this narrative were strangers who had settled temporarily in Swislowitz. One of them came from as far as Vilna. They were young men, fathers of families, who were preparing for the Rabbinate. These ascetics would find some obscure little town where they could devote all their time to study. A more ideal obscurity than Swislowitz could hardly have been imagined. As for the old men who also frequented the House of Study, they were residents of Swislowitz who in their last years had shaken off the worries and temptations of the world and betaken themselves, with all their dreams and hopes, to the world of learning. The ascetics and the old men "ate days" just like the regular Yeshivah students. "Old Meyer" was the dean of them all; no one knew how old he was, but he was certainly above eighty. He had two "days" in my father's house. During week-days he used to conduct a sort of class in the Study House. Workingmen, tailors, shoemakers, raft-binders, shopkeepers, would drop in for an hour or two, and he would read out from the books, with a running commentary of his own. On a certain day he invited me to his "public lecture": "Come with me, Shmeril. You'll like it."

This was a Saturday, during the summer term, when he used to conduct a class in that section of the Mishnah which is known as The Ethics of the Fathers. He reached a certain well-known sentence, which goes, "Who is the mighty man of valour? He that conquers his own inclination"—by implication, of course, the inclination to evil. And there Old Meyer launched into homely illustration.

"As you know, I eat Fridays and Saturdays in the home of Reb Samuel Chaim. In his house it is customary to hand out on Friday some of the *blintzes* (small hot cheese pies) which are left to warm in the oven for the Sabbath meal.

Hot *blintzes* in sour cream. And now imagine, gentlemen, I pick up one of these luscious *blintzes*, I roll it over and over in thick cream, and I put it in my mouth. To swallow such a *blintze* is not one of the most painful sensations in life. It slides, it slips, like a shining sleigh down a snowy hill. And then suddenly, gentlemen, with one of those succulent, slippery *blintzes* half-way down my throat, the first half pulling the second half deliciously downward, I suddenly exert all my will-power: I tear away the second half. Sop enough to the lusts of the flesh! I say sternly to myself. I ask you, gentlemen, is that conquest, or is it not?"

The illustration made a tremendous impression. The audience listened with mouths agape. And I could not make up my mind whether the audience was tasting, with mouths open and eyes half closed, my mother's *blintzes*, or whether it was really overcome by the valour of the old man. Of one thing, however, I am sure. Old Meyer had thought up the story from beginning to end, and only because of my presence. For it is still incredible to me that Old Meyer should ever have been able to overcome his evil inclination for *blintzes* and arrest one midway on its comforting course to his half-starved stomach.

Among the ascetics there was one young man who was celebrated for his piety. He was reputed to be a good scholar, but his religious devotion topped his scholarship. His place in the Synagogue was behind the pulpit, among the poor. He prayed with the fervour of a true saint, and in all matters his bearing was that of a man who had renounced the things of this world. He fasted every Monday and every Thursday, and every night he kept vigil until after midnight and lifted his voice in lamentation for the Destruction, so that the walls of the Study House rang again. There were rumours that he had "taken the exile

262

upon himself," that he knew the lore of the Kaballah, and that he was perhaps one of the "Thirty-Six"—the unknown, unheralded saints of every generation. He was very fond of me, and made me an intimate of his. He told me many stories, particularly of the other world, of Paradise and Hell, of the Fathers, of Moses, and of Elijah the prophet—and every story ended with an allusion to the Messiah. "If the Jews only did what is right, the Messiah would have come long ago." His speech was full of mystic, vague allusions, half phrases, incompleted sentences, and I always left him tantalized and tormented, like a thirsty man to whom the beaker of water has been offered and then withdrawn.

I was in my thirteenth year when our intimacy ripened into close friendship. I was soon to become an "independent Jew," an adult paying for his own sins, gathering the rewards for his own virtuous acts, no longer entered into the account-book of his father. The time had come for me to think of my soul, steeped as it was in evil, and honeycombed with wicked thoughts. I knew too many profane Hebrew books belonging to the secular modernistic "Enlightenment." I read the *Hashachar*, the newspaper of Perez Smolenskin, a publication in which the sacred language of the Bible was applied to mundane affairs. And my ascetic told me unequivocally that this was sin. He told me further to forget all about grammar, for grammar was a plaything of the Devil himself. . . . The Devil, he said, is most effective when he puts on garments of piety, and bids you learn grammar as it were for religious ends. But thus he introduces the spirit of profanity into sacred things. Grammar itself was of no value: nothing mattered but the passion and the intent put into the words.

I do not know whether the ascetic was moved by true piety or by the Evil One himself; for he sought to destroy the world which was so dear to me. And he too began with grammar, but step by step he moved closer to my beloved prophets and stretched his destroying hand toward them. In any case I fell completely under his influence. Judah Artzer faded into the background, and I myself became a changed person. My Rebbi said he no longer recognized me. I began to imitate the ascetic and became fiercely pious. My morning prayers now lasted more than an hour. I counted out the words "as one counts out money"—such is the commandment. I gave up writing, and I turned away from the secular books of the Enlightenment. I spent every moment of freedom in the company of the ascetic, who began to teach me the Zohar and other books of the Kaballah. I became a nuisance at home. I demanded more piety in the bearing of every one: grace after meals was to be said slowly, distinctly, loudly: idle chatter was to cease. If there was nothing to be done in the house, there were always the psalms to repeat. And so on.

My Rebbi Judah took this to heart, and did all he could to restore my common sense to me. My father, in his practical way, reproached me gently—and in very extraordinary terms. He said, "Time enough to become so pious; you're too young to be a saint. A boy of your age must study first—must keep on studying." And the only one who was made happy by the sudden change was my mother. I would catch her looking at me out of eyes filled with admiration. Who knew? Something great might come of all this. My mother lived in a world of dreams—literally. Every other day she would ask to have her dreams interpreted. About me she dreamed in her waking hours. The old Chassidic spirit blazed up in her, and she began to hope for the miraculous.

This was the most pious period of my life, in the mystic and ecstatic sense. But it did not last long.

CHAPTER EIGHTEEN: THE BECKONING OF DESTINY

I CANNOT remember by what method or what path I freed myself at last from the mystic mood into which my friend the ascetic had cast me, and how I crawled out of the labyrinth of tormenting thoughts and emotions and returned to my happy and normal self. But I do remember that the feeling of liberation resembled closely my recovery from typhoid fever. On the other side of the experience it seemed to me that I had been divided into two persons: one of them had been running a high temperature and dreaming wild dreams, and the other had been pulling at him with all his strength to rescue him and restore him to unity; one half of me had been enveloped in thick, heavy clouds, against the background of which fantastic and terrifying pictures had chased each other in crescendo; and one half of me had clung with desperation to the sunlight of reason.

I was freed at length. I do not believe that the episode lasted more than three months. The ascetic lost his hold on me, and the mysteriousness of his bearing no longer attracted me. I went back with renewed delight to the study of the Talmud, and with a feeling of guilt, asking forgiveness for my passing dereliction. I took up my pen again; I plunged once more into the modernistic neo-Hebraic literature. I took revenge on myself, in a violent reaction, and of all things began to write—a novel.

I went the limit: I made the central theme of the novel love. My model was the *Ahavath Zion* of Mapu, and the theme was the story of David and Abigail.

The story, as it is told in the Book of Samuel, had an odd ring about it. Methought the lady did protest too much; she was concerned with loftier matters than become a woman, and somehow David was a trifle too friendly. In a word, I suspected that under the surface of the narrative lurked unspoken things. The idea of casting aspersions at King David did not terrify me: wherein was Abigail better than Bath Sheba, or Nabal than Uriah the Hittite? I set myself to the task of recounting the episode as I conceived it to have been in truth.

The first thing I did was to buy a good supply of white paper and have it bound into a book: bound manuscript was not obtainable in Swislowitz, and my ambition was to write a book forthwith. Then, on the title page, I designed in brilliant black ink the name of the novel and of the author, and of the author's father: David and Abigail, by Shmarya ha-Levi, the son of Samuel Chaim ha-Levi, of Swislowitz. Before plunging into the story, I made up a long preface, in which I sought to prove that in the Book of Samuel the incident had been recounted in very wary terms; but since God has endowed us with reason it was our duty to uncover the entire truth for ourselves. My style was lofty and flowery, heavily interwoven with biblical verses, half verses, and fragments, also with numerous quotations from the Talmud. All of which having been completed, I began the novel.

I worked in secret. I wanted to present my Rebbi with a completed book. I would write out the day's contribution on loose pages and at night, when the family slept, I transcribed it into the volume. Unfortunately, at the twentieth page my imagination gave out. I wrestled with myself, squeezed words from my exhausted brain, but to no effect. I was tormented by my own extravagance in having had an entire volume bound. Here was the greater part of it wholly wasted. The writing of the novel—or of as much as I could do—lasted two weeks. I was ashamed of myself, but in the end author's pride was too strong for me. I carried the novel, such as it was, to my Rebbi.

Concerning the content of the story, my Rebbi said nothing at all. He only criticized the style, praised it, and advised me to abandon novel-writing for the time being. He thought it better for me to confine myself to essays and to poetry. Nobody would print a novel, he said, whereas a short essay or a poem might find its way into a publication, and that was the main thing. My Rebbi's fondest dream was to see something of mine in print. He too used to write brief, stylistic essays, but had not the daring to dream of seeing his own work in print. He looked upon himself as one who still belonged to the old Jewish world: but in me he thought he saw a rising star of the new epoch, and all his hopes were concentrated in me.

During my last *cheder* years I loved and respected Judah Artzer no less than during the first, but I no longer regarded him as a universal authority. He himself boasted everywhere that I wrote the better Hebrew, and that in grammar I could even be his teacher. In the matter of Talmud, the gulf between Rebbi and pupil became narrower with every month. It was therefore impossible for me to look up to him any longer in my studies, but out of love and gratitude I accepted his advice and guidance. I could feel, too, that the years had given him a richness of experience and steadiness of character which set him high above me.

His influence over me was still such, therefore, that *David and Abigail* remained the one novel that I ever attempted.

And I regret the fact to this day. Not that a talented novelist has been lost in me, but that his advice compelled me to return again to the production of empty, flowery little essays, compounded of quotations and twisted phrases, exercises in barren ingenuity, which never touched the springs of the imagination. The truth is that the literature of the Enlightenment, the neo-Hebraic literature, suffered throughout from this intellectual one-sidedness. The trick of "style" was not to find the right, free expression for the idea, but to take the ready-made phrase from the Bible or the Talmud (chiefly from the Bible) and twist it neatly to some sort of purpose. The best pieces of writing were like mosaic, ingenious fragmentation. The tendency was unhealthy, but my Rebbi succumbed to it, and by his influence over me made me a victim too.

By that time, however, my Rebbi knew that I was with him only for one term more; after my Bar Mitzvah (confirmation) I would leave him. He himself openly told my father that he had nothing more to teach me. And therein he illustrated the truth of the Talmudic saying, "There can be envy everywhere, save from the father to the son and from the teacher to the pupil."

The preparations for the great event, when I would take upon myself the responsibility for my own life, began several months ahead. My Rebbi began to teach me the Shulchan Aruch—the accepted codex of Jewish ritual prepared four centuries ago by Joseph Karo—in order that I might be acquainted with all the details of our religious laws. He also spent much time in discussing earnestly with me the course of studies which I would follow after I had left him. My Rebbi now believed that I ought to become a man of letters, and he advised me strongly to write not only Hebrew, but Yiddish too. To this end he read with me *Der Yid-del*—the novel of Mendel Mocher S'phorim, the grand-father of our modern Yiddish literature, and, if I remem-ber aright, *Der Schwartzer Yungermantschick*, by Dinen-sohn. Both books made a deep impression on me, and I even translated part of them into Hebrew. But the Yiddish lan-guage failed to attract me strongly enough. For the time being it was my medium of translation, for it was the only language which I knew besides Hebrew. I began to write Yiddish only after many years. The simple fact is that Yiddish, like Russian, which I learned later, was never as intimate a part of me as Hebrew. The latter language was infinitely more close to me, and I knew its literatures, both ancient and modern, incomparably better. Furthermore, Yiddish literature was at that time still in its swaddling-clothes; its sudden and powerful development still lay in the future.

The Synagogue ceremonies of the Bar Mitzvah held no terrors for me. At the age of seven I had already been called up to the pulpit for the reading of the week's section of the Prophets. And even then I was unafraid. From my earliest years I was wholly at my ease in the presence of a large audience. Fear, as an emotion, was on the whole alien to my nature, and least of all I feared people. For you can talk with people, and when it came to talking I was in my own element.

The banquet which my father prepared on that day was almost as sumptuous as a wedding feast. I think there was hardly a householder in Swislowitz who was not invited; and all of them came, for my father's sake, and, I must add, for mine. At the age of thirteen I was the favourite of the town; and on more than one occasion, both in the street and in the

Synagogue, I would be asked by older Jews to settle a dispute. Such was their faith in my common sense and in my sense of justice.

Four Rabbis came to the ceremony—the Rabbi of our own town and three from neighbouring townlets. I was seated at the head of the table—in the same place where I had sat nine years before, on the day when they smeared the pages of the prayerbook with honey for me, before they carried me off to my first Rebbi, Mottye the bean. My father sat at my side, and my mother helped to serve the guests. But when the moment came for me to deliver my address, my mother took a seat at the side. My Bar Mitzvah address was a complicated and involved treatise on a Talmudic point. I went through it without an error. At the close of it the four Rabbis questioned me closely on the subject matter, and I answered them on that day with unusual ease and skill. When the examination was over they congratulated my father and expressed the hope that I would grow up to be a great man in Israel.

The banquet lasted until late in the afternoon. The importance of the occasion and the success of the ceremonies created a universal mood of happiness. Only one man sat quiet and thoughtful—my Rebbi, Judah. When the guests had withdrawn and only he and the family remained, he asked me to go out for a walk with him. We went downhill out of the town to the colonnade of the state road. I felt that something was weighing heavy on my Rebbi's mind, but I dared not ask him why he had called me out to walk with him. Without a word, each of us sunk in his own thoughts, we walked under the shadows of the trees. When an hour had passed we turned back, still wordless, toward the town. And then my Rebbi, like one who had something to say and had given up the idea of saying it, turned suddenly to me:

"Come, my ex-pupil! We will go to Shuhl for afternoon prayer."

The public acknowledgment of my Rebbi that he himself had nothing more to teach me had created a problem for my parents. Among decent middle-class folk it was the custom to keep a boy in *cheder* at least until his fifteenth year. This had been done with my older brother, Meyer. But Swislowitz had become too small for me. On the one hand my parents were filled with pride; on the other, they were deeply perplexed. What was to be done with me? My father, strong in the idea that I should ultimately become a merchant, did not care to send me to a Yeshivah. He feared that the atmosphere of unworldliness, of pure study, would unfit me for business; I was liable to become a *batlan*, a learned and helpless drifter, like my brother-in-law Asher Shafrai, who was undoubtedly a scholar but utterly at a loss in worldly matters. Finally it was decided that, for the time being, I should receive private lessons from the Rav of the town. As far as I can remember it was the first time in the current history of Swislowitz that the Rav himself became a private tutor. My prestige rose still higher, and I was treated by every one as a person set apart. I had been till then *primus inter pares*, the ablest *cheder* boy in Swislowitz. From that time on, however, I was in a class by myself—in both senses of the phrase.

The new situation was a heavy yoke to me. I had dreamed that with the ending of my *cheder* years I would have a little more time for myself and give freer reign to instincts which had long been suppressed. Without a *cheder*, without the crushing discipline which took every moment of my time, I would be able to divide up the day according to my own wishes. The old passion for the rivers, the meadows, the fields, and the forests of Swislowitz stirred again in me. I wanted to go boating and fishing; I wanted to wander among the trees, many of them so familiar to me that I had watched their yearly growth since my earliest days. And with these dreams were mingled others, in which swam up the faces of girl playmates, and one face more frequent and more friendly than all the others. The other girls called me "Schmerel," simply; her name for me was more affectionate —"Schmereleh." When I heard her calling me a softness flowed through all my limbs, and the verses of the Song of Songs rose to my lips. Now, I thought, I would be able to see her oftener, perhaps in the evenings on Castle Hill, when the sun was setting behind the tangle of the old birch trees. . . .

And suddenly I was singled out to be the only pupil of the Rav of Swislowitz. I would have to be more careful, more grown-up than ever: always serious: tied to books the whole day, and forbidden to leave the Synagogue even between afternoon and evening prayers.

The Rav was not a martinet. It was not for his sake that I had to put on the sober bearing of an ascetic. It was my mother who, more than any one else, kept reminding me that I was a man, that I could no longer compare myself to my schoolmates of yesterday, that in all things I had to conduct myself like the pupil of the Rav of the town. Perhaps she already suspected, in her heart of hearts, that her dream would never be fulfilled; I would never become a Rav. And she snatched what joy she could from the passing illusion that her son had been dedicated to the Torah.

As a matter of fact the Rav was as much given to the study of worldly affairs and of the world's culture as to purely spiritual matters. Apart from his fine Talmudic training he was a good Hebraist (though inferior in this respect—as I have already said—to my uncle, Meyer Wendrow), and this circumstance helped to develop a close friendship between us. Those who have some inkling of the spirit of those times will realize how far he was from being a fanatic when I say that he used to read the *Hashachar* (the secular weekly paper of Perez Smolenskin) with me, and spoke to me at great length about the struggle then on foot in Jewish life— the struggle between the nationalist and the assimilationist forces. Himself a passionate nationalist, he never mentioned the name of Perez Smolenskin, the leader in the war against the assimilationists, save with the deepest affection and respect. Yet he knew well that in orthodox circles Smolenskin was regarded as a dangerous free-thinker, a revolutionary spirit who was corrupting the Jewish youth. The *Hashachar* had been banned from all the Yeshivoth, and woe to the student who was caught with a copy: his dismissal took place on the spot. In spite of this, the influence of this periodical was perhaps greater among the students of the Yeshivoth than among any other class; for them Smolenskin became the prophet of those stormy times. The older folk trembled at the mention of his name; the younger saw in him the pillar of fire which went through the wilderness burning the thorn-bushes in front of it and clearing a path for the new generation.

Smolenskin carried on the war with a double-edged sword and on two fronts. On one side he stormed against all that was rotten and outlived in the old Jewish life; on the other side he hewed the mask from the face of the so-called Mendelssohnian "school." He thundered alike against the obstinate conservatism of the Jewish people, which led to petrifaction, and against assimilation, which led to death.

The quintessence of the Mendelssohnian tendency found expression in that famous phrase, "Be a Jew in thine own tent, and a man when thou goest out." Smolenskin was the first to expose the pitiful, slavish implications of this apparently innocent aphorism. For there is only one construction to place upon it: the contrast between being a Jew and being a man. There is not a civilized man, to whatever nation he belongs, who would not regard the antinomy as a studied insult. Would one dare to say to a Frenchman, a German, or an Englishman, "Be what you are only when you are at home: elsewhere be a man"? And the phrase, "Be a Jew in thine own tent, and a man when thou goest out," has only one meaning, namely, that Jewishness is not a commodity with which you may be seen in public. This was a life-philosophy which would have had all Jews wear a mask, be false to themselves, and become servile imitators of every form of life. It was a life-philosophy which grew out of a false conception of freedom, the bastard child of a shallow emancipation: and against it Smolenskin declared war to the death.

But concerning all these questions of literature and life the Rav would merely talk with me during free hours. Within the circle of his official duties he kept closely to the programme of studies. This was confined wholly to the Talmud and Poskim—the ritualistic and legalistic codes. He declared himself content with my abilities on the two counts which make the good student: a quick grasp of every problem as it arises, and a wide vision of all its implications and ramifications. For the first a sharp mind is needed, for the second a good memory. It was his belief that I bade fair to become a great scholar. And yet, astonishingly enough, he never once tried to persuade me to devote my life only to study. On the contrary, it was clear from his free conversations with me that he looked on the rôle of such a man as Smolenskin as being superior to that of a great scholar. He did not say this outright; his Rabbinic office forbade it. But unguarded phrases, enthusiastic moments, were enough to reveal his sympathies. For all that, he kept me close to my studies, and rejoiced in my progress. Before long I had mastered the greater part of the Yoreh Deoh (the section of the Shulchan Aruch dealing with dietary and other laws), and I had progressed to the point where I could answer questions concerning Kashruth and Tarfuth (ritualistic cleanness and uncleanness of food and utensils) without his help.

A picture rises in my mind: the Rav is sitting with me at table, directing my studies: the door to the adjoining room stands open, and there my mother sits with the Rav's wife. A woman enters, carrying a chicken, or a pot; she has come to find out whether something or other has not made the chicken, or the pot, "unclean." The Rav turns to me, and gives me the honour of rendering the decision. I become grave, and play to perfection the rôle of the Rav's assistant. My mother cannot take her eyes off me. Why should she think of what may come later? Is she not in Paradise already?

But amidst all this I was not happy. Neither the Yoreh Deoh nor the Talmud, nor yet the prospect of answering ritualistic questions on the purity of pots and chickens, excited me any longer. Before me, as in a vision, I saw the modern prophet, Perez Smolenskin, and I heard his call to battle. I did not know what Smolenskin looked like, but I pictured him in the midst of a gathering army of followers, sending out over the increasing ranks the fiery message of the last war for liberation. The forms which the struggle would take, the nature of the liberty we sought, all this was veiled from me. I did not know that a great scholar had already written a book by the name of *Shivath Zion* (The Return to Zion), nor had I ever heard of the thinker, the friend and colleague of Karl Marx, and of his book *Rome and Jeru-*

salem. Yet the latter had appeared in 1862 and in Germany of all places, the classic country of Jewish assimilation. I did not know, either, that both the scholar and the modern thinker had formulated a programme for the national liberation of the Jewish people, a new exodus from Egypt. The names of Zwi Hirsch Kolischer and Moses Hess were never mentioned either by the Rav or by my Rebbi. I had only a dim sense of a vast process of preparation around me.

It is more than likely that my emotions were heightened by the Russian mood of the times. It is true that I had no clear idea of the realities of Russian life; we were, in Swislowitz, as remote from the great centres as if we had been marooned on an island. But the papers brought in vague reports of incipient revolt, and stories of attempts against the lives of the highest in the country. . . . There was dynamite in the air.

Two revolutionary forces were breaking through the framework of the old life. One belonged to a mighty people which on its own soil was preparing to throw off the tyranny of its ruling class; the other to a physically puny people, scattered in exile, preparing to revolt against its fate. To that first force my relationship could not be direct. But I had been prepared by education, by training, and by dreams, for a rôle in the second. The "revolt" of Perez Smolenskin was for me the expression of all that was finest and holiest in my people. It was a revolt against our destiny—against our God. "Thou art eternal, Thou canst wait. *For a thousand years in Thy sight are but as yesterday when it is past and as a watch in the night.* But our patience is at an end. Forgive Thy children, then, if they hasten the day."

It was the eve of Purim in the year 1881. The Jews of Swislowitz were assembled in the Synagogue, prepared for the reading of the scroll of Esther. Suddenly the doors were flung wide open, and at the entrance stood the district commissioner and the sergeant. A shudder ran through the congregation, the hereditary terror, the memory of evil decrees. Without introduction, the commissioner read out the telegram he held in his hand. "Alexander the Second has fallen, a victim of a revolutionary plot. Alexander the Third sits on the throne of all the Russias."

I remember well that I could not quite understand the full meaning of the words. I looked at the faces of the grownups: but they were frozen, expressionless. I found no answer. I did not dream then that on a far-off day the grandson of the murdered Czar would be compelled to open the first constitutional parliament of Russia and that, standing before me—the *cheder* boy of Swislowitz, deputy from the city of Vilna—he would have to read the first address from the throne in the history of his country.

The Modern Jewish Experience

An Arno Press Collection

Asch, Sholem. **Kiddush Ha-Shem**: An Epic of 1648. 1926

Benjamin, I[srael ben] J[oseph]. **Three Years in America**: 1859-1862. 1956. Two vols. in one.

Berman, Hannah. **Melutovna**. 1913

Besant, Walter. **The Rebel Queen**. 1893

Blaustein, David. **Memoirs of David Blaustein**. 1913

Brandes, George. **Reminiscences of My Childhood and Youth**. 1906

Brinig, Myron. **Singermann**. 1929

Cahan, A[braham]. **The White Terror and the Red**. 1905

Chotzinoff, Samuel. **A Lost Paradise**. 1955

Cohen, Morris Raphael. **A Dreamer's Journey**. 1949

Cowen, Philip. **Memories of an American Jew**. 1932

Cooper, Samuel W. **Think and Thank**. 1890

Davitt, Michael. **Within the Pale**. 1903

Dembitz, Lewis N. **Jewish Services in Synagogue and Home**. 1898

Epstein, Jacob. **Epstein**: An Autobiography. 1955

Ferber, Edna. **Fanny Herself**. 1917

Fineman, Irving. **Hear, Ye Sons.** 1933

Fishberg, Maurice. **The Jews:** A Study of Race and Environment. 1911

Fleg, Edmond. **Why I Am a Jew.** 1945

Franzos, Karl Emil. **The Jews of Barnow.** 1883

Gamoran, Emanuel. **Changing Conceptions in Jewish Education.** 1924

Glass, Montagu. **Potash and Perlmutter.** 1909

Goldmark, Josephine. **Pilgrims of '48.** 1930

Grossman, Leonid Petrovich. **Confession of a Jew.** 1924

Gratz, Rebecca. **Letters of Rebecca Gratz.** 1929

Kelly, Myra. **Little Aliens.** 1910

Klein, A. M. **Poems.** 1944

Kober, Arthur. **Having Wonderful Time.** 1937

Kohut, Rebekah. **My Portion** (An Autobiography). 1925

Leroy-Beaulieu, Anatole. **Israel Among the Nations.** 1904

Levin, Shmarya. **Childhood in Exile.** 1929

Levin, Shmarya. **Youth in Revolt.** 1930

Levin, Shmarya. **The Arena.** 1932

Levy, Esther. **Jewish Cookery Book on Principles of Economy Adapted for Jewish Housekeepers.** 1871

Levy, Harriet Lane. **920 O'Farrell Street.** 1947

Lewisohn, Ludwig. **Mid-Channel.** 1929

Lewisohn, Ludwig. **The Island Within.** 1928

Markens, Isaac. **The Hebrews in America.** 1888

Martens, Frederick H. **Leo Ornstein.** 1918

Meade, Robert Douthat. **Judah P. Benjamin.** 1943

Mendoza, Daniel. **The Memoirs of the Life of Daniel Mendoza.** 1951

Meredith, George. **The Tragic Comedians.** 1922

Nichols, Anne. **Abie's Irish Rose.** 1927

Nordau, Max. **The Conventional Lies of Our Civilization.** 1895

Nyburg, Sidney L. **The Chosen People.** 1917

Pinski, David. **Three Plays.** 1918

Roth, Cecil. **A History of the Marranos.** 1932

Roth, Cecil. **A Life of Menasseh Ben Israel.** 1934

Rubinow, I[saac] M. **Economic Conditions of the Jews in Russia.** 1907

Sabsovich, Katherine. **Adventures in Idealism.** 1922

Sachs, A[braham] S. **Worlds That Passed.** 1928

Seide, Michael. **The Common Thread.** 1944

Steiner, Edward A. **From Alien to Citizen.** 1914

Untermeyer, Louis. **Roast Leviathan.** 1923

Weinstein, Gregory. **The Ardent Eighties.** 1928

Yezierska, Anzia. **Hungry Hearts.** 1920

Yiddish Tales. 1912

Zangwill, Israel. **The Melting-Pot.** 1932

Zunser, Eliakum. **Selected Songs of Eliakum Zunser.** 1928